Federalism

FEDERALISM

A Normative Theory and its Practical Relevance

Kyle Scott

continuum

2011

The Continuum International Publishing Group
80 Maiden Lane, New York, NY 10038
The Tower Building, 11 York Road, London SE1 7NX

www.continuumbooks.com

Library of Congress Cataloging-in-Publication Data
Scott, Kyle, 1977-
Federalism : a normative theory and its practical relevance / Kyle Scott.
    p. cm.
Includes bibliographical references and index.
ISBN-13: 978-1-4411-9764-1 (hardcover : alk. paper)
ISBN-10: 1-4411-9764-8 (hardcover : alk. paper)
ISBN-13: 978-1-4411-7714-8 (pbk. : alk. paper)
ISBN-10: 1-4411-7714-0 (pbk. : alk. paper) 1. Federal government.
2. Federal government–Case studies. I. Title.

JC355.S36 2011
320.4'049–dc22   2010032994

ISBN: 978-1-4411-9764-1 (HB)
         978-1-4411-7714-8 (PB)

Typeset by Newgen Imaging Systems Pvt Ltd, Chennai, India
Printed in the United States of America

Contents

Preface

Most defenders of federalism tout its practical advantages. As the famous argument by Tiebout goes, decentralization allows localities to formulate policies best suited for their particular needs and preferences (Tiebout 1956).[1] While I find most of the practical defenses of federalism persuasive, such defenses are not enough as they lack a normative core. What is lacking from federal thought is a normative theory that is prior to policy making and implementation. Without such a theory, federalism can run off course.

In the first three chapters of this book, I develop a theory of federalism that is relevant to, and draws upon, issues related to civil society and democratic theory. In the first chapter I draw upon three philosophers—Althusius, Aristotle, and Tocqueville—to begin a theory of federalism. In the opening account of federalism I argue that there is a proper scale to society, which, when observed, facilitates human interaction that is conducive to a pursuit of the good life.

Chapter 2 takes on one of liberalism's greatest critiques of federalism. According to modern liberalism, what is good should be good everywhere; therefore, federalism violates this liberal pronouncement by allowing variation. In Chapter 2, I draw on Plato and Montesquieu to defend variation against charges of relativism.

While I emphasize the importance of developing a theory of federalism, developing the practical arguments in favor of federalism is necessary as well. The third chapter serves as a bridge between the theory and practice sections. In this chapter I question the modern notion of the sovereign nation-state, and the defense of federalism that adopts the rhetoric of state sovereignty, in an effort to replace it with a notion of popular sovereignty. No matter how the power to govern is divided or distributed, if the government retains sovereignty, it will always be a threat to the people. Sovereignty must stay with the people, and this chapter shows what happens when it does not and introduces measures that can be taken to return sovereignty to the people.

In treating federalism as I do in the first three chapters, I begin to question the institutional mechanisms that modern liberal nations employ to achieve their ends and propose new institutions designed to perpetuate the federal ideal. In so doing, I critique existing notions of liberalism and introduce a new federal-liberty.

Chapter 4 begins the practice section of the book. In this section I develop an argument for nullification, veto, and secession (NVS) in order to create an environment in which the constituent parts can protect themselves against encroachment from a central authority or other constituent parts. In Chapters 4 through 7, I continue the argument that federalism can bring disparate groups together by facilitating a deliberative environment through its ability to function at the proper scale. Traditionally, federalism is thought to diminish conflict because it forms homogeneous communities and keeps them isolated. But, no community can be homogeneous, and if it could be, no community could remain isolated within a federal structure. Thus my support of federalism is the reverse of the prevailing paradigm in that I view federalism as a way of bringing diverse groups together. In doing so I echo the sentiment of the U.S. Supreme Court when it stated that federalism "assures a decentralized government that will be more sensitive to the diverse needs of a heterogeneous society" (*Gregory v. Ashcroft*, 501 U.S. 452, 548 [1991]).

Federal regimes are composed of one central authority and multiple constituent parts. But, being that power tends to centralize, the constituent parts tend to lose much of their authority to the central authority. To prevent a federal regime from becoming a national regime the constituent parts must be equipped with mechanisms to defend themselves. Without these mechanisms the constituent parts will lose authority and the federal structure will cease to produce the positive features of a federal regime. Chapter 4 develops a defense of nullification and provides a recommendation of how it can be implemented. Chapters 5 through 6 do the same for veto and secession respectively.

While the bulk of the theoretical development occurs in Chapters 1 through 3, Chapter 7 provides an additional theoretical layer by drawing on John C. Calhoun. Chapter 7 is the final chapter and it deals with political polarization. The book builds to the final argument that federalism can serve as a means of moderating political preferences and increasing levels of toleration. Federal regimes can reconcile tensions by providing groups with political means by which they can resolve their disputes peacefully. In this final chapter I discuss how Israel and Iraq might benefit from this new view of federalism.

This book is the third that has found its genesis in the teachings of Ross Lence. I am not sure if he would have agreed with what is written or how it is written, but the core ideas come from him. Like all of his students, I learned from the Good Doctor that developing a sense of community is more important than developing government constraints. It is only through community that an individual can reach his highest good. Dr. Lence was a master at bringing people together and creating community.

I would also like to thank my friend Mike Segeren. Through Mike I learned the importance of friendship and that the world is bigger and more complex than what I see immediately around me.

Since this is a book about community I owe the greatest thanks to my most important community: my family. It is in them that I find a purpose for what I do. Each time I look at them I am reminded of the need to make the world better. I lost a great deal of time with them while writing this book. The only way that sacrifice will be acceptable is if this book contributes to improving governments. I would not have embarked on this project had I not thought our lives could be better with it than without it. To Bethany, Braden, and Berkeley, thank you for your love, patience, and acceptance. I hope I have made you proud.

Notes

1. "Devolution can also free residents, teachers, and police officers to imagine and implement innovations that depart from conventional wisdom and routine, and are therefore unlikely to come from the central office" (Fung 2004: 5).

CHAPTER 1

Beginning a Theory of Federalism

Given the frequency of its practice it is shocking how anemic our theory of federalism is. We understand how federal systems operate on a case-by-case basis, but we lack a coherent understanding of how federalism as a concept operates and lack an understanding of what institutions and mechanisms are necessary to make it operate as it should. And while reforms are constantly made in a federal system, we lack an understanding of what reforms are necessary to maintain a federal system so that it is capable of providing what federal systems are intended to provide. These shortcomings exist because there is no theory of federalism. From theory we can improve our understanding of what federalism is, what it ought to be, and what needs to be done to make it so. In the course of developing a theory, this chapter will contrast federalism with deliberative democracy and discuss federalism's relevance to our current understanding of liberalism.

"The test which I apply for federal government is simply this: Does a system of government embody predominantly a division of powers between general and regional authorities, each of which, in its own sphere, is co-ordinate with the others and independent of them?" (Wheare 1964: 62). Wheare's definition of federalism is valid, and offers a good starting point for the development of a theory. What Wheare does not incorporate into his definition is a discussion of scale which would implicate a normative component into the definition thus moving us closer to a theory. Instead, I propose the following: Federalism requires that government authority be divided into constituent parts where each part maintains autonomy within its realm but the possibility of collaboration between constituent parts remains. The proper scale of the constituent parts is determined by human nature so as to create an environment conducive to the pursuit of the higher good. Federalism thus understood relieves the current tension that exists between ancient virtue and modern liberalism.

This chapter will begin to develop a theory of federalism by consulting Johannes Althusius, Aristotle, and Alexis de Tocqueville. Together these thinkers provide what is necessary to begin a theory of federalism. Through these thinkers I will show the importance of scale, human relationships, the balance between rights and obligation, and the proper relationship between public and private. In the course of evaluating these thinkers I will provide a conception of liberty that is distinct from other conceptions because of its dismissal of modernity.

The chapter will conclude with a discussion of deliberative democracy and how federalism can facilitate deliberation while addressing the criticisms that deliberative democracy cannot sufficiently address on its own.

Drawing on Great Minds

Theories of federalism are generally anemic. Even those who set out to construct a theory of federalism generally fail to do little more than point out the strengths of federalism. I attribute much of this deficiency to the lack of attention paid to the great philosophers of federalism. It is without jest that Wayne Norman writes, "It should be noted, historically, that there is at least one great text by a great thinker, namely, Kant's *Perpetual Peace*" (Norman 2006: 80).[1] Such accounts are why it is necessary to revisit some of the strongest arguments for federalism by some of the greatest thinkers in the history of political thought. It is only when this is done that there is any chance of developing a theory of federalism.

In this chapter I focus on Aristotle, Althusius, and Tocqueville; and in later chapters I will turn my attention to Plato, Montesquieu, John Locke, and John C. Calhoun. I do not pretend that this is an exhaustive list of all the great thinkers who have contributed to our understanding of federalism, nor all those with something valuable to say. I have selected those who put forth the most compelling and sophisticated arguments. Alternatively, the inclusion of some of these thinkers may seem odd as they do not directly address the topic, or the topic is not central to their philosophy. By choosing these thinkers I would be able to situate federalism within the broader scope of political philosophy.

Althusius: Introduction and Overview

Johannes Althusius—referred to as "the most profound political thinker between Bodin and Hobbes" (Friedrich 1979: xv)—was born in Diedenshausen in Westphalia in 1557. After studying in Cologne, Paris, Geneva, and Basle, Althusius took a doctorate in both civil and ecclesiastical law at Basle in 1586. In this same year he accepted a position on the law faculty at the Reformed Academy in Hebron. Althusius was not in the academy long. Upon the publication of his most famous work, *Politica*, in 1603, Althusius was offered the position of syndic in Emden, East Frisia, where he guided the city until his death in 1638. Althusius had tremendous influence in this city for 35 years, a city that was one of the first in Germany to accept the Reformed articles of faith.

His appointment at Emden, and its association with the Reformation, reflects his intellectual debt to John Calvin. Like Calvin in the *Institutes*, Althusius argued in *Politica* that all power and government comes from God and civil authorities cannot use their power to serve any ends other than God's. A citizen's first allegiance is to

God. *Politica* was widely embraced by the Dutch as it was thought to be a theoretical justification for their revolt against the Spanish. While not generally recognized in the modern canon, *Politica* was a divisive force during its time. As late as 1757 it was recommended that his books be burned rather than read.

Althusius calls for a unifying covenant, a covenant that is quite different from the social contract of Hobbes. The covenant must be agreed to by all who enter it. Althusius is accused of transforming all public law into private law with his idea of covenant. Althusius preserves this distinction but recognizes the symbiotic relationship between the two.

Althusius finds the origins of his federal design, and understanding of covenant, in the Bible.[2] Althusius creates a federal design based on biblical lessons. (1) The federal design is based upon a network of covenants beginning with the original covenant between God and man that all others are based upon. (2) The classical biblical commonwealth was a federation of tribes which were tied to one another by covenant that functioned as a unifying set of laws between the tribes. (3) The Bible ends with a restoration of the tribal system on a global scale in which each nation is able to preserve its own integrity while supporting a common covenant. Althusius's biblical observations served as the inspiration for his theoretical work that confronted the problem of divisible sovereignty. For a federal system to work, sovereignty must be divided among the constituent parts while still binding the parts to the whole. Althusius addressed this problem by relying on a theory of covenant that would bind the sovereign parts to a sovereign whole. This arrangement mirrors the symbiotic relationship that exists between the private law and the public law.

Althusius wrote in direct refutation of the theory of indivisible sovereignty as understood by Jean Bodin. "Althusius' concept of sovereignty is the opposite of Bodin's. In his system, the state is under the law, which emanates from the social dimension, which is why a sovereign or a magistrate cannot have absolute sovereignty" (Benoist 2000: 45). The idea of a single sovereign and self-determination could not be reconciled until Althusius introduced his theory of federalism, with the covenant as its central feature.

Symbiotics

Althusius introduces the term symbiotic in the opening pages of *Politica*. The term describes the art of politics and the men who live according to that art.

> Politics is the art of associating men for the purpose of establishing, cultivating, and conserving social life among them. Whence it is called "symbiotics". The subject matter of politics is therefore association, in which the symbiotes pledge themselves each to the other, by explicit or tacit agreement, to mutual communication of whatever is useful and necessary for the harmonious exercise of social life. (Althusius 1995: 17)

Symbiotes are similar to citizens, but they have a more intimate role with the political association than the modern conception of citizens. "The symbiotes are co-workers who, by the bond of an associating and uniting agreement, communicate among themselves whatever is appropriate for a comfortable life . . . In other words, they are participants or partners in a common life" (Althusius 1995: 19). For symbiotes there are obligations beyond oneself; there is the community. But the community would not ask a symbiote to do something against himself for the sake of the community. The relationship between the symbiote and the community, and among symbiotes, can be understood in terms similar to those expressed by Aristotle in his discussion of friendship. This understanding stands in stark contrast to both Hobbes and Bodin. For Hobbes and Bodin the sovereign could take any form, and it was the sovereign who had the task and authority to define the means and ends of the state over which he had dominion. Althusius replaces the state with the symbiotes. "The material of politics is the aggregate of precepts of communicating those things, services, and right that we bring together, each fairly and properly according to his ability, for symbiosis and the common advantage of the social life" (Althusius 1995: 24).

"Althusius began with the assumption that the political life was the life of the community, not simply things related to government and the state" (Conyers 2008: 14). Althusius broke somewhat with the Greeks as he argued that "In addition to the state, which is a kind of community, there are also other kinds of human associations." The error here, one that will be exacerbated by later philosophers, is to allow the state to take hold of the debate. One should embrace the opportunity to talk of community without talking of the state. Or if not, one should recognize that the state does not have to be inimical to the community, or other parts of the community, but all sectors can work toward similar goals. Since Althusius does say that the state is but one of many communities, and not necessarily the most important, he does not go as far as the moderns in their admiration of the state, but he does give an opportunity for others to break even further from the ancient conception of the *polis*.[3]

The danger of the modern development is not lost on Althusius, however, as he recognizes that different kinds of associations make up the body politic. In so doing he acknowledges that the body politic is not the most important, or central, part of an individual's life. "It is significant, therefore, that Althusius considered it indispensable to first attend to the function of five 'associations' whose work is different from, and whose goals are distinct from, the state's: the family, the collegium, the city, the province, and the church." Politics serves the individual and the other associations. "Politics is the art of associating men for the purpose of establishing, cultivating, and conserving social life among them" (Althusius 1995: 17). Althusius preserves the Platonic understanding of politics as an art.

For Althusius, the proper beginning of political thought is the recognition that human beings live in natural communities that occur spontaneously and that nowhere do they live alone—or, if they do, they live in an unnatural state. Political life is about living together: "Whence it is called symbiotics." (Conyers 2008: 15)

Thus, it is in error if we say that Althusius left the ancients entirely.

And while the state was not to be the central focus of associations or of the individual, the political man was the ideal state for man on earth. It was the political man that could balance the associations of family, collegium, city, province, and church successfully.

> The end of political "symbiotic" man is holy, just, comfortable, and happy symbiosis, a life lacking nothing either necessary or useful. Truly, in living this life no man is self-sufficient, or adequately endowed by nature. For when he is born, destitute of all help, naked and defenseless . . . he is cast forth into the hardships of this life, not able by his own efforts to reach a maternal breast nor to endure the harshness of his condition, nor to move himself from the place where he was cast forth. By his weeping and tears, he can initiate nothing except the most miserable life, a very certain sign of pressing and immediate misfortune. Bereft of all counsel and aid, for which nevertheless he is then in greatest need, he is unable to help himself without the intervention and assistance of another. (Althusius 1995: 17)

Althusius, like Aristotle before him, considers political life a necessity since man is by nature a social being.

> Truly, in living this life no man is self-sufficient, or adequately endowed by nature . . . Necessity therefore induces association; and the want of things necessary for life, which are acquired and communicated by the help and aid of one's associates, conserves it. For this reason it is evident that the commonwealth, or civil society, exists by nature, and that man is by nature a civil animal who strives eagerly for association. (Althusius 1995: 17 and 25)

Humans, by their nature, come together for it is only through coming together that they are truly human. But, they do not come together merely for the preservation of life, as Hobbes would have them do.[4]

> The symbiotic association does not respond to a collective desire or need; rather, it is defined by a particular quality of life, characterized by justice and pity, without which no individual or collective existence can be sustained . . . A symbiotic relationship is established between those who have the same needs, and who find themselves in neighborhoods of all sorts. This relation cannot be considered voluntary or the result of rational choice. Rather, it constitutes a reality derived from the social character of human existence . . . (Benoist 2000: 32)

Much like contemporary proponents of deliberative democracy, Althusius thought communication was vital for political life. It is through communication that the "things, services, and common rights" of the symbiotes are supplied and the "self-sufficiency and mutuality of life and human society are achieved" (Althusius 1995: 19). The importance of communication derives from his first principle, that humans are social beings, and it also reflects the centrality of Christianity to his political philosophy.

> He [God] did not give all things to one person, but some to one and some to others, so that you have need for my gifts, and I for yours. And so was born, as it were, the need for communicating necessary and useful things, which communication was not possible except in social and political life . . . Consequently, while some persons provided for others, and some received from others what they themselves lacked, all came together into a certain public body that we call the commonwealth, and by mutual aid devoted themselves to the general good and welfare of this body. (Althusius 1995: 23)[5]

Associations

Althusius finds man's natural tendency toward association in the family, and thus lets the family serve as the basis of all other associations, or rather, "these associations are the seedbed of all private and public associational life" (Althusius 1995: 31). From the family comes the basis of civil life. The civil life is arranged by a collegium. The collegium is governed by a leader who is superior to any one individual but inferior to the united colleagues. Thus, he does not superimpose the family structure on the civil structure, which indicates a realist streak within his thought as he recognizes that a single individual with unchecked authority will use that authority against other individuals. Therefore, to prevent tyranny of any type it is necessary that

> all colleagues be considered participants within the common legal structure, not as separate individuals but as one body. So it is not that what the collegium owns is not owed by the individuals separately, and what is owed to the collegium is not owed to the individuals separately. (Althusius 1995: 35)

This line of argument goes along with what was said earlier about the symbiotic relationship as being one of obligation and consideration. This is foreign, or at least objectionable, to modern liberalism which has taken a rights-based approach. The rights-based approach has shifted the focus to the individual in which the individual is superior to the collective. This highlights a limitation of the liberal perspective in that the individual owes the community for its humanity according to Althusius.[6] Althusius, as we see, conceived of a collegium in terms foreign to modern liberalism. "A people is not simply a group of individuals, but a moral, juridical, and political person. Thus, Althusius strongly opposed nominalism, a precursor of liberalism, according to which there is nothing ontologically real outside the lone individual" (Benoist 2000: 31).

Of course there is the strand of liberalism that seeks to make group rights superior to individual rights, but this is merely shifting the seat of potential tyranny from the individual to the group.[7] One goal for Althusius, as it should be, was to eliminate tyranny entirely. Because this was a goal, Althusius has something to say to those who favor individual rights and those who favor group rights. The individual, because of his natural inclination toward association, cannot be conceived of as separate from his group as it helps define who he is and what his values are. Thus it is important to recognize an individual's source of identification in order to recognize the individual and for the individual to be represented. To value the group is to value the individual if the relationship between group and individual is understood correctly. This line of reasoning has valuable import for those concerned with a politics of recognition as Althusius addresses the problem of whether the individual or group has greater value. Also of interest to identity politics and politics of recognition is that Althusius recognizes that an individual is part of different groups and associations. There may be some associations that an individual feels a greater attachment to or identifies more strongly with, but her other associations still condition her attachment and identification with that primary group.[8]

If humans are social, as Althusius posits, then an individual cannot be fully human, or cannot fulfill his human potential, without uniting with other individuals (Althusius 1995: 25; *Politics* 1253a31). Thus, the individual owes its humanity to the community, but owes it to itself to maintain that community since an individual must be in a community to be human.[9] To destroy the community, or aid in its disorder, would be to do the same to the individual. And because of their shared nature, individuals owe it to each individual, not just themselves, to aid in the creation and preservation of the community. Thus, there are three levels of obligation— to oneself, to the community, to other individuals—and the service to all three has identical ends and means. To conceive of the community and individual in this way is to deny a tension between the individual and the community.

A postmodern federalism must reckon with one of the basic principles of post-modern politics, namely that individuals are to be secured in their individual rights, yet groups are also to be recognized as real, legitimate, and requiring an appropriate status. Althusius is the first, and one of the few political philosophers who has attempted to provide for this synthesis. (Elazar 1995: xl)

For Althusius, the covenant forms the basis of all associations. One cannot lose one's identity or sovereignty after the covenant is formed because the covenant is the result of communication among constituent parts, and the purpose of the covenant is to maintain communication between constituent parts. The only way a covenant can fulfill its goal is to facilitate communication. Thus, communication cannot exist if one's authority to express his opinion were stripped from him. If a constituent part lost its identity or sovereignty as the result of covenant, covenant would be self-defeating and contradictory. "Althusius' dual emphasis on federalism as a relationship and on sharing as the basis of federal relationships has turned out to be a basic axiom of federalism . . . The polity, then, is a symbiotic association constituted by symbiotes through communication" (Elazar 1995: xli). In stating the matter more forcefully and directly, Elazar writes,

> Althusius' grand design is developed out of a series of building blocks or self-governing cells from the smallest, most intimate connections to the universal commonwealth, each of which is internally organized and linked to the others by some form of consensual relationship. Each is oriented toward some higher degree of human harmony to be attained in the fullness of time . . . A federalist grand design is one in which the universe is understood in federalistic terms and the comprehensive polity is structured accordingly. (Elazar 1995: xxxviii)

The City

The next stage in political development leads to the city. When associations link together to form a larger political order they create a city, or state. The more associations are linked together the more complicated things become. If it is to maintain the goal of the political, and not just sustain life, the city must protect communication. "Political order in general is the right and power of communicating and participating in useful and necessary matters that are brought to the life of the organized body by its associated members" (Althusius 1995: 39). The relationship between the ruler and the ruled is the same as it was in collegium.

> The superior is the prefect of the community appointed by the consent of the citizens. He directs the business of the community, and governs on behalf of its welfare and advantage, exercising authority over the individuals but not over the citizens collectively. (Althusius 1995: 40)

Althusius does defer to majority rule, but not in absolute terms. Althusius recognizes that there are some decisions that affect the community at large and others that affect the individual. For those decisions that affect the larger community, majority rule is sufficient as the majority serves as the voice of the community, but in those instances in which there are decisions which affect the individuals as individuals— for one does not lose his or her individuality once one joins a community—the consent of each individual is required. Therefore, in elections of public officials a majority is sufficient, but in determining a tax burden, a consensus is required.

The city does not diminish the importance of the other associations. The associations that form the city still exist and one's attachment to, and membership in, those associations still exists.

The community is an association formed by fixed laws and composed of families and collegia living in the same place. It is elsewhere called a city in the broadest sense . . . The members of a community are private and diverse associations of families and collegia, not the individual members of private associations. (Althusius 1995: 40)

The Althusian typology of the city follows the Aristotelian view of the city-state as a composition of other associations (*Politics* 1252a18–22, 1252b10–18, 28–31, 1280b34–5, 1280b40). The city is formed by covenant between associations just as the associations were formed by covenant between individuals. Since the covenant is a form of law, one must turn to Althusius's treatment of law in order to understand his teaching on city and associations.

Laws

The idea that individuals maintain their individuality is extended to family, collegium, and other associations that go in to making up larger associations. Because of this, Althusius anticipates the political sociology of Montesquieu, and follows Aristotle, in recognizing that different regions need different laws and laws should respect the norms and customs of a people or region. Even when there are universal political associations, "this does not prevent separate provinces of the same realm from using different special laws" (Althusius 1995: 67). Here we get an affirmative statement on the question of federalism in that within a federal structure there are laws passed separately by different levels of government. To understand what Althusius means by special law we have to understand how he classifies laws. First there is common law. Common law is akin to universal, or natural law. This law is set down by God, or we come to know it for God has set it down. But, common law is not attained by all people, so proper law is needed. Proper law is based on common law, but it is drawn up with consideration to the "nature, utility, condition, and other special circumstances" of a country (Althusius 1995: 144). "Therefore, proper law is nothing other than the practice of the common natural law as adapted to a particular polity" (Althusius 1995: 144). However, under no circumstance is it acceptable for proper law to be contrary to common law, for then it would lose the force of law altogether. As I will show in the next chapter, Althusius's understanding of proper law is similar to Plato's understanding of just law in that both acknowledge that "Since the nature and condition of these circumstances may be diverse, inconstant, and changeable, it is not possible for proper law to acknowledge one and the same disposition of common law for everything in everything . . ." (Althusius 1995: 145). And in anticipating Montesquieu's conception of law, which will be discussed in the next chapter as well, Althusius quotes Seneca as saying of political prudence, "it orders the present, provides for the future, and remembers the past" (Althusius 1995: 136). Proper law must respect the circumstances in which it exists, for law does not exist in a vacuum. For instance, "common law ... concludes from its principles that evildoers ought to be punished ... Proper law determines specifically that adulterers, murderers, and the like are punished by death, unless the punishment should be mitigated because of further circumstances" (Althusius 1995: 145–6). Therefore, if a legislator is to make good proper law, he must follow Machiavelli's advice and come to know the people and what they value, or Montesquieu's Saint Louis who makes laws consistent with the place, time, and condition of his people.

> The character, customs, nature, attitude, and viewpoints of the people are to be sought and learned from the nature and location of a region, and from the age, condition, circumstances, and education of the people therein ... Then it is advisable that the magistrate accommodate himself for a time to the customs and character of the people that he may learn what things are fitting and appropriate to them, and may propose suitable laws. (Althusius 1995: 149 and 150)

Federalism

Of course, for proper law to be crafted and administered consistent with these ideals, states must be of the proper size. Inherent within any theory of federalism is a specification of scale. Althusius recognizes that there is a proper scale to associations.

> The more populous the association, the safer and more fortunate it is ... On the other hand, a commonwealth or region overflowing with an excess of people is not free from disadvantages, and is exposed to many corruptions ... When the might of a commonwealth grows, fortitude and virtue decline ... From these considerations one may conclude that a commonwealth of medium size is best and steadiest. (Althusius 1995: 68–9)

Not only is it important for a state to be of the proper size so that the lawmakers can know those who they make the law for, but so that one is constrained. One cannot make good law if one's central concern is invasion from neighboring forces—because law then will only be geared toward the production of military power and thus willing to sacrifice liberty for safety—nor if the character of the population is so disreputable that the only focus of the government can be the preservation of order—for then one might be willing to sacrifice liberty for order. For there to be the proper focus and the proper knowledge there must be the proper scale.

   The proper scale goes beyond formal lawmaking in that orders of the proper scale do not demand the extensive and pervasive laws that large-scale orders do because in small-scale orders norms, customs, and a personal connection with others help regulate behavior.

> Their [small-scale societies'] social relationships are more integrated and close-knit than are ours; people interact with one another in a wider range of roles

which requires a more coherent ordering of behavior. Any one relationship has a wider range of functions . . . and its state or condition is correspondingly more important than in our [large] society where many relationships are single-purpose and impersonal . . . But how different it would be if the conductor were also my sister-in-law, near neighbor and the daughter of my father's golfing partner—I would never dare to tender anything other than the correct fare. In a small-scale society every fellow member whom I encounter in my day is likely to be connected to me by a comparable, or even more complex web of strands . . . Their ethics are comparably diffuse. These are not to be found formulated in a unitary doctrine, nor are they necessarily explicitly stated as values or principles. (Silberbauer 1991: 14)

Small-scale societies create sources of identity consistent with Althusius's formulation in which people take on many roles and the construction of identity is complex and dependent upon social interaction as well as individual perception. Large-scale societies tend to isolate individuals from one another in that interactions are usually done for a single purpose so that one individual means only one thing to other people. In large societies the bus driver is only a bus driver to me, I do not see the bus driver as a relative, friend, or colleague. This impersonalization is due to the necessary division and specialization of labor and expertise that make large-scale societies possible.

In complex, large-scale societies like our own, social institutions are highly elaborated and specialized, and, although integrated as components of the whole socio-cultural system, are relatively separate from, and impervious to one another . . . In small-scale societies institutions are versatile, serving many functions simultaneously, and are not readily separable, having high levels of mutual relevance. (Silberbauer 1991: 17)

Thus, economic exchange in large-scale societies is solely concerned with the economic ends, whereas in small societies conformity to social norms and customs is more important in economic exchange.

Relationships are more important in small-scale societies than are the rather casual, comparatively attenuated acquaintances of suburbia or the workplace. We tend to perceive self and personal identity as autonomous, self-contained attributes of individuals. In a smaller society they are seen and felt as including the individuals' kin and friends and enemies. (Silberbauer 1991: 18)

For this reason reciprocity is a more integrated feature in small-scale societies.

Familiarity with the way individuals interact with one another is important given that our identities are shaped, at least partially, by how we interact with others and the role we serve in that interaction. Because in large-scale societies interactions are generally single purpose, identities become oversimplified. In small-scale societies there is less specialization and therefore greater interaction between individuals in different capacities. Therefore, the interactions that exist in small-scale societies are multifaceted, which means an individual's identity is more accurately represented in that society.

The previous discussion on lawmaking did not confront the question of sovereignty, as it is within a discussion of federalism that the relationship between lawmaking and sovereignty is better contextualized. A discussion on lawmaking forces a consideration on sovereignty—for it is the sovereign that makes and administers law—and it is through a consideration of Althusius's conception of sovereignty that we will be brought closer to his idea of federalism. Althusius has already said that majority binds the minority on matters related to the community but not the individual, and that the superior is such in its relation to the individual but not the collective. The power of ruling, and enforcing that ruling, is what gives sovereignty.

> The people, or associated members of the realm, have the power of establishing this right of the realm and of binding themselves to it . . . Without this power no realm or universal symbiotic life can exist . . . This right of the realm, or right of sovereignty, does not belong to individual members, but to all members joined together and to the entire associated body of the realm. (Althusius 1995: 70)

This conception of sovereignty is a conscious contradiction of Bodin, and will serve as an objection to Hobbes.

> He [Bodin] says that the right of sovereignty . . . is a supreme and perpetual power limited neither by law nor by time . . . For this right of sovereignty is not supreme power, neither is it perpetual or above law . . . Indeed, an absolute and supreme power standing above all laws is called tyrannical. (Althusius 1995: 71)

To Althusius, Bodin's conception of sovereignty, as belonging to the king, is contrary to the natural order. First, the king dies, and therefore his sovereignty dies with him. Law does not die with a single person; therefore, its superiority over the king is partly attributed to its longevity. Second, the power of many is greater than the power of one. If the people choose to do so, they can overthrow the king. "Whence it happens that when he exercises tyranny, he is under the united body. When he abuses his power, he ceases to be king and public person, and become a private person. If in any way he proceeds and acts notoriously or wickedly, any one may resist him . . ." (Althusius 1995: 112). Therefore, the king cannot be sovereign if he can be overthrown.

Just as the "king represents the people not the people the king" (Althusius 1995: 73), the community serves the people and not itself. Not only can the king be overthrown, but so too can any community or association. If, as stated above, the community exists as part of the natural order so that humans can live as humans, when a community ceases to fulfill its objective, it may be overthrown.

> Also pertaining to this communication is the right of the vote in the common business and actions of managing and administering the community, and the form and manner by which the city is ruled and governed according to laws it approves and a magistrate that it constitutes with the consent of the citizens. When, on the contrary, these common rights of the community are alienated, the community ceases to exist. (Althusius 1995: 49)

If a structure exists that is not a community, but still exercises authority over people, people have the right to take positive action against it. The ability to end an association extends to collegiums as well, for

> [t]his society by its nature is transitory and can be discontinued. It need not last as long as the lifetime of a man, but can be disbanded honorably and in good faith by the mutual agreement of those who have come together, however much it may have been necessary and useful for social life on another occasion. (Althusius 1995: 33)

We see then, that the same laws that govern the collegium also govern the political, which is consistent since the political is borne out of the collegium. It is the individuals, and constituent parts, through covenant that the larger society exists. The communication of the constituent parts gives the association direction and legitimacy. But, when the association no longer serves its constituent parts, and exists only for itself, the constituent parts are free to disband.

> When it follows that the use and ownership of this right [sovereignty] belong neither to one person not to individual members, but to the members of the realm jointly. By their common consent, they are able to establish and set in order matters pertaining to it. And what they have once set in order is to be maintained and followed, unless something else pleases the common will. For as the whole body is related to the individual citizens, and can rule, restrain, and direct each member, so the people rules each citizen. (Althusius 1995: 70)

It seems that there is a just war component to his argument of disbanding an association as well. The constituent parts of an association may bring an end to an association even if it precipitates violence.

> The third cause [of just war] is the necessity for preserving liberty, privileges, rights, peace, and tranquility . . . The sixth reason is contumacy, which occurs when any prince, lord, or city has so contemptuously and repeatedly scorned the

decisions of courts that justice cannot otherwise be administered and defended. The seventh just cause of war occurs when agreements are not implemented by the other party, when he does not keep his promises, and when tyranny is practiced upon his subjects. (Althusius 1995: 88–9)

Not only does Althusius justify revolution and civil disobedience, he justifies secession, the focus of Chapter 6 in this book.

One of the estates, or one part of the realm, can abandon the remaining body to which it belonged and choose for itself a separate ruler or a new form of commonwealth when the public and manifest welfare of this entire part altogether requires it, or when fundamental law of the country are not observed by the magistrate but are obstinately and outrageously violated . . . Thus also subjects can withdraw their support from a magistrate who does not defend them when he should, and can justly have recourse to another prince and submit themselves to him. (Althusius 1995: 197–8)

We can see this develop earlier in his account of associating in that each constituent part maintains its identity with the previous association. That is, a family does not cease to be a family when it joins with other families. It would be just as ridiculous to say that a father is no longer a father when a tribe is formed as it would be to say a mayor of a city is no longer a mayor when a city joins with another to become a state. The only way secession could be disavowed is if we say that once a constituent part joins with another it ceases to have its former identity. Bound up in this conception of identity is sovereignty. A father has dominion over his children regardless of whether there is a city or nation. A city or nation may take action that affects the father's relationship with his children, such as outlawing abuse, but the father still has the ability to be a father. What Althusius maintains is that if the city or state takes illegitimate action against the family, such as forcing the family to sacrifice its first born, the father may withdraw his family from that association. This is because he maintains his sovereignty which is defined by his identity. The same is true for any constituent part and association.

This discussion of civil disobedience, revolution, and secession further shows that sovereignty lay with the individual, who through covenant communicates the means and ends of association. When there is error, or a move away from the good, the association that was the result of covenant can be brought to an end when it violates the purpose of the covenant.

All power is limited by definite boundaries and laws. No power is absolute, infinite, unbridled, arbitrary, and lawless. Every power is bound to laws, right, and equity. Likewise, every civil power that is constituted by legitimate means can be terminated and abolished. (Althusius 1995: 115)

So while there is obligation on behalf of the individual to the association, there is an obligation that runs the other way as well. Remember the individual is a constituent part of the family; the family is a constituent part of the collegium, the collegium to the city, and the city to the province. Obligation does not exist merely between the constituent part and its most direct association, that is, city to province, but rather there is an obligation from every constituent part to every association. Equally important, there is an obligation on behalf of each association that extends to each constituent part. Obligation runs in multiple directions.[10] "Symbiotic association involves something more than mere existence together. It indicates a quality of group life characterized by piety and justice, without which, Althusius believes, neither individual persons nor society can endure" (Carney 1995: xv). The importance this has for a theory of federalism is clear: the relationship between various governing levels is only legitimate if there is cooperation and communication. The sovereignty of one level cannot be violated by the other, for if it does, it violates the covenant and the system is then weakened to a point where tyranny can enter.

Althusius's theory of federalism, while not a fully developed theory of federalism, incorporates a justification for varying laws, divided sovereignty, and a focus on nonstate actors. The emphasis is not on rights but on obligation and collaboration as a means for bringing about liberty.[11] In Althusius I find a solid foundation for developing a theory of federalism as well as a theory of liberty that is distinct from the various conceptions of liberty currently available (e.g., positive, negative, republican). Federal liberty is distinct from the other variants in that it—among other things—escapes the trappings of modernity, particularly modernity's hubris. In order for federalism to function, the different subnational actors, and the national regime, must be willing to allow variance in policy. To accept variance is to accept that what is appropriate for one regime is not appropriate for all, even if they are under the same national regime. To refrain enforcing one's policy preferences on another one must maintain a certain amount of humility that modernity lacks. Modernity, specifically modern liberalism,[12] assumes that it contains the answers, and therefore cannot allow variance for then it must admit it does not have the answers.

Another distinguishing feature of federal liberty is that it reconciles the tension between obligation and rights. Whereas rights are generally recognized as one's positive claim against another, namely a right to repel another's intrusion upon oneself or upon one's autonomy, obligation implies a certain level of concern for the collective that may require one to act against one's right in order to better the community. However, as seen in Althusius, this does not require that the individual must sacrifice herself to the community. There is a reconciliation that occurs in federalism as one recognizes that one owes his or her humanity and improvement to the community, but the community recognizes that without the individual maintaining individuality the community is acting to destroy what it has set out to protect and improve: the individual.

Aristotle: Man as a Political Animal

Like any good theorist, Aristotle begins with human nature which dictates individuals must live together (*Politics* I.2). With this fact, Aristotle discusses the various levels of human association: the first being the family, the second being a village—which is a composition of families—third he gives us the *polis* which is comprised of villages.[13] For Aristotle the city falls into the class of things that exist by nature because man is a political animal. Any man that lives alone is either a beast or a god (*Politics* 1253a2, 1253a25; see also *NE*[14] 1097b10). Man is a political animal, but he and his associations are superior to other animals and associations because while a city "comes into existence for the sake of mere life, it exists for the sake of a good life" (*Politics* 1252b27). This is partly attributable to man's second characteristic: speech, which "man alone of the animals is furnished with the faculty of language" (*Politics* 1253a7).[15] Though, reading on, it is not just his language that separates him from other animals, but his ability to declare what is good and bad because humans alone have the ability to perceive, and therefore discuss, what is good and evil or just and unjust. Human associations, for Aristotle, are built around the discussion and pursuit of the good life (*Politics* 1253a7). The good life is contingent upon another characteristic unique to humans: reason (*NE* 1098a5).[16] In the *Nicomachean Ethics* Aristotle argues that "The proper function of man, then, consists in an activity of the soul in conformity with a rational principle or, at least not without it" (*NE* 1098a5).

Despite the logical progression from the individual through the various associations, Aristotle concludes that the city is prior to the individual and the family. This seems an odd conclusion, but what he seems to mean is that man's full nature cannot be realized outside of the city, and neither can the family's nor the village's; therefore, the city is essential for the existence of humans and the lower associations, for it is necessary for the individual, family, and village to be in a city to properly discharge their functions (*Politics* 1253a18). Perhaps, a human can be a human outside of the city, but it would be only in name as it is not part of its nature to exist outside of the city and a human cannot reach its *telos*[17] outside of the city.[18]

> There is therefore a natural impulse in all men towards an association of this sort . . . Man, when perfected, is the best of animals; but if he is isolated from law and justice he is the worst of all . . . The virtue of justice belongs to the city; for justice is an ordering of the political association, and the virtue of justice consists in the determination of what is just. (*Politics* 1253a25)

But more than providing a place for a human to be the best possible person he or she can be, the city allows a person to be human, for a person is inherently a political animal; therefore, needs to associate in order to be human, or to do what is natural (*NE* 1098a10–15).

Aristotle presses this point when he writes, "When great issues are at stake, we distrust our own abilities as insufficient to decide the matter and call in others to join us in our deliberations" (*NE* 1112b10). Aristotle is particular about what he means by deliberation as deliberation must be a rational discussion, "man is the source of his actions, deliberation is concerned with things attainable by human action, and actions aim at ends other than themselves" (*NE* 1112b30). His defense of deliberation incorporates the earlier argument that speech and reason are natural and peculiar to man, and joining the two together is what justifies deliberation as deliberation incorporates these two traits and aids in the pursuit of reasoned conclusions.

> Since, then, the object of choice is something within our own power which we desire as a result of deliberation, we may define choice as a deliberate desire for things that are within our power: we arrive at a decision on the basis of deliberation, and then let the deliberation guide our desire. (*NE* 1113a10)

A government would need to have a space for deliberation and public input so as to respect that natural order of things.[19]

A city is not a mere aggregation of people and associations, but it is a compound whole. (*NE* 1094a; *Politics* 1258a18, 1274b39). Aristotle's view of the city shares characteristics with the idea of subsidiarity in which

> [t]he basic idea is that each community [family, school, church, club, state, etc.] should be allowed to make its own distinctive contribution to the common good without improper interference from the governing institutions of the other communities, yet at the same time with the appropriate help or aid from the other institutions where assistance is warranted. Notably, the principle of subsidiarity within Roman Catholic thought is generally traced to Aquinas and, before him, to Aristotle. (Aroney 2007: 163)[20]

Good Citizen/Good Person

A person must fulfill different roles throughout one's life. One can be simultaneously a mother, daughter, CEO, volunteer, and citizen. However, the traits that define one as a good mother may be different than those that define a good CEO. For Aristotle this problem arises when he asks what it means to be a good citizen because,

> [t]he conclusion to which we are thus led is that the excellence of the citizen must be an excellence relative to the constitution. It follows that if there are several different kinds of constitution there cannot be a single absolute excellence of the good citizen. But the good man is a man so called in virtue of a single absolute excellence. (*Politics* 1276b16)

The city may make demands of a person that render him or her a good citizen but a bad person. The potential is that there are bad constitutions, and for one to be a good citizen, one must act in congruence with that constitution, but acting thusly may make one a bad person. But, the choice of whether to be a good person or a good citizen seems to be eliminated when there is a good constitution, as a good constitution does what is best for the individual and the community, or places demands on its citizens that are consistent with being a good person.

> [T]hose constitutions which consider the common interest are right constitutions, judged by the standard of absolute justice. Those constitutions which consider only the personal interest of the rulers are all wrong constitutions, or perversions of the right forms. Such perverted forms are despotic; whereas the city is an association of freemen. (*Politics* 1279a8)

If we place the restraint of consistency around Aristotle then we are forced to the conclusion that it is possible to be a good citizen and a good person if a person must live in a city, the existence of the city is inevitable—and prior to— the individual since people are by nature political animals (*Politics* 1278b15). Aristotle, in order to remain consistent, cannot say that one must come into a city to reach his *telos*, but the demands of the city make it impossible for him to do so. For Aristotle, there must be good cities and bad cities, or good and bad constitutions for it is "only in such a constitution that the good man and the good citizen be absolutely identified . . ." (*Politics* 1293a35). Positioning what he writes at *Politics* 1293a35 with *Politics* 1279a8 as cited above—"[s]uch perverted forms are despotic; where as the city is an association of freemen"—and the later comment that "[r]uling over freemen is a finer thing and one more connected with goodness, than ruling despotically" (*Politics* 1333b29), we are left with the possibility of being a good person and a good citizen, but it is dependent upon the constitution. A good constitution is one that allows the individual to be good in both capacities.

It is especially important to understand the relationship between the citizen and the city, since for Aristotle, politics is a contributing factor to the moral development of the individual.

> Aristotle knew and rejected a view of the city which seems to foreshadow the modern view of political society and hence the distinction between state and society. According to that view, the purpose of the city is to enable its members to exchange goods and services by protecting them against violence among themselves and from foreigners, without it being concerned at all with the moral character of its members. (Strauss 1964: 32, with reference to *Politics* 1280a25–b35 and Augustine's *De Civitate Dei* II.20)

This distinction also makes the later discussion about the similarity between the city and friendship more pertinent.

Scale

In criticism of Plato's political associations in the *Republic* and *Laws* he writes,

> [t]o handle everything well is perhaps a difficult thing. Take, for example, the number of citizens which has just been mentioned. We cannot overlook the fact that such a number will require a territory the size of Babylon or some space which is similarly unlimited in extent. It will need all that to support 5,000 people in idleness, especially when we reflect that they will be augmented by a crowd of women and attendants many times as great as themselves. It is rights to assume the most desirable conditions but not to assume anything which is plainly impossible. (*Politics* 1265a10)

But without giving a definitive number, Aristotle offers guidance when he writes in the *Nicomachean Ethics* that "Ten persons do not make a city, and when there are a hundred thousand it is no longer a city. The right number is perhaps not some specific number, but anything that lies between certain fixed limits" (*NE* 1170b30–1171a1).[21]

The concern over size links directly to the discussion on being a good person and good citizen as the proper scale is required, as seen in the discussion of Althusius, for the production of good constitutions and laws.

> Most people think that the happiness of a city depends on its being great. They may be right; but even if they are, they do not know what it is that makes a city great or small. They judge greatness in numerical terms, by the size of the population; but it is capacity, rather than size, which should properly be called the criterion . . . for a great city is not the same as a populous city . . . (*Politics* 1325b33)

The capacity to which he speaks in the cited passage is a city's ability to help an individual or association to reach its *telos*. "Cities, like other things, have a function to perform; and the city which shows the highest capacity for performing the function of a city is therefore the one which should be counted greatest" (*Politics* 1325b33). Unfortunately, the achievement of the function is not easy as it is restricted in a number of ways, one of which is size. Experience shows that it is difficult, if not impossible, for a very populous city to enjoy good government (*Politics* 1326a25). We may therefore conclude that the best city will be one which combines scale, as a city cannot be too small or too large, with the principle of goodness just mentioned (*Politics* 1326a25).

Since Aristotle cannot be pinned down to a definitive number we must turn elsewhere to supplement our understanding of what the proper scale might be. That is, our understanding of scale must be sensitive to the ends and practices rather than formulaic since governments must be sensitive to the physical and cultural characteristics of a place, characteristics that offer too many variations to allow for a simple formula to be adopted. The reader of the *Nicomachean Ethics* gains insight into the discussion of scale through its discussion of friendship. Since the discussion of the city, and its scale, is essentially a discussion about the relationship between men, we would do well to see what Aristotle says about relationships in another context to see if anything can be transferred between the two discussions. This is not just conjecture. Turning to Aristotle's discussion of friendship to shed light on his discussion of the city is a natural turn given his incorporation of the city in his discussion about the proper number of friends one ought to have (*NE* 1170b30–1171a5). But more directly, Aristotle states that

> All communities are like parts of the political community. Men combine with an eye to some advantage or to provide some of the necessities of life, and we think of the city as having initially come together and as enduring to secure the advantage of its members . . . Now, all other forms of communities aim at some partial advantage . . . But all these communities seem to be encompassed by the community that is the political community . . . Thus all communities seem to be parts of the political community, but the kind of friendship prevalent in each will be determined by the kind of community it is. (*NE* 1160a10–30)

This, along with *NE* 1161a10–1161b10, substantiates the claim that Aristotle's discussion of scale as it regards friendship provides relevant insight into the discussion of the political community and scale.

In discussing the proper number of friends, Aristotle says that one should not have too many if we are to take the view that friendship is for mutual usefulness given that one cannot give back to too many people what they are given in turn (*NE* 1170b25). The number of friends one ought to have is simply a matter of practicality at this point, a point made even more salient just a few lines later when he writes,

> It is also difficult to share the joys and sorrows of many people as intensely as if they were one's own, for it might well happen that one would have to share the joy of one friend and the grief of another all at the same time. So the right course is perhaps not to seek to have as many friends as possible, but as many as are sufficient for living together. (*NE* 1171a5–10; see also *NE* 1097b10–15)

Aristotle argues that for people to be friends, they must have consistent contact which makes living in close physical proximity to one another a requirement of friendship, otherwise, "But if the absence lasts for a long time, it apparently also causes the friendship itself to be forgotten . . . For nothing characterizes friends as much as living in each other's company" (*NE* 1157b5–10). Aside from the fact that Aristotle suggests we ought to consider friendship and political life on the same terms (*NE* 1170b20–30), it would be wise to apply the standard of friendship to the *polis* given that friendship is a social relationship in which both people act consistently with their own, and the other's, pursuit of virtue (*NE* 1157b30–35, 1171a15–20). Not to stretch the connection too far at this point, but it is important to recognize the potential import of a discussion of friendship on a discussion of politics because in political life one needs a certain recognition of another's desires and needs relative to one's own in order to create a policy which does not sacrifice one for the other. If this is the case, then a city cannot have too many people for fear of diminishing the connection between individuals that is necessary for justice. Thus, in the city, and just as in friendship, "It is natural that the element of justice increases with the closeness of friendship, since friendship and what is just exist in the same relationship and are coextensive with range" (*NE* 1160a5).

In discussing friendship even further, Aristotle writes,

> [t]o be friends with many people, in the sense of perfect friendship, is impossible, just as it is impossible to be in love with many people at the same time . . . Also, one must have some experience of the other person and have come to be familiar with him, and that is the hardest thing of all. (*NE* 1158a10–15; see also *NE* 1157b5–20, Book IX, 12)

Compare this with what he says about representative government, and the connection between friendship and political scale becomes undeniable.

> Both in order to give decisions in matters of disputed rights and to distribute the offices of government according to the merit of candidates, the citizens of a city must know one another's characters. Where this is not the case, the distribution of offices and the giving of decisions will suffer. Both are matters in which it is wrong to operate by guesswork; but that is what obviously happens where the population is too large. (*Politics* 1326b7)

Just as a person cannot have too many friends for then he will be unable to be a friend, a government cannot have too many citizens for then it will not be able to work in its citizen's best interests.

We can look also at what Aristotle has to say about the affects on individual character and behavior to get a better sense of what he considers the proper scale of government. Aristotle argues that individual character is partly shaped by external factors, such as geography, and regimes must vary as these conditions vary.[22] Aristotle acknowledges that citizens must have a natural endowment, and that a citizen's endowment is partly determined by geography and other physical conditions. Mountainous people have different characters from those who live in valleys, there are differences between people who live in cold, hot, and temperate environments, and those who live inland and those who live by the coast (*Politics* 1327b18). On this point there are obvious connections between Aristotle, Althusius, Plato, and Montesquieu. For instance, Althusius writes, "Then, as the customs of regions often express diverse interests and discernments, so persons born in these regions hold diverse patters in their customs" (Althusius 1995: 150).

As will be discussed in greater detail in the next chapter, Montesquieu's political sociology is commonly recognized to be grounded in this understanding of the individual and its relation to geography, mores, and customs.[23] For these philosophers, a regime must be familiar with the individual and what affects individual behavior in order to make good laws.[24] Plato shows just how complicated it can be to make laws that take these factors into consideration and why one must have a personal relationship with each citizen in order to make good laws.

> Because a law would never be capable of comprehending with precision for all simultaneously the best and the most just and enjoining the best, for the dissimilarities of human beings and of their actions and the fact that almost none of the human things is ever at rest do not allow any art whatsoever to declare in any case anything simple about all and over the entire time. (*Statesman* 294b)

Plato is suggesting that law, and written law in particular, is insufficient for directing humans as it tries to do something which is impossible. Since law is static, and humans are dynamic, law is contrary to human nature. For this reason, Plato suggests that the law is the second best regime and the rule of the statesman is the best, for it is under the statesman—who is someone with knowledge of what is best and can direct each person individually toward it (*Statesman* 295b)—that the ideal city will be ruled.[25] But rule by the statesman is unlikely; therefore, we should do our best to create laws that approximate statesmanship. But, if laws are to be good, as the statesman is, the people in charge of making laws must have an intimate familiarity with those they make laws for, so that they can make laws consistent with the needs and nature of those who will live under the laws. This sort of familiarity only comes when people live in close physical proximity with one another.

Scale also has an impact on how we shape our conceptions of morality.

> If there is a difference between the moralities of small-scale societies and those of societies like ours, I suggest it stems from the greater importance of interpersonal relations in the former. In these, morality is less of an end in itself but is seen more clearly as a set of orientations for establishing and maintaining the health of relationships. Morality, then, is a means to a desired, enjoyed end. In complex, large-scale societies relationships are less intense and less significant in the lives of individuals and in the structures of the societies. (Silberbauer 1991: 27)

Silberbauer's argument is consistent with Aristotle's discussion of friendship in which the relationship itself is valuable in addition to the ancillary benefits it provides the participants. The point, however, is that relationships can only generate the proper moral outlook and constraint if there is the proper scale.

Aristotle's discussion of scale can supplement contemporary discussions of federalism.

> But we may also note that cities, like all other things have definite measure of size. Any object will lose its power of performing its function if it is either excessively small or of an excessive size . . . A city composed of too few members is a city without self-sufficiency. One composed of too many will indeed be self-sufficient in the matter of material necessities but it will not be a city, since it can hardly have a constitution. (*Politics* 1326a35)

The struggle over the proper size and scope of a city, or nation, is not unique to Aristotle, and those who have been charged with creating nations have had to confront this problem. The solution, in some instances, has been the adoption of a federal structure. Ideally a federal system will allow a nation to be large enough to protect its borders and provide necessary services to its citizens while at the same time preserving the benefits of a smaller system. In the United States this discussion occurred in public when the Federalists and Anti-Federalists debated whether the Constitution ought to be ratified. But, the United States is not the only country to consider federalism as a remedy to these problems.

Aristotle enriches our understanding of politics in a number of ways, but with regard to federalism, he enriches our understanding by showing the relationship between the individual and the political realm and the importance of scale.

Alexis de Tocqueville

Tocqueville is a commentator on the American regime, but his insights into how government functions provides universal insight. With regard to federalism, Tocqueville recognizes that there needs to be a divide between the lawmaking arm of government and the administrative arm of government.

> Certain interests are common to all parts of the nation, such as the formation of general laws . . . Other interests are special to certain parts of the nation, such as, for example, the undertakings of the township. To concentrate the power to direct the first in the same place or in the same hand is to found what I shall call governmental centralization. To concentrate to direct the second in the same manner is to found what I shall name administrative centralization . . . I cannot conceive that a nation can live or above all prosper without strong governmental centralization. (*DIA*[26] 1.1.5[27])

Tocqueville is not a radical decentralist, for he recognizes the importance of a strong central government.[28] But, he also acknowledges that the application of laws must be allowed to vary as circumstances and people vary. Similar to Montesquieu's evaluation of England, Tocqueville writes of the United States, "the laws contribute more to the maintenance of the democratic republic . . . than do physical causes . . . [but] . . . mores contribute more than the laws" (*DIA* 1.2.9). Tocqueville here is stating a common refrain, man and their governments are limited in how much of nature they can control. A government and its laws must conform to the external environs and the mores of the people. Culture and history are what mores are built upon. This type of thought runs counter to modernity as modernity embraces the idea that man can be in complete control of his destiny if only he is good enough at creating institutions and laws.[29]

Tocqueville, like the others already discussed in this vein, recognized that laws must conform to the particular circumstances of the people in order for them to be just. To this end, the divide between central lawmaking and provincial administration is essential, for the effect of tyrannical laws need not be felt by the people who are insulated via the provincial administrators. A problem arises when both the lawmaking and administration becomes centralized.[30]

> If the power that directs American societies found these two means [governmental and administrative] of government at its disposal, and added the capacity and the habit of executing everything by itself to the right of the commanding everything if, after having established the general principles of government, it entered into the details of application, and after having regulated the great interests of the country it could descend to the limit of individual interests, freedom would soon be banished from the new world . . . This deserves to be thought about. If a democratic republic like that of the United States ever came to be founded in a country where the power of one alone already have established administrative centralization and made it pass into habits as into laws, I do not fear to say, in a republic like this, despotism would become more intolerable than in any of the absolute monarchies of Europe. (*DIA* 1.2.8)

Tocqueville holds out hope that this will not occur in the American regime for it has provincial administration. Thus, the capacity for tyranny does not exist in America to the same degree that it exists in the countries of Europe.

> When the central government that represents it has sovereignty ordained, it must rely for the execution of its commandment on agents who often do not depend on it, and whom it cannot direct in each instant. Municipal bodies and the administrative of counties form so many hidden shoals that delay or divide the popular will. Were the law oppressive, freedom would still find shelter in the manner in which the law was executed . . . (*DIA* 1.2.8)

He may be correct in his estimation of how this should work but Tocqueville appears a bit naïve. Tocqueville underestimates the permissiveness of these "shoals" and the pervasiveness of central government. Even at the time of his writing he admits that the shoals he puts so much faith in have become compromised. Although he does not recognize it as such at the time of his writing.

The patriotic sentiment attaching each American to his state has become less exclusive . . . Commerce goes up and down the rivers of the interior with unexampled rapidity. To the opportunities created by nature and art are added to the instability of desires, the restiveness of spirit, the love of wealth that constantly push an American out of his dwelling, putting him in communication with a great number of his fellow citizens. He travels through his country in all directions; he visits populations inhabiting it . . . At the same time that Americans mix together, they assimilate to one another, the differences in climate, origin, and institutions have put between them diminish. More and more all are brought together into a common type . . . As the industry of Americans makes progress, one sees the commercial bonds that unite all the confederated states tighten . . . (*DIA* 1.2.10)

The differences he describes as breeding distrust between people of different states, and thus tying people to their state rather than the nation earlier in 1.2.10, are overwhelmed by the drive for economic prosperity. Why he does not connect this development with the potential for centralization of administrative power goes unexplained. But even more elementary than economic prosperity is the rise of individualism. While there is much that drives economic prosperity, a singular focus on oneself allows for one to pursue nothing more than wealth. And individualism, as seen below, is a deft foe.

Individualism occurs naturally in democratic regimes. The rise of individualism is a common theme among French philosophers, as Montesquieu argued that "[i]f they are so great in number that the majority are unknown to one another, the desire to distinguish oneself redoubles because there is more hope of success . . ." Ironically, however, "Where everyone wishes to make himself noticed, no one is noticed at all." Size is the culprit. On Montesquieu's understanding of the problem, as the number of people within a society increases the pull toward individuality increases as everyone aspires to set themselves apart. The consequence is that a sense of community and common identity is lost. Moreover, one loses all identity as one fails to be recognized by others because the focus of the individual in such a society becomes the individual. In the search for identity one continually turns inwards in search of that identity, thus giving up any hope of finding it in the relationships she or he has with others. No longer does one identify as a citizen of a country, member of an organization, church, or community; but as an individual only. Montesquieu seems to anticipate many of the problems faced by those working in identity politics and the politics of recognition.

What Montesquieu attributed to size, Tocqueville attributed to equality. For Tocqueville individualism arises from equality, and from individualism arises isolation and the destruction of community.

Individualism is a sentiment, well thought out and conducive to peace, which disposes each citizen to isolate himself from the mass of those who resemble him and to retire apart with his family and his friends in such a fashion that, after having created a little society for his own use, he willingly abandons society at large to its own devices.

With the rise of individualism the sovereign state will come to replace voluntary community. The consequences of an empowered state have never been more acutely articulated than by Tocqueville.

> [T]he sovereign extends its arms about the society as a whole; it covers its surface with a network of petty regulations—complicated, minute, and uniform—through which even the most original minds and the most vigorous souls know not how to make their way past the crowd and emerge into the light of day . . . [the sovereign power] . . . softens [wills], bends them, and directs them; rarely does it force one to act, but it constantly opposes itself to one's acting on one's own . . . it reduces every nation to nothing but a herd of timid and industrious animals, of which the government is the shepherd. (*DIA* 2.4.6)

This growth of the sovereign state is contrasted with a life in which the state is not the primary form of association and where a reliance on community is preferred to a reliance on the government.

> One of the happiest consequences of the absence of government is the development of individual strength that inevitably follows from it. Each man learns to think, to act by himself, without counting on the support of an outside force—which, however vigilant one supposes it to be, can never answer all social needs. Man, thus accustomed to seek his well-being solely through his own efforts, raises himself in his opinion as he does in the opinion of others; his soul becomes larger and stronger at the same time. (*DIA* 1.4.10)

Tocqueville has quite a bit to say on this problem, as it is provincial government and community associations that he considers vital for the preservation of liberty. But, with the rise of individualism which inevitably gives rise to governmental authority, the people seem willing to give up their community and perhaps are unaware of what is happening.

> Each of them, withdrawn apart, is a virtual stranger, unaware of the fate of the others: his children and his particular friends form for him the entirety of the human race; as for his fellow citizens, he is beside them but he sees them not; he touches them and senses them not; he exists only in himself and for himself alone, and, if he still has a family, one could say at least that he no longer has a fatherland . . . Over these is elevated an immense, tutelary power, which takes sole charge of assuring their enjoyment and of watching over their fate. It is absolute, attentive to detail, regular, provident, and gentle. It would resemble the paternal

power if, like that power, it had as its object to prepare men for man hood, but it seeks, to the contrary, to keep them irrevocably fixed in childhood; it love the fact that the citizens enjoy themselves provided that they dream solely of their own enjoyment. It works willingly for their happiness, but it wishes to be the only agent and the sole arbiter of that happiness. It provides for their security, foresees and supplies their needs, guides them in the principal affairs, directs their industry regulates their testaments, divides their inheritances . . . In this fashion, every day, it renders the employment of free will less useful and more rare; it confines the action of the will within a smaller space, and bit by bit it steals from each citizen the use of that which is his own. (*DIA* 1.4.13)

Tocqueville recognized that life could not be compartmentalized and that political society could not remain sequestered from civil society (Rahe 2009: 158). The consequence would be that people would come to be dependent upon government and abandon civil society as the strength of the government grew. This is what he meant by "soft despotism" as people would be less likely to fight for themselves and against government encroachment (Rahe 2009: 165). Tocqueville astutely recognizes that certain factors will lead to the destruction of the provincial regimes that, he argued, were invaluable for preventing a slide into tyranny and despotism; but, oddly, he does not seem to think that it will happen in America.

The common recourse to the travails of individualism is forced community recognition, but Tocqueville shows that the state-centered response to this problem only exacerbates it and that we should recognize—with some help from Montesquieu—that size and forced community is part of the problem. There should be a (re)focus on the community, but it cannot be artificial, and the system which allows for it to occur naturally is fragile.

The importance of provincial institutions, for the purpose of administering laws, is undeniable for Tocqueville. While it has been discussed above why administration needs to be decentralized, it is useful to look again at why it should be done by provincial institutions specifically in a representative system of government.

I believe provincial institutions useful to all peoples; but none seems to me to have a more real need of these institutions than one whose social state is democratic . . . A democracy without provincial institutions possesses no guarantee against such evils [despotism] . . . Those who fear license and those who dread absolute power should therefore equally desire the gradual development of provincial freedoms. I am convinced, furthermore, that no nations are more at risk of falling under the yoke of administrative centralization than those whose social state is democratic. The permanent tendency of these nations is to concentrate all governmental power in the hands of the sole power that directly represents the people, because beyond the people one perceives no more than equal individuals confused with the general mass. (*DIA* 1.1.5)

Again we see an identity crisis that contributes to the rise of individualism. This crisis can be avoided if the provincial governments are maintained, most specifically the New England Town Hall meeting of which he is so fond.

> [O]ne sees reign a form of political life that is active, entirely democratic, and republican . . . Within the township in New England, the law of representation is not admitted. As in Athens, it is in the public square and within the bosom of the general assembly of citizens that matters which touch the interest of all are dealt with by all . . .

For Tocqueville representation occurs with direct participation, which can only occur at the local level. Moreover, the type of governing that occurs in the township is the most natural to man, as the township is "the only association which is so much in accord with nature that everywhere men are gathered, the township takes form by itself." Associating is natural to man, and when he associates he finds that there is sometimes need for the making of rules and cooperation. In the township this is voluntary, and citizens have a direct role in the government. Because of its size, method of representation, and voluntary nature, the township preserves the proper balance between individual and community for, "it is in the township that the strength of the people resides." This is not to say that people are by themselves feeble, but when they come together in a noncoercive environment to deliberate and govern themselves, the power of the people is truly realized and is increased more than it can be on its own. While Tocqueville does not adopt the Aristotelian language, it is clear that he sees man as a social creature as it is necessary for him to associate to survive and prosper.

In order to prosper, individuals must exist in small-scale communities that help develop their character, and townships provide an educative function. It is because they are communities of the proper scale that they are able to serve that function.

> Communal institutions are for liberty what primary schools are for science; they place it within reach of the people; they make the people taste its peaceful employ and habituate them to its use. Without communal institutions a nation is able to give itself a free government, but it lacks the spirit of liberty . . . in this restricted sphere, which lies within his reach, he attempts to govern society . . . he is penetrated by the spirit, he gets a taste for order, he comprehends the harmony of powers, and in the end he gathers together clear and practical ideas with regard to the nature of his duties as well as the extent of his rights. (*DIA* 1.1.5)

The identity crisis that he warns of in democratic governments does not exist in the township because of the direct involvement by the people and the lessons they learn as a result.

> [W]hen citizens are forced to occupy themselves with public affairs, they are drawn of necessity out of the milieu of individual interests and, from time to

time, they are wrenched away from looking at themselves . . . [and he sees] . . . that he is not as independent of those whom he resembles as he at first imagined . . . [and thus sees] . . . the value of public good will . . .

For Tocqueville, man began going to government only for the things he had to have and could not provide on his own. But, as power became more centralized man went to the government more often thus reinforcing the centralizing tendency. As a result, the intermediary institutions disappeared—such as town hall meetings and voluntary associations[31]—that tempered government power. But the soft despotism set in, and people cared no longer for active participation and the virtues that entailed. Thus, government was able to involve itself in more private interests than ever before which further enfeebled the citizens and attached them even more strongly to the government.

Here I will express a thought which will recall what I said elsewhere with regard to communal liberty: there is no country in which associations are more necessary to prevent the despotism of parties or the arbitrary rule of the prince than those where the social condition is democratic . . . if individuals are unable by artifice and on the spur of the moment to create something which resembles them, I no longer perceive a dike of any sort against tyranny, and a great people may be oppressed with impunity by a handful of the factious or by a single man.

Tocqueville adds a layer to the Althusian and Aristotelian account of federalism. Althusius and Aristotle both speak about the need of a healthy civil and political life, the sanctity of the individual, the need for social life to fulfill the individual's ends, and scale; but from Tocqueville we can draw a more exacting account of how all these themes intertwine. Provincial government is necessary for people to be engaged and energized in political matters, and provincial government allows the people a check on the government to keep it from creeping into areas it does not belong. Furthermore, provincial government allows people to organize and govern through means other than the government. The challenge is to protect provincial governments. Tocqueville assumed there was some built-in mechanism that would protect them, though he identified some of what would come to undermine those mechanisms without attributing them to the downfall of the provincial governments. What Tocqueville teaches is not just the need for provincial government, but that provincial governments must be properly equipped to defend themselves against the forces of centralization.

Another unifying thread between these three thinkers is the commitment to nature. Each of the three draws on what he considers man's natural state and condition. In doing so each recognizes that positive government action is limited in what it can accomplish. There is an inherent humility in their commitment to decentralized government. This formulation perhaps seems alien to an audience that is accustomed to government intervention. Whether it is health care, American college football, or the prevention of financial collapse; it is positive government action that is sought after to provide whatever ails us. The assumption we make when we turn to the government to make laws and implement regulations is that it can provide better answers than we can on our own. And when we go to the national government, we assume that it can provide better answers than our local governments are capable of providing. This is the modern turn. We do not recognize that some things are out of government's control, and when it is proper for things to be brought under government control, it ought to be done at the most local level, for variation in conditions demand such a response. Positive government action is most often uniform; this is an inevitable extension of the modern turn. Therefore, in developing a theory of federalism, modernity must be critically evaluated.

Modernity

A commanding and critical appraisal of modern political man is given by Peter Augustine Lawler.

> The autonomous self cannot help but be proud. His pride, oriented in the direction of unprecedented political reform, surpasses that of any aristocrat. This proud tyrant readily or ideologically comes to believe that he can remake the world as he pleases. (Lawler 1999: 36)

For Lawler, modernity is the rational attempt to eradicate the mystery of being and human misery is rooted in material deprivation (Lawler 1999: 109). The elimination of mystery and the institution of predictability is what we see in thinkers such as Alexander Hamilton[32] and Jean-Jacques Rousseau.

> According to Rousseau, through the foundation of society, natural inequality is replaced by conventional equality; the social contract which creates society is the basis of morality, of moral freedom or autonomy; but the practice of moral virtue, the fulfillment of our duties to our fellow men is the one thing needful . . . But it cannot be a duty to respect that natural inequality, for morality means autonomy, i.e. not to bow to any law which a man has not imposed upon himself . . . In such a society, which is rational precisely because it is not natural . . . [natural inequalities] will gradually disappear since, as one can hope, the acquired faculties can also become inherited, to say nothing of human measures which may have to be taken during the transition period in which coercion cannot yet be dispensed with . . . For Aristotle, natural inequality is a sufficient justification for the non-egalitarian character of the city and is as it were part of the proof that the city is the natural association *par excellence*. (Strauss 1964: 40–1)

What Aristotle, Althusius, and Tocqueville recognize, and Rousseau and other moderns do not, is that man is the proper measure of those things that apply to man, thus reinforcing the importance of scale.

But, this is not to say that man is the final arbiter of the good, or that man is capable of defining for himself what is natural or that he has the ability to construct reality in his own image. Part of what makes humans what they are is their relationship to, and dependency upon, their external environment. So while I draw on Locke extensively in developing certain aspects of my view of federalism, Lawler is accurate in characterizing Locke as a modern when he writes,

> Everything of value, including knowledge, human beings have made for themselves. Locke's very comprehensive labor theory of value . . . is really a doctrine of free or historical self-creation in opposition to nature. And Locke presents no limits that can be determined in advance to such self-creation. The only guidance nature gives to human beings is negative: They should do everything they can to overcome it. (Lawler 1999: 7)[33]

In essence, modernity entails a diminished sense of limits.

The point of modern thought is to recognize that man is separate from nature and that in order to be free man must free himself from nature.

> What is peculiar to modern thought is not this conclusion by itself but the consequent resolve to liberate man from that enslavement by his own sustained effort. This resolve finds its telling expression in the demand for the "conquest" of nature: nature is understood and treated as an enemy who must be subjugated. (Strauss 1964: 42)

The state indeed has limits, although this fact is not recognized by modernity, yet it is acknowledged in its most accurate form in Plato's *Republic*.

> The *Republic* then indeed makes clear what justice is. As Cicero has observed, the Republic does not bring to light the best possible regime but rather the nature of political things—the nature of the city. Socrates makes clear in the *Republic* of what character the city would have to be in order to satisfy the highest need of man. By letting us see that the city constructed in accordance with this requirement is not possible, he lets us see the essential limits, the nature, of the city. (Strauss 1964: 138)

Recall Tocqueville's critique of individualism and one will gain insight into my critique of modernity. A. J. Conyers writes,

> The latitude given to the individuals is increased with respect to the social connections that once demanded a certain loyalty and discipline of them, but whose authority is now diminished. All belong to the state, and to that extent they belong less to the church, the guild, the regional culture, and the family. (Conyers 2008: 9)

But Conyers's observation goes beyond Tocqueville and touches on my notion of federal liberty in that it requires not just protection of individual rights, but an understanding of obligation. Tocqueville and Conyers understood what Althusius and Aristotle understood, the individual and the community are inseparable as being social is a fundamental part of being human. To paraphrase Althusius, the two have a symbiotic relationship. This is why Daniel Elazar's introduction to *Politica* can be read as a critique of modern federalism.

> It remained for the Americans to invent modern federalism on the basis of individualism and thus reintroduce the idea of the state as a political association rather than a reified entity, an artifact that is assumed to have an existence independent of the people who constitute it. (Elazar 1995: xxxviii)

My estimation of the American regime is quite different from Elazar's as I think it falls into the category that Elazar says it escapes from, but I do agree with his estimation of the modern state in that it is built upon the foundation of individualism and is independent of the people who constitute it. In assessing why Althusius remained outside the canon for so long, Elazar speculates it is because of the formulation of the modern state, to which Althusius runs counter.

> They [Althusian ideas] remained a peripheral event to students of modern federalism since modern federalism was so strongly connected with the principle of individualism that there was no interest in considering the Althusian effort to deal with the problems of family, occupation, and community along with individual rights in establishing political order. (Elazar 1995: xxxix)

A federal system cannot be implemented into a state that is grounded in modernity as such a state lacks the humility to allow constituent parts to act on their own. Federalism entails a certain amount of experimentation and autonomous action that cannot be allowed by modernity as modernity is too certain of its solutions to allow for trial and error. At the heart of modernity is the thought that we, humans, have the answers—or at least the capacity—for answers. Once an answer has been achieved, it must be the right answer and the right answer must then be adopted by all for otherwise it would not be right. Thus, federalism rightly understood requires a return to pre-modern modes of thinking which means we must humble ourselves. Federalism allows us to create a regime consistent with liberalism, if not entirely liberal, without the trappings of modernity.[34] Federal-liberalism is distinct from other strands of liberalism as it embraces the community and individual in a non-contradictory way and incorporates humility into its understanding of proper government action.[35]

Deliberative Democracy

What I find missing in contemporary treatments of liberalism and federalism, I also find missing in discussions of deliberative democracy. Humility is implied by most deliberative democratic theorists but never discussed except when giving a passing reference to John Stuart Mill.[36] Modern deliberative democrats have then, because they have not taken humility seriously, fallen into a modernist trap which is inimical to their enterprise. By introducing humility into a discussion of deliberative democracy, federalism can also be introduced as a way to make deliberative democracy practical.

In what follows, I will discuss the similarities between deliberative democracy and federalism in an effort to show that federalism produces outcomes similar to deliberative democracy without opening itself to the same criticisms deliberative democracy is open to. But, this is not to say that my view of federalism and deliberative democracy are the same thing, only that there is a convergence between the two theories. Deliberative democracy is used as a rhetorical device, for lack of a better term, in order to relate to the reader already versed in democratic theory, my theory of federalism. Because I seek to maximize deliberation, of the sort that some deliberative democratic theorists seek to maximize, it is convenient to speak of federalism and deliberative democracy together. The goal of deliberative democracy, which is to create an environment in which citizens engage in a rational dialogue to influence government policy, is one that is shared by my conception of federalism. My aim is not to create a deliberative democracy proper, but merely to show that federalism can approximate—or possibly mimic—the positive attributes of deliberative democracy. The outcome of my federal theory and institutional design only converges with deliberative democracy.

A discussion of deliberative democracy at this point may seem like another odd turn in developing a theory of federalism, but we see in Aristotle an essential starting point for deliberation and a justification for federalism to be discussed in conjunction within a deliberative framework. Those who partake in deliberation must have a shared common end, and come to recognize the competing groups as having a common end.

> We deliberate not about ends but about the means to attain ends: no physician deliberates whether he should cure, no orator whether he should be convincing, no statesman whether he should establish law and order, nor does any expert deliberate about the end of his profession. We take the end for granted, and then consider what manner and by what means it can be realized. (*NE* 1112b10–15)

It may be difficult to see a shared common end in the Israeli-Palestinian debate or in the conflict between the North and the South that precipitated the U.S. Civil War, but if there were a deliberative structure in place in which ends could be expressed independent of the means each side saw as necessary in producing the ends, then the shared common end would be easier to realize. Thus, deliberation about ends must come prior to policy formulation. Policy deliberation—which can be called means deliberation—should only be pursued after ends deliberation.

For Aristotle, the proper end exists whether it is recognized or not, and is independent of human agency; however, the attainment of the end is dependent on human agency. The end, for Aristotle, must be a natural condition of a given being and the means must be a natural function of that condition. The natural condition (social) of man is realized through the natural function (language, reason) of man. Man can still associate without reason, just as surely as one can blabber on incoherently, but that is not being social in the humanistic sense if we take the highest form of sociability to be the only form of human sociability—

> The proper function of man, then, consists in an activity of the soul in conformity with a rational principle or, at least, not without it. In speaking of the proper function of a given individual we mean that it is the same in kind as the function of an individual who sets high standards for himself . . . the full attainment of excellence must be added to the mere function. (*NE* 1098a5–10)

—and to reason without language would be to reason in isolation which is inherently inhuman; therefore, one cannot reason fully in isolation. The use of language and reason can lead to an understanding and attainment of the proper end as it brings man together socially in his most humane capacity.

The means by which the proper end is pursued must be sensitive to the condition in which each individual resides. A nation may agree on the end it wants, but disagree about the means by which that end can be realized. The adoption of a uniform set of means can inhibit the pursuit of the proper end if the conditions of a particular region or area are not conducive to the adoption and implementation of a particular policy. Federalism allows for each governing unit to adopt a means most appropriate for it to pursue the proper ends. Federalism allows for variation in means adoption in a way that does not inhibit each governing unit's ability to decide for itself the best means. Federalism provides a framework in which differences of means can be deliberated at the national and subnational levels without the risk of domination.

Since some readers may be less familiar with deliberative democracy, I will provide a simple definition before moving on to more sophisticated concerns. "Broadly defined, deliberative democracy refers to the idea that legitimate lawmaking issues from the public deliberation of citizens" (Macedo 1999: iv). Another general definition is proposed by Joshua Cohen, "By a deliberative democracy I shall mean, roughly, an association whose affairs are governed by the public deliberation of its members" (Cohen 1997: 67). Deliberative democracy refers to a theory of democracy in which the citizens deliberate over the issues, and their deliberation is what determines public policy. Deliberation forces citizens to formulate arguments for their position that are better reasoned than they would otherwise need to be if they were simply asked to vote. Moreover, by forcing citizens—some of whom presumably hold competing views—to engage in a dialogue more legitimacy is bestowed upon these decisions since each citizen will have voiced his or her argument which means they have input. Most importantly, from a legitimacy standpoint, no action is taken until the citizens have come to an understanding of what policy is in the best interest of the community. This forces citizens to come to a reasoned agreement. "When citizens or their representatives disagree morally, they should 'continue to reason together to reach mutually acceptable decisions'" (Wertheimer 1999: 171). This is substantially different from the practice of politics in which pork barrel and vote swaps are the norm.

> If people affected each other only by tripping over each other's feet, or by dumping their garbage into one another's backyards, a social choice mechanism might cope. But the task of politics is not only to eliminate inefficiency, but also to create justice . . . This suggests that principles of the forum must differ from those of the market. A long-standing tradition from the Greek *polis* onwards suggest that politics must be an open and public activity, as distinct from the isolated and private expression of preferences that occurs in buying and selling. (Elster 1997: 10)

When Stephen Macedo asks, "What can deliberative democracy do for us?" he replies by saying that deliberative democracy, "should help promote the legitimacy of collective decisions" and "promote mutually respectful decision-making" (Macedo 1999: 9–10). While he supplies other reasons to pursue deliberative democracy, these two seem to be the most important as they are the ones to which most attention is given.

The first purpose is grounded in Aristotle's view of human nature.

> Aristotelian views, for example, endorse the claim that the exercise of the deliberative capacities is a fundamental component of the good life, and conclude that a political association ought to be organized to encourage the realization of those capacities by its members. (Cohen 1997: 80)

Aristotle's observations have been repeated by more recent observers, for it was Hannah Arendt who wrote, "neither exclusively because of duty nor, and even less, to serve their own interests but most of all because they enjoyed the discussions, the deliberations, and the making of decisions" (as quoted by Elster 1997: 24). Because deliberation is inherently natural, it is no surprise that proponents of deliberative democracy push the argument further and say, "laws that are adopted after mutual consideration of conflicting moral claims are more likely to be legitimate than those enacted after only strategic calculation of the relative strength of competing political interests" (Gutmann and Thompson 1999: 247).

The second purpose is more of an empirical claim. There is support for the claim that decisions derived from the deliberative process will be mutually respectful.

Since chapters 4–7 of this book will provide a more detailed discussion of this point and how federalism is able to make this possible, I will save the discussion.

Federalism offers a remedy for some of the common criticisms of deliberative democracy lobbed from its liberal critics. For instance, "[o]ne difficulty is that public reason often allows more than one reasonable answer to any particular question" (Rawls 1999: 114). Federalism is designed to accommodate multiple reasonable answers to questions, particularly in the application of the answers to specific circumstances. Another criticism is that there is no way to "specify when a question is successfully resolved by public reason" (Rawls 1997: 114). The job of governing is never done, but an issue is resolved, at least temporarily, when the law is passed. What is revealed in Rawls's latter criticism of deliberative democracy is his adherence to the modern attachment to the capacity of humans to permanently resolve their problems. Federalism acknowledges the need for constant revision as humans and conditions are in constant motion, so those things which seek to govern their behavior must remain in constant motion as well. Moreover, we allow ourselves to improve policy by being open and adaptable. The moment we assume that our problems are solved and there is no need to pursue the matter further— that is, once we realize Rawls's goal—we put a suffocating restriction around human action and choice.

Cass Sunstein (1999) argues that people can know that something is true without knowing why it is true. Also, there is no need for people to have a full account of why something is true, have fully theorized judgments, or operate at a high level of abstraction. Since deliberative democracy, according to Sunstein, requires people to give reasoned accounts of their position and that consensus can be formed through competing reasoned accounts, which also means that participants must be open to persuasion through reason, Sunstein's empirical evidence shows that it is unlikely people will act as deliberative democracy needs them to.

Iris Marion Young argues that reasoned responses will naturally arise because "[p]olitical actors should promote their own interests in such a process, but must also be answerable to others to justify their proposals. This means that actors must be prepared to take the interests of others into account" (Young 1997: 400). Young's argument rests, partly, on Kant's observation that when one argues one must "think from the standpoint of everyone else" (Kant 1987: 160). Young, following Kant, provides a refutation of Sunstein. If people are to be successful in a deliberative environment, which means they are to be persuasive, they must become good at formulating arguments, which means they must develop a reasoned account of their position which takes into account the strongest arguments of the other position. This is a more realistic assessment of how people argue as it still allows for individuals to be self-interested actors.

Also, Young's argument rests upon the idea that people, for whatever reason, will not simply come out and say, "I want this just because" or "This is what is good for me which is the only reason why I want it." When engaging in a public debate, people will try to craft arguments that will appeal to others, and in the process seek to develop some sort of theory for their ideas, or at least ground their ideas in some sort of overarching theory of the good. Of course, this does have the potential of turning into ideological banter, but in a well-designed environment it can move beyond that sort of small-minded discourse. Young continues,

> [i]f differently positioned citizens engage in public discussion with the aim of solving problems with a spirit of openness and mutual accountability, then these conditions are sufficient for transformative deliberation . . . their stance of openness and mutual accountability requires them to attend to their particular differences in order to understand the situation and perspective of others . . . Plurality perspectives motivates claimants to express their proposals as appeals to justice rather than expressions of mere self-interest or preference . . . Confrontation with different perspectives, interests, and cultural meanings teaches individuals the partiality of their own, and reveals to them their own experience as perspectival . . . Expressing, questioning, and challenging differently situated knowledge adds to social knowledge. (Young 1997: 402–3)

While these visions of deliberation may seem naïve, or even utopian, the fact remains that dialogue does decrease polarization and increase the likelihood of achieving a better understanding of competing interests. If deliberation is not encouraged, and politics is simply acting on a will to dominate, then the potential for resolution and the achievement of a higher good is terminated.

Federalism does not succumb to what might be perceived as naiveté and can still foster deliberation. For instance, if a national government wants to see a law adopted at the subnational level, and consent from subnational governing units is required, then there will have to be deliberation between the national and subnational levels. The only way in which the subnational governing units will cooperate is if they are persuaded. Of course there is the possibility of coercion and backroom negotiations that work against the public good, but, by following the outline I provide in chapters 4–6, these things can be avoided.

According to Elster's reading of Habermas, "[t]he core of the theory, then, is that rather than aggregating or filtering preferences, the political system should be set up with a view to changing them by public debate and confrontation" (Elster 1997: 10). My view of the deliberative process, as incorporated into the federal design outlined in chapters 4–6 is less ambitious, in that I expect people to engage in debate, but do not require them to be reasoned in their discussion. While such reasoned dialogue is sought after and anticipated by my federal system as the mechanisms I outline will produce those affects, my system does not require a reasoned dialogue—as it is often construed to be altruistic dialogue or dialogue devoid of private interest. Within a properly constructed federal system there are accountability checks at each turn that force deliberation among policymakers and between citizens and policymakers. But, if deliberation fails to actualize, these checks will still be able to thwart majority tyranny, preserve the virtues of small-scale societies, and prevent the centralizing and homogenizing tendency of large-scale governments. Thus, the system takes into consideration that the ideal may not be achieved, and prepares for failure in such a way that the private and public good can still be approximated successfully.

Deliberative democrats seem to ignore other practical concerns.

> Voting en masse is no substitute for deliberating in forums that permit representatives to challenge and respond to the views expressed by citizens and allow citizens to engage with representatives and with one another . . . But while voting cannot substitute for deliberation, it is also true that deliberation cannot substitute for voting . . . (Gutmann and Thompson 1996: 142)

This observation brings to light a valid criticism of deliberative democracy: There is no proposed system that would allow deliberative democracy to be implemented on a large scale. "Despite the vast outpouring of work . . . there is little instruction for the neophyte on just how such a theory work on the ground" (Hardin 1999: 112). This is not true, however, of my federal design. In chapters 4–6 I outline how nullification, veto, and secession can be used to create the sort of environment necessary for producing the positive effects deliberative democracy seeks. Those chapters do not stop at presenting the ideas, but they show how they can be put into practice and incorporate empirical studies to show they can work to produce the desired effects.

Critics of deliberative democracy who oppose it on the grounds that it is unworkable are working under the paradigm that the scale at which governments currently operate is the only scale available. We may effectively shrink the size of government by enhancing federalism. Creating smaller, more localized governing units allow for a workable model of direct democracy—with direct democracy being a vital component of deliberative democracy.

> Direct democracy can work, but it must be moderated and of the proper scale. For instance, the Quaker and New England communities work because the communities are small and because the government is not the primary focus. Direct democracy can become burdensome when everything that needs to be done is requested to be done by the government, when special interest groups co-opt the system, and when the people involved are not part of a community but merely citizens under the state. (Sale 1980: 40)

Because the scale is smaller, people have greater contact with fellow citizens, policymakers are more within reach and access to methods of participation is made easier. Participation is self-reinforcing as well. The more people participate, and see the effect of their participation, the more likely they are to continue participating. Moreover, participation serves an educative function in that people learn more about how to participate effectively and become more informed about policy the more they participate. Furthermore, direct democracy gives people a greater sense of fulfillment. But, direct democracy—and thus deliberative democracy—can only be realized when government operates on a small scale.

> [T]here has been an expansion of representative democracy and direct democracy at the sub-national levels of government. Access is easiest when government is within practical reach of the citizenry. Furthermore, people participate because they feel a sense of belonging to a community, which creates a public spiritedness that transcends narrow self-interest. From this perspective, institutions are held accountable by public sentiment and the direct participation of concerned citizens, rather than by market competition. Public participation is both a privilege and an obligation of citizenship, but only a small and immediate community can act in such a public-spirited and active manner. Institutions must be decentralized to the level at which a meaningful participation can be sustained. (Ansell and Gingrich 2003: 140)

Federalism should be seen as, and can become, a method by which deliberative settings can be created because federalism localizes decision making.

In addition to the well-worn benefits of federalism, the ability for a federal structure to foster a deliberative environment that produces psychological and practical benefits should be recognized. It is in this context that federalism is discussed throughout this book. I argue that because of its ability to create a deliberative environment it is better able to reconcile ethnic and cultural tensions, produce policy-consensus, maximize the legitimacy of government action, and place proper limits around government authority. But before we can move into a discussion of how to make federalism work to achieve these goals, the theory of federalism must be flushed out more fully.

Conclusion

Modern liberalism is one of the reasons interest in the theoretical development of federalism has dropped off. Modern liberalism searches for universals, and the assumption is, if something is true in one place then it is true in all places. By extension then, federalism can be seen as a threat to the liberal premise of universal justice since it authorizes policy variation across constituent parts. However, when combined with an ancient understanding of virtue we can alleviate modern liberalism's concern about federalism being an instrument for relativism. This is the objective of the next chapter.

The idea is to develop a theory of federalism that can rectify tensions between ancient virtue and liberal values, in some sense it may be conceived as liberalism independent of modernity. To do this one must emphasize scale, motion as being the natural state of man and his environment, and arguing against the liberal critics of federalism who have discounted its value due to their inability to separate it from relativism.

Notes

1. "The Federalists, Tocqueville, Montesquieu, and Mill all make the best of the big, best of the small argument for federalism . . ." (Norman 2006: 84). In supposing to develop a theory of federalism, Norman goes on to write, "Federalism promises to combine the democratic advantages of small republican communities with the military and economic advantages of imperial powers, while avoiding the worst defects of either" (Norman 2006: 84). This is insufficient grounds for advocating federalism as it only rests on con-sequentialist grounds. That is fine for purely empirical studies seeking to find out which regime is best in terms of providing services and benefits, but what is needed now is a more sophisticated justification of federalism that builds on a theory and not predictions of its advantages.

2. The idea of covenant did not end with Althusius. The tradition was carried through to David Hume.

   > Justice, therefore, is not, for Hume, a product of rational analysis but rather derives from tradition, is based on the invention or artifice of humans in particular social contexts, and serves the purposes of the community. The basis of the artifice for developing a particular notion of justice is not a conscious contract among people but is the deeper level of agreement that can better be called convention or covenant. (McCoy and Baker 1991: 93)

3. Althusius follows Aquinas on this point who also wrote of various forms of communities as comprising the state. Aquinas adopted

   > Aristotle's political thought to a very different social context and intellectual milieu in which Aquinas lived and worked. And it was this great plurality of communities that later jurists, such as Johannes Althusius took for granted when constructing the first recognizably 'modern' theories of federalism. Accordingly . . . the basic conceptual apparatus for a theory of federalism was at least latent within Aquinas's legal and political thought . . . (Aroney 2007: 165–6)

4. "In modern terms, his politics is derived from the concept of the social. It is a sort of sociology, even economy (in the Aristotelian sense of the term). Its objective is to study all groups, natural and social, from the standpoint of a general physiological community, allowing the possibility to identify the primary properties and essential laws of its association. Its goal is the conservation of social life, which means that it is no longer only a result or consequence of the state, but also concerns all groups participating in this social life" (Benoist 2000: 30–1).

5. The sociability of man is also reflected in subsidiarity.

   > It assumes that the basic aim of societal structures . . . is to promote human dignity and, hence, genuine freedom. It views the human person not as an instrument, but as an end-in-himself. At the same time, persons are irreducibly social and realize their most authentic humanity is only in community with others. (Duncan 2006: 68)

6. In response to the individualist premises of modern liberalism, "Catholic social teaching reminds us that the ultimate objective of subsidiarity is not an individual's achievement of autonomy for autonomy's sake, but the facilitation of authentic human flourishing" (Vischer 2007: 187).

7. While an individual may reach her *telos* in a group, the group is not prior to the individual and cannot exist without the individual in the same way that the individual can exist without the group, albeit to a lesser standard than had she been part of a group.

8. Those who fail to recognize the influence of different group affiliations on one's identity,

> fail to recognize that each of us is born into a community with a given history, set of traditions, and meaning. The particular relations in this community give texture to our social affiliations, and in particular condition the value frameworks within which we develop our ability to make particular decisions, including decisions to change some of the community's practices or to leave the community. (Young 2000a: 150)

Althusian identity has similarities to the cosmopolitan version as well. "Cosmopolitanism is more wary of traditional enclosures and favours voluntary affiliations. Cosmopolitanism promotes multiple identities, emphasizes the dynamic and changing character of many groups, and is responsive to the potential for creating new cultural combinations" (Hollinger 1995: 3).

9. This does not mean an individual without a community becomes some new species, but that person is denying what it is to be human and is not acting in accord with human nature. The person would, in a sense, become alienated from himself.

10. "In federal theology this dynamic element is affirmed by viewing the creation of the world and humanity, not as complete, but as developing toward ever greater fulfillment within the unfolding of economies of the covenant of God. God's covenant is not a static order but a pattern of changing relations in the world toward greater justice and love. Both humanity and history are understood developmentally, as moving toward fulfillment, and humans are understood as social covenantally shaped and committed. The mix of good and evil in history and the compound of original goodness and fallen sinfulness in human nature eliminates the possibility of an easy optimism or a notion of automatic progress with reference to the future" (McCoy and Baker 1991: 14).

11. This is similar to Iris Marion Young's analysis of Iroquois Federalism. "What federalism meant to the Iroquois, then, was an assumption of self-determination for the member nations at the same time as a commitment to procedural unity with the other five nations and the willingness to have any issue considered for federal decision making" (Young 2000b: 241).

12. Take the unrealistic, yet proposed as realistic, view of modern liberalism expressed by Kant as but one illustration of modernity's hubris. "Any action is right if it can coexist with everyone's freedom in accordance with a universal law, or if, on its maxim, the freedom of choice of each can coexist with everyone's freedom in accordance with a universal law" (Kant 1993: 24). In putting this forth as a workable model Kant ignores the fact that such a universal law is impossible to achieve as there can never be knowledge of everyone's freedom and what that entails. Kant's model does not even provoke a useful framework as it requires us to forget what is true of human nature and force a uniform vision of the good over human conduct.

13. Like Aquinas's view of subsidiarity, "This means that political communities consist of parts that in some respects have an operation independent of the whole community, while in other respects participate in the operation of the whole" (Aroney 2007: 176).

14. *NE* refers to *Nicomachean Ethics*.

15. "Aristotle goes to the end of this road by asserting that the political association is by nature and that man is by nature political because he is the being characterized by speech or reason and thus capable of the more perfect, the most intimate union with his fellows which is possible: the union in pure thought" (Strauss 1964: 17, referencing *Politics* 1253a1–18, 1281a2–4).

16. Note the similarities between what Aristotle and Aquinas had to say.

    It is natural to man that he live in partnership with many . . . It is therefore necessary, if man is to live in an association, that one should be helped by another, and that different people should be occupied in discovering different things through reason. (On Princely Government I.1)

17. "For, as Aristotle insisted, humanity is by nature a political animal, an animal whose end is fulfilled only in the *polis*" (Aroney 2007: 176).

18. "Understood strictly within this context, Aquinas affirms with Aristotle that political science considers the ultimate end of human life. But Aquinas is careful to point out that 'the ultimate end of the whole universe is considered theology, which is the most important without qualification. Absolutely speaking, says Aquinas, our highest good is in God" (Aroney 2007: 170–1).

19. "Aquinas derives from Aristotle the proposition that 'all should have some share in the government', for this is conducive to peace among the people and thus all will love and defend the constitution" (Aroney 2007: 213–14).

20. In Encyclical letter *Quadragesimo Anno* par. 79 (1931), Pope Pius XI writes of subsidiarity,

    Just as it is gravely wrong to take from individuals what they can accomplish by their own initiative and industry and give it to the community, so also it is an injustice and at the same time a grave evil and disturbance of right order to assign to a greater and higher association what lesser and subordinate organizations can do. For every social activity ought of its very nature to furnish help to the members of the body social, and never destroy and absorb them.

21. "Since Aristotle, no one has more forcefully stated an objection to large-scale systems than the economist Leopold Kohr. His 'unified political philosophy . . . suggests that there seems only one cause behind all forms of social misery: bigness. Oversimplified as this may seem, we shall find the idea more easily acceptable if we consider that bigness, or oversize, is really much more than just a social problem. It appears to be the one and only problem permeating all creation. Wherever something is wrong, something is too big'" (Sale 1980: 82).

22. "It is more urgent to point out that partly as a consequence of the modern notion of 'growth,' the classical distinction between nature and convention, according to which nature is of higher dignity than convention, has been overlaid by the modern distinction between nature and history according to which history (the realm of freedom and of values) is of higher dignity than nature (which lacks purposes and values) . . . The confusion is caused by the desire for a kind of clarity and simplicity which is alien to the subject matter" (Strauss 1964: 16–19 in reference to *Politics* 1267b30–1268a6, 1368b3–4, 11; *NE* 1094b11–27).

23. This formulation is familiar to students of Edmund Burke as well. According to Gertrude Himmelfarb, Edmund Burke adopted a similar philosophy, "by making the 'sentiments,

manners, and moral opinions' of men the basis of society itself, and, ultimately, of the polity as well'" (Himmelfarb 2004: 92).

It is his recognition of varying temperaments and conditions that allowed him to reject the French revolution and embrace the American.

> In his speeches on America, he had said that the issue should be decided not in terms of "abstract speculation" and "metaphysics," but of the particular "circumstances" of the people and the times . . . The circumstances are what render every civil and political scheme beneficial or noxious to mankind. (as quoted in Himmelfard 2004: 84–5)

24. It is not evidence of weakness that these philosophers have concluded that there are some things outside the control of man, for David Hume also concluded something similar "[d]espite being able to 'dismantle the metaphysical systems of rationalistic philosophers and the dogmatic systems of theologians,' Hume was unable to 'touch the power of natural sentiments and convictions that shaped communal traditions and common sense . . .'" (McCoy and Baker 1991: 93).
25. Plato's Statesman should not be confused with Leo Strauss's critique of the modern lawmaker.

> The conventions originate in human acts, and these acts are as necessary, as fully determined by preceding causes, as natural as any natural event . . . hence the distinction between natural and convention can only be provisional or superficial. Yet this "universal consideration regarding the concatenation of the causes" is not helpful as long as one does not show the kind of preceding causes which are relevant for the explanation of conventions. Natural conditions like climate, character of a territory, race, fauna, flora appear to be especially relevant. This means, however, that in each case the "legislator" has prescribed what was best for his people or that all customs are sensible or that all legislators are wise. Since this sanguine assumption cannot be maintained, one is compelled to have recourse also to the errors, superstitions, or follies of the legislators. (Strauss 1964: 15–16)

26. *DIA* refers to *Democracy in America*.
27. Numbering refers to Volume. Part. Chapter.
28. Tocqueville's theory of lawmaking may seem contradictory to the method of lawmaking I adopt in the next chapter, but his advocacy for decentralized administration and townships have the same effect I advocate through my reading of Montesquieu and Plato.
29. It is with the enlightenment that modernity receives its political justification and in it we too see the government reach its full potential. It is through the principles founded in the enlightenment that government authority is able to reach its hands into "private interests" (Rahe 2009: 186). To this end I cannot whole-heartedly embrace either Montesquieu or Tocqueville as each contains a strand of modernity that I reject. That does not mean either of the two should be entirely dismissed either. The usual objection to my characterization of modernity usually comes from practitioners. Edmund Burke, both philosopher and practitioner—who is sometimes characterized as a modern himself, stated, in March 1775, in his "Speech on Conciliation", that "the issue could not be solved by abstract ideas of right or theories of government, but by consulting the nature of the people and the circumstances of the time" (as quoted by Himmelfarb 2004: 80).

30. "Tocqueville stressed that democracy is constantly threatened by state centralization, which deprives intermediaries of their autonomy by reducing their jurisdiction. He lectures about decentralization and the revitalization of provincial and regional institutions as means for achieving 'political life in every part of the territory, in order to multiply infinitely the opportunities of citizens to act collectively, and to make them feel mutually dependent on a daily basis'" (Benoist 2000: 56).
31. See Putnam 2001.
32. See Scott 2008.
33. "According to the modern project, philosophy or science was no longer to be understood as essentially contemplative and proud but as active and charitable . . . it was to be cultivated for the sake of human power; it was to enable man to become the master and owner of nature through the intellectual conquest of nature" (Strauss 1964: 3–4).
34. This conception of the self, the modern conception of the self, "has been carried forward by . . . political liberalism . . ." (Feeley and Rubin 2008: 8).
35. Because an extended treatment of my position on humility and its relationship to politics is outside the purview I cannot dedicate as much space to the issue as I would like. Thus, it is sufficient for now if the reader would see my position as consistent with that of the Socrates of the *Euthyphro* in that it would be arrogant of us to think we can rightly understand the gods—or nature—and not respect the importance of custom and tradition. This point is similar to that expressed by Socrates in *Alcibiades II* as well.
36. We see the humility of Mill, and the origin of deliberative democracy, when he writes:

> The whole strength and value then of human judgment, depending on the one property, that it can be set right when it is wrong, reliance can be placed on it only, when the means of setting it right are kept constantly at hand. In the case of a person whose judgment is really deserving of confidence, how has it become so? Because he has kept his mind open to criticism on his opinions and conduct. Because it has been his practice to listen to all that could be said against him; to profit by as much of it as was just, and expound to himself, and upon occasion to others, the fallacy of what was fallacious. Because he has felt that the only way in which a human being can make some approach to knowing the whole of a subject, is by hearing what can be said about it by persons of every variety of opinion, and studying all modes in which it can be looked at by every character of mind.

Mill's account of deliberation seems to undervalue human emotion. Certain issues elicit emotionally based responses that can overwhelm an otherwise rational individual. These issues generally have moral undertones, such as abortion, the death penalty, gay marriage. Ian Shapiro, a consistent critic of deliberative democracy, sees this problem as a major obstacle to the effectiveness of deliberative democracy.

> In my view, Gutmann and Thompson's emphasis on deliberation attends too little to the degree to which moral disagreements in politics are shaped by differences of interest and power. I think they give a plausible account of the nature of some moral disagreements and of possible argumentative strategies for constructive responses to them when protagonists are appropriately inclined. It is as response to moral disagreement in politics that their account seems to me to be lacking. (Shapiro 1999: 29)

Ian Shapiro's account takes away any idealism and shows that people do not react rationally, or are even willing to debate an issue, but sometimes just end up yelling at one another. Town hall meetings designed to discuss health care reform in the summer of 2009 illustrate this point. In an effort to gain support for, and give details of, the health care proposal initiated by President Obama, Democrats would hold town hall meetings. What usually happened was opponents in the crowd would simply yell objections and insults and the proponents would generally retaliate in kind. These meetings did little to advance the dialogue as they ended with opponents and proponents yelling at one another in the most uncivil and primitive manner one could imagine. Hardly deliberative democracy's finest hour. Deliberative democracy cannot occur without some structure, which includes mechanisms designed to direct deliberation and keep it productive. How this can be done is seen in Archon Fung's (2004) seminal work on deliberative and participatory democracy.

CHAPTER 2

Saving Federalism from Relativism

A theory of federalism in general, and one that deals with its seeming resemblance to relativism in particular, is still lacking. Because of a deficiency in theory, federalism has been twisted in such a way that there appears to be no distinction between it and relativism. Federalism appears to be nothing more than a weak form of relativism. One consequence of such a deficiency in theory is reflected in the public statements of the U.S. political party that proclaims its allegiance to federalism. During the Republican debates preceding the 2008 presidential election I found it startling that whenever the candidates were asked a question about a policy with obvious moral implications each candidate would embrace federalism as a way out of the question, saying something to the effect that it would not be the role of the president to decide such a matter. To say that because of federalism a national official does not have to consider questions on abortion or the death penalty is to abandon federalism and embrace relativism. But, given the anemic state of federal theory we should expect this from political officials.

Sheldon Wolin wrote over 40 years ago that "relatively few theoretical treatises [on federalism] of lasting significance have emerged," which explains "the failure of theory to keep pace with practice" and it seems little has changed (Wolin 1964: vii). "In light of its prominence as a governing arrangement and of the many varied benefits advocates claim for it, one might expect there to be a vast and robust theoretical literature on federalism. Yet there is not" (Feeley and Rubin 2008: 1). Jacob Levy is an astute observer and theorist of federalism. He cites a lack of a theory of federalism and recognizes that the "failure of theory to keep pace with practice is in part because theorists have been looking in the wrong places, when they have looked at all, to understandings of federalism" (Levy 2007: 459). He blames political philosophy for not taking federalism seriously as an area of inquiry. "The dominant tendency in contemporary normative theory has been to ignore federalism altogether . . . the dominant mood in political philosophy since the early 1970s has been one of disdain for questions of institutional design . . ." (Levy 2007: 463). While Levy's observations are important and instructive, I depart from Levy when he makes the argument that theory should be dictated by practice. "We do not, however, have a political theory to match the real federalist practice of a large share of the world's constitutional democracies" (Levy 2007: 459). Perhaps I could agree with Levy if he was referring to positive theory, but I understand him to be discussing normative theory. I contend that practice should conform to theory on normative matters. Or, at the very least, we should judge the goodness of a system by how well it conforms to independently derived objective standards of justice. I agree with Levy's call for a theory, but disagree with his argument that theory should reflect practice as that could potentially lead to a theory lacking in normative value. Such a theory would be merely descriptive. Political theorists need to create a richer account of federalism, one that provides normative guidance for practitioners and allows observers to critique federalism, in an effort to correct practical missteps, based upon objective standards of justice.

Few dispute the idea that federalism, when implemented in the proper manner that takes into account scale, can have benefits that are lacking in a centralized system. Like Levy, Gertrude Himmelfarb attributes some of the lack of federal theory to the rise of liberalism. But, political philosophy—because of the pervasiveness of liberalism—has tended to ignore federalism for the conclusion is that if something is just in one place then it must be just everywhere. "A good law Condorcet protested ought to be good for all men, just as a true proposition is true for all" (Himmelfarb 2004: 161). Immanuel Kant is probably more of an influence than Condorcet, and it is Kant's categorical imperative that simply says that if something is right, then it is right for everyone in all times and in all places (Kant 1993: 25–7, 30). Therefore, in developing a theory of federalism, one must overcome the objection from liberalism by first separating federalism from relativism and then showing how that different times and places sometimes require different treatment to meet the rigors of justice, even justice that is universally applied and objectively derived.

To develop a theory of federalism that is distinct from relativism along practical and theoretical dimensions, I will draw upon Plato[1] and Montesquieu. I will use the ancient understanding of law, government, and the human condition as enunciated by Plato, and Montesquieu's more empirically driven account of federalism. This chapter will show that one can embrace federalism without embracing relativism, and to do otherwise would distort the meaning of federalism. A secondary outcome of this chapter will show that Montesquieu's political theory was closer to that of the ancients than it was to the moderns. This chapter will show that Plato and Montesquieu were realistic without sacrificing an objective standard of justice or morality.

Protagoras holds that, although law and morality are human creations which vary from society to society, they are nevertheless binding for human beings. For Plato, however, even Protagoras' non-skeptical form of conventionalism is inadequate. He holds instead that there is an unchanging moral reality, but one of which human societies, with their great variety of conventional practices, are largely ignorant. Like all knowledge, knowledge of goodness depends on being able to penetrate beyond the veil of appearances to the hidden, unchanging reality of the Forms. (Buckle 1991: 162)

Plato allows variation because each should be allowed to pursue the Form in accordance with its nature. For Plato, every just society reaches for the same Form, but must be allowed to chart its own path toward that Form. This is not all that different from Aristotle's account of change in that so long as the change is consistent with a being's inner purpose then the change is acceptable and necessary.[2] We can create a thicker defense of variation by incorporating Montesquieu's defense of subtle change that requires respect for customs, norms, and mores. This chapter will focus on Montesquieu and Plato, but Mill's defense of free speech as being the only way to reach a true opinion should be remembered.

It needs to be said that because I am using Plato and Montesquieu to formulate a defense of federalism I do not intend to show that either was a particularly strong proponent of federalism. Moreover, I do not make the argument that Montesquieu drew from, or intentionally built upon, Plato. Rather, I intend to show, that if we take from Plato that law must respect human nature in order to be just, and we take from Montesquieu that government ought to do the same, we can create a theory of federalism that embraces an objective standard of justice and thus rejects relativism.

Plato

While Plato is not generally drawn on for a defense of federalism, it is not such a stretch that he would have some opinion on the matter given that he was familiar with the defeat of the Persians by a Greek confederacy. However, circumstantial evidence is not what interests this discussion. This chapter draws on Plato's understanding of just law to facilitate our understanding of federalism. For Plato, laws, like a regime, must be made and administered rationally in order to be just. This allows Plato some flexibility in the design of the regime in that the achievement of just laws is more important than a commitment to a single regime type. This same flexibility will be seen in Montesquieu.

For this chapter, my concern with federalism is its relationship to the making and administration of law. Because of this, I will first turn to Plato's *Minos*, which is the only dialogue whose only theme is the definition of law. The *Minos* defines law as the pursuit to discover the truth (*Minos* 315a), which is similar to his definition of good writing in the *Phaedrus* (*Phaedrus* 278d). A law is only legitimate if it is pursuing the discovery of the truth (Strauss 1987: 70).[3] According to the *Minos*, good law can only be accomplished by kingly law, meaning law generated from good men, as only good men deserve the name kings (*Minos* 317b–c). Because men are infinitely variable, laws too must be infinitely variable in that they must adapt themselves to different men in order to pursue the truth of things (*Minos* 318a–c). Infinitely variable does not mean unstable or capricious.[4] As is seen in the example of the *aulos*, the laws must be wise and stable (*Minos* 318c). So, while the *Minos* is clear on the point that law must be stable, variable, and wise; it is not clear on how to accomplish this mighty task unless one were to have a king who was deserving of the name—which is a man who is in charge of handing down laws and has a wise soul (*Minos* 317b–d).

We cannot ignore the obvious fact that manmade laws are composed of words, and therefore Plato's primary work on writing and speeches is instructive in a discussion of laws. The point of words is to lead the soul (*Phaedrus* 261a, 271d). Therefore, one must not misuse words. In order to use words correctly so as not to mislead the soul, one must understand the soul and the difference between good and evil (*Phaedrus* 258d, 260a–c). This is true for laws as well.

Composing speeches and laws well is an art that requires one to divide things up and bring them back together. Socrates mentions specifically his preference for dialectical works as they are the only form that can divide things into their natural classes and bring them back together (*Phaedrus* 265d–e, 266a–b). Dialectic provides what all great arts provide, a discussion and high speculation about nature (*Phaedrus* 269e). Socrates refers to dialectical speech as an art (*Phaedrus* 266d).

"But evidently the man whose rhetorical teaching is a real art will explain accurately the nature of that which his words are to be addressed, and that is the soul, is it not?" (*Phaedrus* 270e). The good rhetorician must be able to classify men and speeches and know which speeches go with which man. The good rhetorician will be able to describe the soul accurately, the direction and action of the rhetoric, and adapt the speech to the differing needs of different souls in order to persuade the soul to virtue (*Phaedrus* 271a–c).[5] The rhetorician must know how to speak to each man and possess the knowledge of when to keep silent (*Phaedrus* 271d–272b). And while all discourses are different, all have the same ends, and all are organized as a living thing with a body, head, and feet. The middle, according to Socrates, must fit in relation to the whole (*Phaedrus* 264c). Only philosophy can give someone the knowledge to categorize men and speeches and to organize discourses correctly (*Phaedrus* 261a). The discussion of the best rhetorician began with a discussion of knowledge of what is best for the whole (*Phaedrus* 270b–c), which sets up the argument that follows that in order to serve the whole one must be able to serve the individual, which cannot be done without understanding the whole.

Like the *Phaedrus*, Plato's *Statesman* is concerned with the proper division and classification of things as seen in the discussion on weaving. In the *Statesman*,

> [t]he art of weaving finally emerges as the most important model for statesmanship, which 'rules all of these, and the laws, and cares for every aspect of things in the city-state, weaving everything together in the most correct way'. The statesman is also a weaver of souls. (Miller 2007: 97; quoting *Statesman* 305e2–4)

The true statesman then weaves together different citizens into a cohesive whole. The weaving does not diminish the value of the individual or ask the individual to sacrifice for the greater good.

In the *Statesman*, we see that Young Socrates and the Stranger agree that statesmanship is necessary (*Statesman* 292d); for only a statesman can, "distribute to those in the city that which with mind and art is most just, and can keep them safe and make them better for worse as far as possible" (*Statesman* 297b).[6] The true statesman, who rules in accordance with art, is therefore free to act in the absence of, or contrary to, the written laws (*Statesman* 293a–b, 293c–d, 295b).[7] The Stranger gives the example of a doctor who leaves written instructions for his patients to follow while he is away. If the doctor returns and finds that things have changed and there is a better way to treat the patients than the written instructions provided, the doctor ought to be free to change his treatment (*Statesman* 295c–d). To do otherwise would endanger the health of those who are under his care. The same is true for the statesman.[8] Even when a law is in force, if the statesman deems it not in the best interest of the city, he may violate it and provide for the city what is best.

Unfortunately, statesmanship is the most difficult human science to acquire and a multitude is unlikely to acquire it (*Statesman* 292d). Nevertheless, the state ought to be ruled by the highest *available* intelligence, for it is always better for the wise to rule the unwise (*Statesman* 290d, 296b). If there is a city with no true statesman there must be an alternative to rule by a statesman. If a statesman is absent the highest *available* intelligence is the law. Rule of law is the second best regime.[9]

The second best regime is not a just regime, but it is attempting to become just, just as the definition of law in the *Minos* is trying to become the discovery of what is just. (*Minos* 315a). The just regime, that which is ruled by a statesman, does not need written laws, but all other regimes do, simply because absent a statesman and absent laws tyranny will reign (*Statesman* 301a–b; Cairns 1942: 361).[10] In the discussion devoted exclusively to the second best regime that begins at 297e and continues to 299e, the reader finds that the second best regime is imitative, much like the written word in the *Phaedrus* was found to be imitative of true wisdom (*Statesman* 299d; *Phaedrus* 275a–b). Written law is consistently referred to as imitative (*Statesman* 301a).

In the *Phaedrus*, written speeches were unable to target their audience and appeal to individuals individually, the same is true with written laws in the *Statesman*.

> Because a law would never be capable of comprehending with precision for all simultaneously the best and the most just and enjoining the best, for the dissimilarities of human beings and of their actions and the fact that almost none of the human things is ever at rest . . . (*Statesman* 294a–b)

The law treats everyone the same (*Statesman* 294b–c, e). Human nature is dynamic and varying, therefore nothing static can decide anything in all cases at all times. Written law treats humans as something less than human.

While it is determined that something never simple cannot be governed by something that is always simple, that is precisely what the law tries to do (*Statesman* 294b–c). This is almost an identical point to that made at *Phaedrus* 271d–272b that written speeches are inferior to spoken ones, as it is the job of the rhetorician to divide men and speeches according to their nature and apply the proper speeches to the proper man, something the written word could never accomplish.[11] Moreover, men—who have souls—are always changing because they are in constant motion, as all living things are, so the speech that was proper for a man at one time in his life may not be so at another.

Every soul is immortal. That is because whatever is always in motion is immortal, while what moves, and is moved by, something else stops living when it stops moving. So it is only what moves itself that never desists from motion, since it does not leave off being itself. In fact, this self-mover is also the source and spring of motion in everything else that moves; and a source has no beginning. (*Phaedrus* 245c–d)

The law must be adaptable, or account for motion, since the things which it governs are in constant motion.

Plato sets up a scenario in which the only option absent a statesman is federalism. A law must address every individual individually since the individual's condition changes the needs an individual has. A law given to one person may not be appropriate for another if the two people exist in different conditions, just as the doctor's prescription may be different for two different patients depending upon their ailments and their individual constitution. But, a person's condition may change, which means the law should change with it as well. Plato's ideal law giver would be one with a wise soul that was in continuous contact with the law receiver so that he could be familiar with the condition of the law receiver. This demands a small-scale society and a ruler with a wise soul. The second condition cannot be guaranteed—though perhaps through deliberative decision-making procedures it can be approximated—but it can be manufactured in a federal regime. In a federal regime, laws can be adapted to the changing needs of a society more consistent with the direction of the change. And more generally, federal regimes, by placing the law-making body closer to the people, can be more familiar with the condition of the society and the individuals within it, thus it is in a better position to assess the needs and demands of the people for which it makes laws.

A turn now to Montesquieu is appropriate as he helps show how, absent a statesman, good laws can be made. Montesquieu's theory of government takes into account Plato's assessment that because in the second best regime a fixed law must govern what is always changing, conflict will inevitably result (Cairns 1942: 362). The limitations of the written law make the statesman necessary, but if a statesman is not available there must be an alternative. Montesquieu attempts to explicate an alternative.

Montesquieu

In writing in objection to Montesquieu, Condorcet—who seemingly embodies political philosophy's primary objection to, or reason for ignoring, federalism—writes,

As truth, reason, justice, the rights of man, the interests of property, of liberty, of security, are in all places the same; we cannot discover why all the provinces of a state, or even all states, should not have the same civil and criminal laws, and the same laws relative to commerce. A good law should be good for all men. A true proposition is true everywhere. (Condorcet 1814: 274)

The last sentence of this statement seems unobjectionable, but it can be objected to on the grounds that universal does not mean uniform.[12] For Montesquieu, uniformity is the hobgoblin of small minds.

> He [Montesquieu] thought, however, that the logic of uniformity was a danger to liberty—both indirectly, because uniformity was likely to be coercively enforced and diversity stamped out, and indirectly, because uniformity tended to weaken the loyalties and attachments that could perpetuate the intermediate bodies that guarded the fundamental laws against despotic rulers and assemblies. (Levy 2007: 470)

Plato, who argues that motion is the natural state of all things good[13] criticizes uniformity when he writes,

> there will be no motion in a state of uniformity. For it is difficult, or rather impossible, for something to be moved without something to set it in motion without something to be moved by it . . . And so let us always presume that rest is found in a state of uniformity and to attribute motion to nonuniformity. The latter, moreover, is caused by inequality . . . (*Timaeus* 57e–58)

For Plato, uniformity is unnatural as it stops motion, which means a thing's value has ceased; it has died.

Perhaps Montesquieu is not the most obvious choice for insight on federalism and my focus here should be on someone like Lord Acton or a modern writer like Daniel Elazar or Donald Lutz. But because Montesquieu is overlooked as a thinker of federalism does not mean he is without valuable insight on the topic, and this oversight on behalf of federalism scholars is but one justification for using him here.

> The common perception that Montesquieu is not a major theorist of federalism is due both to the peripheral nature of his account of confederate republics and his praise of the unitary British Constitution . . . [but] his most significant reflections on federalism were not contained in his brief treatment of confederate republics, but rather in his lengthy discussion of Gothic constitutionalism. (Ward 2007: 563)

In defending Montesquieu as a federal theorist, Lee Ward has done most of the heavy lifting.

> While Montesquieu praises the English judiciary and regional representation in the lower house as the preservation of some aspects of the Gothic original,

he mourns the loss in England and France of the intermediary regional institutions that were once distinctive features of the Gothic Constitution. It is in his detailed treatment of medieval France that Montesquieu brings to the fore a largely forgotten constitutional system in which the relationship between the center and the periphery was ideally one of ongoing accommodation between the primary local communities and the central government. Montesquieu presents the federal principles embedded in the decentralized Gothic Constitution as a vital supplement to the separation of powers, and a corrective to the problem of concentrated power in modern England and France. (Ward 2007: 564)

While his theory of, and philosophical justification for, federalism need to be extracted with great care due to its being bound up in historical examples, his practical reasons for supporting federalism are quite straightforward. These reasons are listed in *Spirit of the Laws*.

A republic of this kind, able to withstand external force, may support itself without any internal corruption; the form of this society prevents all manner of inconveniences.

If a single member should attempt to usurp the supreme power, he could not be supposed to have an equal authority and credit in all the confederate states. Were he to have too great an influence over one. This would alarm the rest; were he to subdue a part; that which would still remain free might oppose him with forces independent of those which he had usurped, and overpower him before he could be settled in his usurpation.

Should a popular insurrection happen in one of the confederate states, the others are able to quell it. Should abuses creep into one part, they are reformed by those that remain sound. The state may be destroyed on one side, and not on the other; the confederacy may be dissolved, and the confederates preserve their sovereignty.

As this government is composed of small republics, it enjoys the internal happiness of each; and with regard to its external situation, by means of the association, it possesses all the advantages of large monarchies.

It is, therefore, very probable that mankind would have been, at length, obliged to live constantly under the government of a single person, had they not contrived a kind of constitution that has all the internal advantages of a republican, together with the external force of a monarchical, government. I mean a confederate republic.

This form of government is a convention by which several small states agree to become members of a larger one, which they intend to establish. It is a kind of society of societies, that constitute a new one, capable of increasing by means of further associations, till they arrive at such a degree of power as to be able to provide for the security of the whole body.

It was these associations that so long contributed to the prosperity of Greece. By these the Romans attacked the whole globe, and by these alone the whole globe withstood them; for when Rome had arrived at the highest pitch of her grandeur, it was the associations beyond the Danube—associations formed by the terror of her arms—that enabled the barbarians to resist her.

These advantages of federalism seem as accurate today as they did during Montesquieu's time: federalism provides all of the advantages of small and large republics with none of the defects.[14] In Book VIII, it is essentially the size of the state that determines what type of laws and government structure it ought to have. Small states should be republics, medium should be monarchies, and large states ultimately end in despotic authority. (VIII.16, 17, 19). As aptly noted by Ana Samuel, "The federal republic does not fit into any one of the three archetypes. It is an anomaly, a union of many republics, and it is said to overcome internal and external political threats . . . " (Samuel 2009: 309).

Montesquieu also turns his attention to the philosophical to further justify federalism. As I have argued above, federalism brings government policy closer to justice because it is more consistent with human nature and condition. Montesquieu is here combined with Plato to show the full promise and practicality of federalism.

In Montesquieu's *Spirit of the Laws* (*SL*) we see that moderation is the key to a nation's ability to preserve liberty without sacrificing security (Scott 2008; Ward 2007). As Montesquieu writes, "[p]olitical liberty is found only in moderate governments" (XI.6). For there to be moderation there must be a separation between the people and the rulers, and intermediaries are required to bridge the separation. But the intermediate body must be able to enforce, administer, and make laws. Montesquieu writes,

> It is not enough to have intermediate ranks in a monarchy; there must also be a depository of the laws. The depository can only be in the political bodies, which announce the laws when they are made and recall them when they are forgotten. (II.4)

Montesquieu's teaching is based partly on the lessons of history. His understanding of history is one of the legs on which his political philosophy stands. In Montesquieu we see an effort to derive political truths from history. "It is in the thought of Montesquieu that the need to derive some moral and political standards from history, history understood as opposed to, or as the replacement for nature, comes into the foreground of the tradition of political philosophy" (Pangle 1973: 9). The lesson of history is moderation. History resolves itself by balancing extremes and achieving moderation, and it is the moderate resolutions that are desired by Montesquieu. Montesquieu presents history to us in such a way that we see that history achieves moderation by destroying those nations that lie at the extremes.

Athens and Marseilles were destroyed when they abandoned their moderate base. When Rome became an empire, it too was destroyed as a result of abandoning its moderate principles of republicanism. This reading of history leads Montesquieu to conclude that the proper political order is the order which is moderate.

Montesquieu does not follow Hobbes who looks only at human nature as being the determiner of events and the dictator of how a political system should be ordered, but instead builds on a foundation of human nature and historical events since "Nature always acts, but it is overwhelmed by social customs."[15] Montesquieu draws this conclusion from his reading of history, and transmits these lessons to the reader by providing historical examples in such a way that shows the different defects of each system and how the defects could have been corrected had the nations better understood the effects of custom, tradition, and history; and Montesquieu then shows how failed nations might have directed the effects of custom, tradition, and history through the proper implementation of laws. A nice example of this is when he shows that the effects of wealth are not the same in all circumstances. While wealth worked wonderfully in modern England, it led to destruction in both Carthage and Rome. On this point, Montesquieu echoes Althusius who wrote,

> The magistrate should know the nature and attitude of his own people, of neighboring peoples, and of people in general. The nature, condition, and attitude of his own people, or the people subject to him, ought to be perceived, explored, and learned by him in order that he may know in what things and by what means he may lead, motivate, offend, and rule his people, and what sort of laws and manner of governing are consequently most appropriate. (Althusius 1995: 150)

The dialectic—and sometimes deterministic—progression of history must be derived from his use of historical examples, as he does not make an explicit statement about his view of history.[16] When he describes Athens in Book V, Montesquieu draws the reader's attention more to the internal conflict taking place within Athens than he does to the external war with Sparta. Athens, as with all commercial republics, must find the balance between anarchy and republicanism (V.6). It was the fate of Athens to fall as it had not properly balanced the positive and negative benefits of a commercial republic, which resulted in corruption from within. Within Athens it was not the fault of the leaders, but the people who, "applied themselves more to eloquence than to military arts" (VIII.2). The people of Athens had turned lazy and inequality resulted from their commercial success, despite the best efforts of Solon to reform the laws in such a way that would encourage equality.[17] Inequality led to greed, laziness, and excess. Contrast this with Sparta whose prudence was captured by Montesquieu in his citation of Plato, " 'We offer common things,' said a Spartan, 'so that we have the means for honoring the gods every day' " (XXV.7). Internal unrest in Athens did not begin with its domestic policies, but with its foreign agenda. As a commercial republic Athens was not built to be a military empire, its expansion would have to be due to its commercial success if it was to be successful. One of the responsibilities of the laws in a republic is to keep the people humble, and the people cannot remain humble if their nation's success is attributed to their involvement.

> Great successes, especially those to which the people contribute much, make them so arrogant that it is no longer possible to guide them. Jealous of the magistrates, they become jealous of the magistracy; enemies of those who govern, they soon become enemies of the constitution. In this way the victory at Salamis over the Persians corrupted the republic of Athens; in this way the defeat of the Athenians ruined the republic of Syracuse. (VIII.4)

Athens fell because it was unable to balance its ambition for external greatness with the need for domestic tranquility. The laws of Athens were unable to produce a people that were consistent with the requirements of a republican government. Athens was unable, perhaps unwilling, to recognize and support its true spirit through its laws. It failed to recognize the "spirit of the laws." Montesquieu's states-man is much like Plato's "Many things govern men . . . climate, religion, laws and the maxims of government, examples of past things, mores and manners; a general spirit is formed as a result" (XIX.4). "A legislator is to take his or her cues from the general spirit." The environ external to the individual, whether it be geography, climate, customs, mores, or history, shapes an individual's character and the character of the people. A law cannot operate in a vacuum as these forces are more powerful than a manmade law. To guide human behavior within the confines of the external environment is what the goal of law should be. The law needs to respect the individual and what affects the character of the individual. This is why moderation is important to Montesquieu as moderation allows for subtle change that respects these factors. Althusius provides a similar account when he writes,

> The enactment of law is the process by which the magistrate, with the consent of the optimates and estates of his imperium and realm, legislates what is fair, useful, and necessary to the commonwealth. The magistrate shall especially see that the customs, temperament, and ancient rights of the nation are respected, and that new laws are accommodated to them. Moderation is thus to be exercised in writing new laws and edicts, and the wishes of those who must maintain these laws . . . are to be ascertained. (Althusius 1995: 176)

Montesquieu balances the picture he paints of Athens with that of ancient Marseilles. In Athens, success bred jealousy, and this jealousy contributed to its downfall, as jealousy runs counter to the positive effects of commerce. "Jealous of the magistrates, they become jealous of the magistracy; enemies of those who govern, they soon become enemies of the constitution" (VIII.4). In some sense it was the greatness of Athens that led to its downfall, and Marseilles then, was protected from the same fate since, "The republic of Marseilles never underwent these great shifts from lowliness to greatness; thus, it always governed itself with wisdom; thus, it preserved its principles" (VIII.4). Marseilles is an example of a commercial republic which was able to balance its competing forces in order to endure. Marseilles, during its high point, was moderate. Montesquieu acknowledges that the general purpose of each state is to preserve itself, each state having a purpose peculiar to it, which in the case of Marseilles was the preservation of public tranquility (XI.5). Like all nations, Marseilles is restrained by factors it cannot control, such as climate and geography. But what a nation can control is how it reacts to the uncontrollable elements, and a government that reacts correctly to its environment will be able to preserve itself.

> Marseilles, a necessary retreat in the midst of a stormy sea, Marseilles, where all the winds, the shoals, and the coastline order ships to put in, was frequented by sea-faring people. The barrenness of its territory made its citizens decide on economic commerce. They had to be hardworking in order to replace that which nature refused them; just, in order to live among the barbarian nations that were to make their prosperity; moderate, in order for their government always to be tranquil; finally, of frugal mores, in order to live always by a commerce that would the more surely preserve the less it was advantageous to them. (XX.5)

But like Athens, Marseilles fell, and fell because of internal strife, a civil war that was the result of an inadequate constitution and governing system that could not prevent the citizens from becoming lazy and being overtaken by the Gauls and civil war. It was the inability to establish a balance between industry and power. Marseilles chose to focus its attention and resources internally by being a commercial giant which would bring it riches. It did not balance the need to be a force in foreign affairs with its desire for domestic tranquility. Marseilles, like Athens, did not recognize the proper character of its government or people, or in Montesquieu's terms, it did not adhere to the "spirit of the laws." Placing these two governments side by side, one can see the dialectic between Athens and Marseilles develop. If one were to match the negative features of one, with the positive features of the other, one would have a properly balanced commercial republic. Such a state would exhibit moderation as a result of the interaction between ambition and priorities.

The examples of Athens and Marseilles show that when a state moves to the extreme, and ignores its history, it loses stability, which then leads to a loss of liberty. The examples of Athens and Marseilles set up another interesting teaching as well. All states contain within themselves the seed of destruction; all regimes have some virtue that can become a vice, and therefore a state is better off figuring out how to remedy the vices of its own system and capitalize on the virtues rather than trading it in for an all new system. Montesquieu begins Book IX of the *SL* by writing, "If a republic is small, it is destroyed by a foreign force; if it is large, it is destroyed by internal vice" (IX.1). The solution is to mix the two forms of government by creating a federal republic, a government which has the advantages of both while controlling for the vices of both. If difficulties arise in one of the areas, the others can help pacify or let that area break off and thus internal stability is maintained. And because federal republics can draw together their military forces, their ability to stave off military attack is equal to large monarchies. A federal republic checks the central authority while providing an institutional check on the common people in a way the noble class does under a monarchy.

In order to understand why such a system is the solution to the problem Montesquieu sees, one must go beyond the historical examples and look to his description of human nature and see that human nature is what makes creating a government that preserves liberty and security so difficult. Montesquieu's system is one that understands human nature cannot be made to conform to a political system, instead, a political system must meet human nature on its own terms and adapt to it without allowing it to run unchecked, or without stifling it. The reader quickly learns from Montesquieu what laws are and how they must function relative to human nature. In the first chapter of the first book Montesquieu writes, "Laws, taken in the broadest meaning, are the necessary relations deriving from the nature of things; and in this sense, all beings have their laws . . ." (I.1). And again, in the beginning of the third book, Montesquieu clearly states that the laws of a government should be relative to both its structure and the human passions. Laws, for Montesquieu, are not as restrictive as we may typically think of laws as being. Laws should conform to the nature of a thing in order to be as unobtrusive as possible when directing something to a desirable end. A law should never attempt to change the nature of a thing, but should instead conform to it and guide it.

Having a clear understanding of this allows one to see why Montesquieu adopts the ancient flexibility toward governmental structure (II.1). Montesquieu never commits to a single government structure as being the best for all people. And while he does seem partial to the English model, or any model which derives from the Germanic tribes (XI.6), he knows that government structures are not one size fits all. His refusal to name a single system as best is instructive when crafting a theory of federalism based on his writing.

Given the connection between laws and government (I.1 and II.1) it is not hard to find support for the claim that if there is no single government system that is right for everyone then no law can be either. But such a conclusion would be false. Montesquieu's theory of law is more nuanced than his position on government. For Montesquieu, as it was for Plato, there is at least one universal law: a just law is one that is made in accord with human nature and does what is best for the individual and the collective simultaneously. And because people are variable, laws must be as well. "And does not the greatness of genius consist rather in knowing in which cases there must be uniformity and in which differences? When the citizens observe the laws, what does it matter if they observe the same ones?" (XXIX.18).

In Montesquieu we see the attempt to institutionalize Plato's statesman in the form of a federal republic. The localities are supposed to govern the people well since they are close to them and know them. This allows for local officials to have a better idea of what policies are best for its people. The national government monitors the local governments—in a similar manner as the local monitor the people within its jurisdiction—and seeks policies that are best for each locality in relation to the whole.

Why This Is Not Relativism

The motion inherent in human activity, which is one cause for the infinite variation in human behavior, cannot be tracked or reacted to by a distant governing body. Take this lighthearted, and oversimplified, example to help get the point across. Anyone whose children receive gifts from grandparents who live far away knows how disappointed a seven-year-old boy would be to receive a toy fire engine for his birthday. On his third birthday it would have been great, and to his grandparents he still is three in some respects, due partly to the fact that they rarely see him. But the boy's preference in toys has changed. Put this in the context of government policy. Malcolm Gladwell makes mention of the government's inability to keep up with real time. The software developer featured in the story criticizes the Federal Reserve for making decisions in 'batch' while the world operates in real time. The Fed uses data from weeks and months past, while the current economic climate has already changed. Therefore, its reaction to control money supply through interest rate changes could be seriously out of date. "For roughly a century, government and private economic data in the United States and Britain has usually been behind the times rather than ahead of them in spotlighting the major changes overtaking the two nations" (Phillips 2008: liii). Even with new technology, it seems that failing to keep up with the lives and needs of its citizens is the inevitable fate of a centralized body charged with overseeing such a large system. While these are but a few examples, one could imagine how the bureaucratic filter through which Washington—or Moscow, or Beijing, or Mexico City—makes its decisions could lead it to make poor policy decisions. This is why governing needs to be done on a local, more human, scale.

Plato makes note of this in the instances I have already cited, in addition to his discussion of motion in the *Laws* when he writes if

> the whole course and movement of the heavens and all that is in them reflect the motion and revolution and calculation of reason, and operate in a corresponding fashion, then clearly we have to admit that it is the best kind of soul that cares for the entire universe and directs it along the best path. (*Laws* 10.897c)

The political application of this passage becomes relevant when one refers back to an early passage in which Plato argues that the statesman must understand the motion of the human body relative to itself and other bodies as the astronomer understands the orbit of the planets and stars (*Laws* 7.821–822c). The statesman, or government, must be able to put the citizens—when necessary—into proper motion which is that motion which brings them to their highest state of goodness (*Laws* 7.789c–d; *Timaeus* 89e–90). But, let us not forget, the government does not bear the whole burden of making man good, nor can it (*Laws* 7.790b).

The variation in human behavior is simply far too great for a central, distant government to govern justly. As shown in my treatment of the *Statesman*, Plato takes the position that all things human are in motion, even wisdom and knowledge.[18] Because motion is natural to man, and to the virtues, a political system and laws that attempt to be just must take into account the natural condition of man and the virtues.

This may sound as if morals are manmade, which if that is the case, morals are relative. However, there are laws of nature found in Montesquieu and there are universal laws, perhaps derived from nature, found in Plato as well. Montesquieu and Plato recognize that humans vary, and therefore laws must vary. A law limiting the number of cars that drive in downtown Manhattan makes sense given the congestion and pollution. But, a similar law in Manhattan, KS, would do nothing more than create public backlash for an unreasonable and indefensible policy. A policy by the national government to give each state ten million dollars to build infrastructure to protect against natural disasters makes some sense. But if that money could only be spent on infrastructure that deals with lake effect snow, people in Galveston, Texas, and New Orleans would be understandably upset. These are examples that nearly everyone can recognize as being a necessary reason for having a federal system and do not force one to be a relativist either. But on questions of morality, can federalism, with help from Montesquieu and Plato, avoid being relativistic?

What Montesquieu and Plato show is that there is a universal idea of justice but its attainment is conditioned upon individual circumstances and character. Different routes can lead to the same place. Because there is a universal idea of justice, that is also objective, Plato and Montesquieu are not relativists, but rather humanists. The justified path to justice is one that does not coerce action but directs it to a higher good in a manner consistent with its nature and character. Allowing variation in application, while holding the value of justice constant, separates Plato and Montesquieu from relativists. A theory of law and government, if justice is its goal, must respect human nature; Plato and Montesquieu do.[19]

This theory of federalism does not exempt national officials from having an opinion on morally charged matters either. For Plato and Montesquieu laws must be made in accord with human nature, just as regime types must be those which best fit with the culture and history of a people. Thus, any law that runs contrary to the natural order of things is unjust and should not be implemented. Therefore, if a law passed by one governing unit in a federal system would upset the natural order in another, the law should not apply to the second governing unit; and the same applies to laws passed by the national government as well. Likewise, if a law is passed by a local governing unit that only affects the people of that local governing unit is contrary to the natural order within that local governing unit, the national government is obliged to intervene. While it would be ideal for local governments to always make laws in accord with nature, all governments are prone to error, and there must be some agent with the authority to step in. So even though certain decisions are better made at the state level, a nationally elected official must still have an opinion on the matter as the lower level can act contrary to nature, which would then require the national official to intervene.

In this theory of federalism, justice is the metric by which all things are measured, and authority is divided among the governing parts in order to provide a system which forces deliberation and allows for intervention on behalf of justice when such action is warranted. So while we may say that policies on abortion or the death penalty are best left to the local governing units, this does not offer a national official a pass on the question as it is his or her duty to make sure the states are making just laws and to stop them when they are not. While this could be construed as a threat to state authority, by the theory I have sketched, such a threat is justified given that the preservation of justice is more important than professing one's loyalty to a particular government structure. Also, in the practice of federalism that I will sketch, the states have the right to veto or nullify a national law. Politics and lawmaking, like all living things, are constantly in motion. It is rare in politics, if not impossible, to get things right the first time through. Justice can be achieved through iteration only,[20] which is why policy deliberation and the resulting adjustments are so important. Let us not forget that man's ever changing condition in relation to his physical surroundings means that what is just at one time and place may not be just at another. Justice is unchanging, but the making of law, which can only try to approximate justice, must change and adapt if it has any hope of realizing justice.

Conclusion

Having sufficiently dealt with one hurdle on the path to developing a theory of federalism, separating it from relativism, the next chapter—and in some ways the rest of this book—will continue to develop a theory of federalism that was begun in the first chapter. Chapter 3 will discuss the topic of sovereignty and how federalism ought to place sovereignty with the people for if left with the government, at any level, there will always remain a threat to self-determination and identification. The next chapter serves as a bridge between the theory and practice sections as it employs case studies in support of the point that sovereignty placed in the government poses a threat to the people.

Notes

1. "In ancient Greece at least some of the Sophists defended a version of moral relativism, which Plato attempted to refute" (Wong 1991: 442). See also *Theaetetus* 172ab.
2. See also Thomas Aquinas who wrote that law must "adapt to time and place [and] can be rightly changed on account of the changed condition of man" (Aquinas *ST* 1a2ae

97.1, see also 1a2ae 104.3 ad. 1.). David VanDrunen sums the position up nicely when he writes, "Though justice itself is a universal goal for human law, the substance of justice depends upon the particular conditions in which it is applied" (VanDrunen 2002: 322). In elaborating upon his reading of Aristotle, VanDrunen writes, "political writers must reflect not only upon what form of government is best absolutely but also upon what form or forms are possible under given social circumstances" (VanDrunen 2002: 318).

3. The law's pursuit of truth is also consistent with art in that art pursues the discovery of things (*Minos* 314b; *Phaedrus* 269e).

4. Also, one should not confuse variable with different, as the unnamed interlocutor does. The unnamed interlocutor uses the different strategies of burial and sacrifice across cultures to show that laws are different (*Minos* 315b–d). Socrates does not respond directly to this rebuttal but offers to embark on the discussion through a different manner of speaking.

5. What one finds in the *Phaedrus* one also finds in *Timaeus*.

> So once we have come to know them and to share in the ability to make correct calculations according to nature, we should stabilize the straying revolutions within ourselves by imitating the completely unstraying revolutions of the god. Likewise, the same account goes for sound and hearing—these too are the god's gifts, given for the same purpose and intended to achieve the same result. Speech was designed for this very purpose—it plays the greatest part in its achievement. And all such composition as lends itself to making audible musical sound is given in order to express harmony, and so serves this purpose as well. And harmony, whose movements are akin to the orbits within our souls, is a gift of the Muses, if our dealings with them are guided by understanding, not for irrational pleasure, for which people nowadays seem to make use of it, but to serve as an ally in the fight to bring order to any orbit in our soul that has become unharmonized, and make it concordant with itself. (*Timaeus* 47c–d)

6. This follows the lesson learned from following the dramatic action of the *Phaedrus* that the good speech—which is the unwritten speech—can only exist outside of the city's walls.

7. Fred Miller writes of the *Statesman*,

> [t]he rule of reason is a central theme of the *Statesman* in three important ways: it provides a criterion for distinguishing the true statesman from the counterfeit; it is indispensable for the proper aim of politics; and it is a standard for comparing and evaluating constitutions. (Miller 2007: 93)

Perhaps it might be a worthwhile project to search for the relationship between Plato's statesman and what Nietzsche meant by being beyond good and evil with respect to the act of creation.

8. But we should heed the warning that not all rulers are statesmen. Look to *Cratylus* and one finds, "By god, presumably some rule-setters are good and others bad, especially if what we agreed to before is true, and they are just like other craftsmen" (*Cratylus* 431e).

9. We should heed the warning that the distance between the second best and the best regime can be quite substantial. "Or haven't you noticed how far images are from having the same features as the things of which they are images?" (*Cratylus* 432d).

10. Even with written laws there can be tyranny, but more importantly is the distinction between what a law is, and what poses as a law.

> But look here. Don't lawmakers make law to be the greatest good to the city? Without that, law-abiding civilized life is impossible (*Greater Hippias* 284d) . . . So when people who are trying to make laws fail to make them good, they have failed to make them lawful—indeed, to make them law (*Greater Hippias* 284d) . . . But I suppose people who know the, at least, believe that what is more beneficial is more lawful in truth for all men. (*Greater Hippias* 284e)

11. This link between speeches and politics is found in *Timaeus* as well.

> Furthermore, when men whose constitutions are bad in this way have bad forms of government where bad civic speeches are given . . . no studies that could remedy this situation are at all pursued by people from their youth on up, that is how all of us who are bad come to be that way—two causes both entirely beyond our control. (*Timaeus* 87b)

12. Also evident is that Condorcet seems fine with coercion. That is, so long as the system is good, it can be forced upon the people. We see the ridiculousness of such conformity, and the departure from justice with the willingness to coerce, when we read Plato's *Republic*.

13. *Timaeus* 36c. Or, one could even press the argument further and say that all things, even the bad, are in motion. "Then since they must be in motion, and there is no such thing anywhere as absence of motion, it follows that all things are always in every kind of motion" (*Theaetetus* 181e–182).

14. "Throughout much of the history of federalist thought—sometimes explicitly, sometimes implicitly—the answer to the question 'Why federate?' has been because it gives a self-governing political community the best of both worlds: the advantages of being a relatively small, homogenous polity, along with the advantages of being part of a stronger, more secure larger state or alliance; while at the same time avoiding some of the worst disadvantages of being either too small or too large" (Karmis and Norman 2005: 8).

15. This comes from *Pensees*, but I found it initially in Judith Shklar (1986): 55.

16. Montesquieu makes very little explicit in fact, as he wants to make the reader work. "But one must not always exhaust a subject that one leaves nothing for the reader to do. It is not a question of making him read but of making him think" (XI.20).

17. It may not have been Solon's fault entirely for it takes time to reform a people's character. Or, because Solon tried reforms that were too radical too quickly it might have been his fault. For as Althusius writes,

> For it is important that not everything be corrected at once, but gradually. For Cicero says, none of us can be changed quickly. Nor can one's life be altered or his character transformed suddenly. Some evils the prince can remove more easily if he is patient with them. (Althusius 1995: 180)

18. *Cratylus* 411d.

19. For both Plato and Montesquieu the people's allegiance must be to the common good without sacrificing individual liberty. In a small republic, so small that there is little

variation in views from one citizen to another or when there is variation the human connection and communal interdependence that exists in small-scale communities will allow the differences in opinion to be reconciled humanely, the difference between the common good and the individual good is almost indistinguishable. But each time geographic size and population size increases the variation in views increases, and the ability to bridge the gap between differing views decreases as a result. From a practical level, it is easier to manage and easier to know the tension between the individual good and the common good. "People are more likely to have neighbors, friends, and family in state than in federal offices or employment" (Levy 2007: 464). That is, people will not have to be coerced into following the orders of the state because their allegiance is natural. And as a matter of policy formation and implementation, "State governments will tend to immediately feel local needs, whereas the federal government's primary business will seem far off and relatively unimportant. State politics will simply be more familiar and comprehensible" (Levy 2007: 464).

20. I have in mind something like the Fibonacci sequence.

CHAPTER 3

Resituating Sovereignty

Nancy Fraser, while not intentionally an advocate of federalism, makes a strong argument in favor of a federal system when she writes,

> [g]iven the increased salience of both transnational and subnational processes, the Westphalian sovereign state can no longer serve as the sole unit or container of justice. Rather, notwithstanding its continuing importance, that state is one frame among others in an emerging new multileveled structure. In this situation, deliberations about institutionalizing justice must take care to pose questions at the right level, determining which matters are generally national, which local, which regional, and which global. (Fraser 2003: 88)

Fraser, despite her criticism of the Westphalian sovereign state, neglects to question its legitimacy in that she ignores the possibility that there can be questions relating to family or community that do not have to fall into the formal-political sphere. Not all issues must come under government regulation and consideration as her formulation presupposes. Rather, we can allow for nonstate actors to provide some of the solutions.

Federalism should not be state-centric. By giving sovereignty to an entity other than the people means that entity is superior to the people. The people ought to remain sovereign, and it is only when people retain their sovereignty that a workable federal system can exist.[1]

This chapter will discuss federalism within the U.S. context by focusing on the doctrine of sovereign immunity. This chapter serves as a transition between the theory and practice sections of the book. It adds an additional layer to the theory of federalism I developed in the first two chapters, but shows what happens in practice when a state-centered view of federalism is adopted.

Sovereign immunity insulates the government and government officials from legal recourse. This means that a government or government agent is immune from legal recourse. There are three broad categories of sovereign immunity in the United States: federal sovereign immunity, state sovereign immunity, and tribal sovereign immunity. This chapter will consider each type of immunity in the context of federalism.

The case for sovereign immunity at the subnational level presents an interesting challenge for proponents of federalism. Those who want to reserve state sovereignty must, it appears, support sovereign immunity for without it states can lose their strength relative to the national government. If states, or Indian tribes, lose the power of sovereign immunity and the national government retains it, then citizens are free to sue the state government but not the national government thus weakening the position of the state if only in perception. However, sovereign immunity reinforces the state dominance that federal theory and practice seeks to limit. The grant of sovereign immunity to any level of government limits the extent to which the people can hold their government accountable. If sovereign immunity is in place, the legal consequences the government may be exposed to are limited, which then limits accountability and places the citizen in a subordinate role.

This chapter will progress in four sections. It begins by outlining some of the problems with a state-centric view of government and federalism before providing an analysis of the sovereign immunity doctrine in the United States. This is followed by a theoretical critique of sovereign immunity to supplement the practical critique. The theoretical critique will be grounded in the political theory of John Locke. Finally, it will show, based upon the discussion of sovereign immunity, that something other than an unelected judiciary should be the final arbiter of the law and the protector of majority and minority rights.

Federalism and the State

Federalism is often equated with the ability of subnational governing units to govern themselves. In the United States this often means that preserving federalism means preserving states' rights. McGinnis and Somin correctly recognize that "federalism is too often confused by both admirers and detractors with state autonomy" (McGinnis and Somin 2004: 89). Federalism does place an emphasis on the ability of subnational governing units to govern themselves, but it does not grant any level of government sovereignty over the people. To make federalism a state-centered enterprise is to adopt a Hobbesian view of government that federalism opposes. To contrast the federal view with the modern-nation state view is to contrast the view of contract and covenant as put forth by Hobbes and Althusius respectively. As shown in Chapter 1, the Althusian covenant is communal and communicative in which each association communicates its needs with other associations to form a covenant.[2] Each association is bound to that covenant in so far as it provides what it was designed to provide. It is not the larger association that defines the common good, but the constituent members of the association that define the common good. As it relates to the state, "the state does not define the common good, but safeguards and promotes it, in the sense of making up for the natural incapacities of social groups, who are themselves capable of working for the common good" (Duncan 2006: 75).

Associations covenant with other associations which then leads to the creation of larger associations. These associations serve as a link between the individual and the state.[3] As a matter of course, each associating body retains its identity and original authority. It does not give up its ability to decide matters within its sphere when it forms a larger association. The reach of the larger association is limited, and only extends to those things that cannot be dealt with by the smaller association alone. This is consistent with the notion of subsidiarity in so far as "subsidiarity seeks to nourish these intermediate social groups, whether by protecting them from government interference, empowering them through limited government intervention, or coordinating their various pursuits" (Duncan 2006: 67).[4] This formulation stands in stark contrast to the Hobbesian formulation in which the Leviathan is superior to the individuals who constitute it and whose reach is unlimited.

For Hobbes the covenant is ever-binding and individual. An individual enters into a contract to turn his power over to a governing body so that there is only one sovereign. That sovereign has the absolute authority to rule. Associations outside state control—or leagues or covenants that are made in addition to that made with the state—are dangerous in the Hobbesian formulation for they decrease the importance of, and the reliance upon, the Leviathan. In contemporary terms, civil society is a threat to the state and should therefore be disallowed. As it relates to federalism more literally, granting the right to rule to subnational governing units should be disallowed as it threatens the sovereignty of the national government. The point to remember with Hobbes is that sovereignty remains in the hands of government for it is sovereignty which was turned over to it when the social contract was signed. So not only does Hobbes stand in contrast to Althusius, but to the idea of federalism more generally. The following is the antithesis of Hobbesian thought, and brings forth the idea similar to what I have tried to articulate.

> There is a natural law structure of society in which families, vocational associations, communes and provinces all exist as necessary and organic members intermediate between the individuals and the state and in which the wider union is consolidated from the corporative unities of the narrower unions and thereby obtains its members. These narrower unions as real and organic communities create by themselves a distinct common life and a legal sphere of their own, and at the same time give up to the larger union so much as it needs in order to fulfill its specific purposes. (Sobei 1931: 29–30)

Within a federal structure sovereignty remains with the people. A state-centered approach places the people in an ancillary—if not a subordinate—role. In reference to the U.S. system, Supreme Court Justice Sandra Day O'Connor wrote, "the Constitution does not protect the sovereignty of States for the benefit of the States or state governments as abstract political entities [but] for the protection of individuals."[5] Regardless of whether her interpretation of the U.S. Constitution is correct,[6] her argument about federalism more generally is correct. Subnational governing units serve as intermediary institutions that protect the people from the national government. Thus, the intermediary institutions must be protected for without them a buffer of protection is lost. Subnational governing units exist so that they will help thwart tyranny, not because they are in and of themselves good. Proponents of states' rights often miss the point that even states can act against the people. No level of government is exempt from tyrannical tendencies.

I make the argument below that under the current state-centered view of federalism all things not the state are made subordinate to it. This is a turn away from Althusius with repercussions envisioned by Tocqueville. If citizens allow their fate to be determined by the state, Tocqueville predicts devastating effects (see Chapter 1 and Rahe 2009: 187–9). Tocqueville recognized that civil society must thrive, for if too much is given to the government, too much will be lost. Therefore, federalism is not simply about limiting the power of government, but limiting people's reliance on government. Not all grievances and disputes need to find their remedy through government action. People need to be empowered, and feel empowered, to take charge of the everyday problems they face as individuals and as a community.

Tocqueville sees an additional problem when sovereignty is granted to the nation-state. As the reliance on the nation-state increases so too does a rise in individualism. The common recourse to the travails of individualism is forced community, but Tocqueville shows that the state-centered response to this problem only exacerbates it and that we should recognize that forced community is emblematic of the larger problem. Thus, there should be a (re)focus, and (re)validation of nonstate associations, points made earlier in Chapter 1.

Adding J. S. Mill to the discussion broadens the reach of Tocqueville's observation.

> Sometimes it is the effect of identity of race and descent. Community of language and community of religion greatly contribute to it. Geographical limits are one of its causes. But the strongest of all is identity of political antecedents: the possession of a national history and consequent community of recollections; collective pride and humiliation, pleasure and regret, connected with the same incidents in the past. (Mill 1953: 229)

What Mill is suggesting is that there are things that go into cultural identity that cannot be manufactured or accounted for by the state. As Kyle Duncan writes, "Human personhood requires a kaleidoscope of associations for its full expression" (Duncan 2006: 67). To overcome individualism with a manufactured sense of community will fail to unite a people beyond a superficial level as they will lack the necessary sinew. Tocqueville is not far removed from Mill when he writes,

> [w]hat keeps a great number of citizens under the same government is much less reasoned desire to remain united than the instinctive and, in a sense, involuntary accord which springs from like feelings and similar opinions; only when certain men consider a great many questions from the same point of view and have the same opinions on a great many subjects and when the same events give rise to like thoughts and impressions is there a society. (*DIA* I.2.10)

Mill's and Tocqueville's observations anticipate Iris Marion Young's argument that allowing the state to determine classification is tantamount to who is granted rights as it is through recognition that rights are granted. Therefore, if a certain group fails to gain recognition in a state, that group will lack legitimacy which leads to a lack of rights. "[T]he reason to draw a clear distinction between a nation and an ethnic group is to determine which groups have rights of self-government and which do not . . ." (Young 2000a: 153). Reading together Tocqueville, Mill, and Young we come away with a vision of the nation-state that is rather unappealing. The nation-state forces individualism but strives for a manufactured patriotism as a way of binding people to the state. The state fails to reproduce a natural sense of community and in the process eliminates some natural communities, associations, and identities.

Part of what motivates my theory of federalism is the failure of modern nation-states. If a federal structure operates according to the parameters which I set—which include scale and mechanisms for preserving scale and deliberation—it will be more likely that a nation-state will avoid some of the failures that have come to define its existence. By emphasizing local governance a sense of community will increase along with civil society. As a result, people will be less reliant on the government and the government will tend to be less overbearing, for it will be given less opportunity. The mechanisms that are necessary for preserving federalism will also be able to overcome the nation-state's tendency to force groupings and identities that are unnatural. By equipping groups and local entities with the federalism preserving mechanisms I discuss in Chapters 4 through 6, groups will be able to use formal channels to protect themselves against the tendencies of the nation-state.[7]

Because government is needed there can be no call for an end of the state and there need not be a need for a call to end the nation-state. What is needed is a revision of sovereignty. Althusius provides the most straightforward account of how a nation-state can be formed without becoming the nation-state of modernity. There are other philosophers who help clarify Althusius and give depth to areas in which he is thin, but the point he makes that there need to remain levels of association that maintain their importance, and members of those associations need to maintain their identity, is a lesson that needs to be learned by modern governments.

In the next section is an account of what happens when the people are no longer thought of as sovereign.

Sovereign Immunity

This section will provide a general outline of sovereign immunity jurisprudence in the United States. The analysis shows that government actors work consistently toward an expansion of their authority. When the national government is in competition with the state government the Supreme Court acts to restrict state authority and increase national authority, but when a state is in competition with a nonstate actor (e.g., individual, Indian tribe) it will work to the advantage of the state. The general lesson is that federalism should not be focused on devolving power to a lower level of government, or any level of government, for government at all levels is capable of abusing power. Federalism should grant sovereignty to citizens. This is a view consistent with Althusius and subsidiarity as discussed in the first chapter.

State sovereign immunity was formerly established in the United States by the Eleventh Amendment as a way of protecting states from civil lawsuits. Malcolm Feeley and Edward Rubin praise the Eleventh Amendment for its ability to promote federalism because it has an identifiable core, something they argue the Tenth Amendment lacks.[8] In Article III of the U.S. Constitution the national courts are given diversity jurisdiction in order to create a neutral forum in case a citizen and a state enter into a dispute. The Eleventh Amendment precludes such diversity jurisdiction when a defendant is a state. The Eleventh Amendment has been expanded.

> While the amendment, by its literal terms, seems to apply only to diversity suits, the Court has extended it to federal question suits as well. It has applied the amendment not only to citizens suing another state in federal court but to citizens suing their own state on a federal claim in federal court. In addition and perhaps most remarkably, it has barred citizens from suing their own state on a federal claim in their own state court. (Feeley and Rubin 2008: 145)

According to Feeley and Rubin the national government has placed some restrictions on state sovereign immunity that extend beyond the restrictions it has placed on national sovereign immunity. First, the federal government may bring suit against a state. Second, the national government can authorize actions against the state to enforce the Civil War Amendments. Third, the U.S. Supreme Court can overturn state court decisions. Feeley and Rubin's description of the Eleventh Amendment and its evolution leave one to wonder why they would suggest that it is worthy of more praise than the Tenth in terms of having an identifiable core. Feeley and Rubin are in a small minority of scholars who consider Eleventh Amendment jurisprudence coherent. Look for instance to 2006 when the Court exhibited the seeming-schizophrenia it has become known for in state sovereign immunity cases. Having decided in 1996 that states were immune from suits seeking money damages,[9] the Supreme Court seemed to reverse itself by deciding that Congress could abrogate a state's sovereign immunity under the Bankruptcy Clause.[10] This is not a reversal of the Court's jurisprudence as some have suggested,[11] but the continuation of a policy in which the Court is willing to restrict state sovereign immunity if it means increasing national power, and its willingness to increase sovereign immunity of the state if it comes at the expense of nonstate actors. For most commentators, the Supreme Court is inconsistent in its application and has expanded the sovereign immunity protections further than they were ever intended. But, I agree with Feeley and Rubin that the Court has been consistent in at least one aspect, and that is in increasing the authority of the national government through sovereign immunity.

Modern defenders of state sovereign immunity trace the origins of the doctrine in the United States to Alexander Hamilton who wrote in *Federalist* #81,

> It is inherent in the nature of sovereignty, not to be amenable to the suit of an individual without its consent. This is the general sense and the general practice of mankind; and the exemption, as one of the attributes of sovereignty, is now enjoyed by the government of every state in the union.

In this instance, however, Hamilton strips individuals of their sovereignty and turns it over to the states. In so doing he redefined federalism.

State sovereign immunity came later than national sovereign immunity, and it is less extensive even now. But its threat to individual liberty is still daunting. Before the passage of the Eleventh Amendment, the delegates at the Constitutional Convention in Philadelphia recognized that the states needed some sort of protection against law suits. But, fears materialized early on in the absence of a formal restraint on the ability of private citizens to sue state governments. In *Chisholm v. Georgia*[12] two citizens from South Carolina, acting as executors of a British creditor, filed suit against Georgia. In 1793 the Court decided that the suit was consistent with Article III, Section 2, which gave the federal courts jurisdiction over controversies "between a State and Citizens of another State." To protect state sovereignty against the centralizing tendency of the federal courts, and to protect the states against an onslaught of citizen suits, Congress and the states ratified the Eleventh Amendment which overturned *Chisholm*. Initially directed only at a narrow range of cases, state courts—with support from the U.S. Supreme Court—have consistently expanded the meaning of the Eleventh Amendment to include any suit filed against a state. Of course, this is to be expected. States, no matter what size, will utilize the tools at their disposal to increase their authority.

Equally disconcerting is the Court's willingness to break away from the text of the Constitution and the Eleventh Amendment, something it did in *Seminole Tribe*. "Although the text of the Amendment would appear to restrict only the Article III diversity jurisdiction of federal courts, we have understood the Eleventh Amendment to stand not so much for what it says, but for the proposition . . . which it confirms."[13] The Court has been willing to expand the application of the Eleventh Amendment beyond the text, which conflicts with Article III, Section 2 as well as the historical background. The Court suggests that because the U.S. inherited the common law tradition from England, and because the common law prohibited the Crown from being sued, that the same courtesy should be extended to the states.[14] What the Court, in invoking this reasoning, forgets is that the U.S. rebelled against a government that could not be held accountable by the people.

> [T]hat "the King can do no wrong" has always been absurd; the bloody path trod by the English monarchs both before and after they reached the throne demonstrated the fictional character of any such assumption. Even if the fiction

has been accepted in Britain, the recitation in the Declaration of Independence of the wrongs committed by King George III made the proposition unacceptable on this side of the Atlantic.[15]

Moreover, as I have shown in my two previous books, the common law was not adopted wholesale, but only those features that provided a basis for the protection of individual liberty were incorporated into the U.S. constitutional tradition.[16] I find support for my conclusion that sovereign immunity has little to do with justice, federalism, or original intent in Kenneth Culp Davis. Rather that being grounded in justice, federalism, or original intent, the "strongest support for sovereign immunity is provided by the four horse team so often encountered—historical accident, habit, a natural tendency to favor the familiar, and inertia" (Davis 1970: 384).

Had the ratifiers of the Eleventh Amendment wanted broader sovereign immunity protections they would have adopted the earlier amendment that was never voted on that read,

> [t]hat no state shall be liable to be made a party defendant in any of the Judicial Courts established or to be established under the authority of the United States, at the suit of any person or persons, citizens or foreigners, or of any body politics or corporate whether within or without the United States.

But instead they adopted an amendment that read, "The Judicial power of the United States shall not be construed to extend to any suit in law or equity, commenced or prosecuted against one of the United States by Citizens of another State, or by Citizens or Subjects of any Foreign State." The Supreme Court is correct in citing precedent dating back to *Hans* that supports its expansive reading, but *Hans* was without precedent[17] and the Court's expansive reading is judicially constructed as a result, something it is only willing to do when it is in its favor to do so.[18]

The Supreme Court has expanded state sovereign immunity for various reasons, but the Rehnquist and Roberts Courts have expanded state sovereign immunity in their effort to strengthen federalism. "Dual sovereignty is a defining feature of our Nation's constitutional blueprint. States, upon ratification of the Constitution, did not consent to become mere appendages of the Federal government. Rather, they entered the union with their sovereignty intact."[19] This may be true to some degree, but the Court denies the existence of citizen sovereignty, for it was the citizens of each state who were called upon to ratify the new Constitution through conventions, not the state as an autonomous actor.[20] The Court, in trying to improve federalism, has only followed Hamilton.

In *Alden v. Maine* a similar statement was made by the Court in addressing two of the ways the Constitution provides for state sovereign immunity.

> First, it reserves to them a substantial portion of the Nation's primary sovereignty, together with the dignity and essential attributes inhering to that status. Second,

even as to matters within the competence of the National government, the constitutional design secures the founding generation's rejection of "the concept of a central government that would act upon and through the States" in favor of "a system in which the State and Federal Governments would exercise concurrent authority over the people . . ."[21]

If the *Alden* Court's reading of the American founding is accurate, then not only does that Court adhere to a threatening form of federalism, but so too did the American founding. That is, such statements only reflect Hamilton's thought, and misstep, when it comes to federalism. Sovereign immunity is about insulating the states from the people, not preserving federalism. Federalism seeks to create proper spheres of authority within government while leaving the people sovereign. Federalism understands that a state government should be a buffer of protection for the people against the national government. When sovereign immunity is granted to the states that buffer is lost and the threat to the people comes from the state and the national government.

State sovereign immunity has increased, just as federal sovereign immunity has. But, relative to federal sovereign immunity, state sovereign immunity has declined. The Court has never been shy about exerting national superiority in matters of sovereign immunity nor in abrogating the sovereign immunity of state actors when it competes with the national government. But, when competing with nonstate actors, state sovereign immunity has expanded consistently.

If what we want is a clear example of how the national government has used the sovereign immunity doctrine in its favor we should look to *Pennhurst State School & Hospital v. Halderman*[22] as this is where the Supreme Court took from the states their ability to define what a state agency is in order to limit sovereign immunity protections afforded to states. The Court argued that because of how the agency was created, the Eleventh Amendment did not apply. The Court stated, here and elsewhere, that Congress has the power to abrogate the Eleventh Amendment and allow for states to be sued in federal court without the state's consent.[23] In his objection to the majority holding in *Pennhurst State School & Hospital*, Justice Stevens shows how state sovereignty has come under attack from the federal government. This decision had the affect of saying that states cannot decide for themselves what is and what is not a state actor. This means it is up to the Court and the national government to decide the matter.

But, the abrogation of state sovereign immunity looks less serious when compared to how Native American tribes have been treated, particularly with regard to sovereign immunity. Justice Kennedy's opinion in *Idaho v. Coeur d'Alene Tribe* reflects the preference for states over communities and individuals as he emphasizes the importance of maintaining the dignity of the state even at the expense of individuals and communities. Such an interpretation is, as he admits, judicially constructed and not based on the Eleventh Amendment or Article III. The Court's recognition of sovereign immunity has not been limited to the suits described in the text of the Eleventh Amendment.

> To respect the broader concept of immunity, implicit in the Constitution, which we have regarded the Eleventh Amendment as evidencing and exemplifying, we have extended a State's protection from suit to suits brought by the State's own citizens. Furthermore, the dignity and respect afforded a State, which the immunity is designed to protect, are placed in jeopardy whether or not the suit is based on diversity jurisdiction. As a consequence, suits invoking the federal-question jurisdiction of Article III courts may also be barred by the Amendment. (Doernberg 2005: 112)

Kennedy's concern with state dignity echoes *Hans v. Louisiana* when the majority wrote, "The preeminent purpose of state sovereign immunity is to accord States the dignity that is consistent with their status as sovereign entities."[24] In the Court's view, the dignity and sovereignty of the individual, or the people, is subordinate to that of the state. James Wilson, writing from a Lockean—rather than an Hobbesian or Hamiltonian—perspective in *Chisholm* shows how far the *Hans* and *Coeur d'Alene* decisions have extended sovereign immunity protection.

> I know, and can decide upon the knowledge that the citizens of Georgia, when they acted upon the large scale of the Union, as a part of the 'People of the United States,' did not surrender the Supreme or sovereign Power to that State; but, as to the purpose of the Union, retained it to themselves . . . Let a State be considered as subordinated to the People . . . [25]

Communities and people have become subordinate to the state as examples from sovereign immunity cases show.

The Supreme Court has an accomplice in Congress. Congress acts when the Court will not, to restrict tribal immunity which then allows the Court to restrict tribal immunity without breaking away from the law too far. In *California v. Cabazon of Mission Indians*[26] the Court was unable to permit California to regulate gambling on tribal lands as it would infringe on the sovereignty of the tribal government. This prompted Congress to pass the Indian Gaming Regulator Act (IGRA) which allowed the states to regulate gaming on tribal lands. The pertinent portion of the law reads,

> Indian tribes have the exclusive right to regulate gaming activity on Indian lands if the gaming activity is not specifically prohibited by Federal law and is conducted within a State which does not, as a matter of criminal law and public policy, prohibit such gaming activity.[27]

So, Indian tribes can only have gaming which is not prohibited by the state. Moreover, even if a gaming type is not prohibited by a state, the Indian tribe must enter into a compact with the state to allow it to have said gaming. This simply means that the tribes have only as much authority over their lands as the state chooses not to take.

When a tribe seeks to enter into a compact under the IGRA the state must negotiate in good faith with the tribe. Under the IGRA, should the state refuse to negotiate, the tribe has standing in a U.S. District Court. The remedy the court can offer is a 60-day extension for negotiations. If negotiations are not held within this timeframe, the Secretary of the Interior is authorized to settle the matter even without the consent of the state. This statute gave rise to *Seminole Tribe of Florida v. Florida* in which the state of Florida refused to enter into negotiations with the Seminole Tribe and the tribe sought remedy through the means laid out in the IGRA. The Supreme Court decided that Congress did not have the authority to abrogate state sovereign immunity in this instance and therefore the tribe could not file suit in district court nor seek a remedy with the Secretary of the Interior. In *Seminole Tribe* the Court declared a new, forceful immunity theory by rejecting a suit brought by a sovereign Indian tribe against a state that was authorized by federal law. The Court has decided that state sovereign immunity seems to be impervious to Congress's enumerated powers in matters related to a state's relationship with Indian tribes.

> Eventually, the Supreme Court held in *Seminole Tribe v. Florida* that the Eleventh Amendment immunized the states from suit in federal court; this decision effectively eradicates a significant feature of the gaming statute, and hands over most of the bargaining power the tribes had taken from *Cabazon* to the recalcitrant states. *Seminole Tribe* meant that states could negotiate terms much more favorable to them in the compact negotiations. (Fletcher 2005: 77)

Seminole Tribe is thus important for understanding the present argument about why states' rights should not be considered synonymous with federalism and for the argument developed in the following chapters that subnational entities need to be equipped with sufficient power to limit the threat to their authority from other levels of government. Without a veto power, or some tool to force deliberation, deliberation will not occur. If there is an asymmetric power distribution, the entity which has a disproportionate share of power will use it to strengthen its position, and can do so at the detriment of the other actors. This is why I advocate the legitimization of nullification, veto, and secession in federal schemes. These mechanisms will empower the subnational units in such a way that will force deliberation, maximize consensus, and minimize threats to sovereignty and minority rights.

Before the event of *Seminole Tribe*, tribal lands were free to have gaming as they thought fit. After the episode, tribes were only allowed gaming that was explicitly allowed elsewhere in the state unless the state was willing to grant an exception. And if the state was unwilling to abide by federal law, the tribe had no recourse except through appeal to the state because remedy through the executive branch, the federal judiciary, and the legislative branch was cut off.

The IGRA provided remedial relief to Indian tribes in cases where the state was unwilling to negotiate in good faith. But due to the Courts' reading of sovereign immunity, any provision granting relief to Indian tribes has been read out of the statute by *Texas v. U.S.*,[28] *Seminole Tribe, Davis v. U.S.*,[29] and *U.S. v. Spokane Tribe of Indians.*[30] In *Davis*, the federal court wrote,

> [T]he Supreme Court's recent statement that the judicial concept of tribal sovereign immunity developed 'almost by accident' and the Court's admonition that, at least in the commercial context, the doctrine should be curtailed by Congress, casts doubt on any past notion that tribal sovereign immunity could be an interest compelling in itself.[31]

Referring to *Davis*, Fletcher writes, "Given the high Court's criticism the court appeared to be saying that the weight given tribal immunity was drastically reduced, in comparison with the weight given federal or state immunity" (Fletcher 2005: 59).

In addition to these cases, the tenth circuit held in *Mescalero Apache Tribe v. New Mexico*[32] that IGRA abrogated tribal immunity from a state suit, seeking declaratory and injunctive relief for an alleged violation of the IGRA. This means under the IGRA a state may sue a member of a tribe that has entered into a contract in accordance with the IGRA. The circuit court decided that absent an express declaration from the Supreme Court or Congress that alters tribal immunity, the court is unwilling to do so itself. But the circuit court acknowledges that both Congress and the Supreme Court have, and have the authority to, limit and alter tribal immunity. This raises the question of how immune or sovereign tribes really are if their sovereign immunity can be curtailed at the hands of some other entity.

One of the most perplexing features of the tribal immunity cases is that Indian tribes are treated as private citizens. Tribes, at least historically, have not been treated so in any other arena. Indian tribes were often treated as sovereigns in that the U.S. government would make treaties with, and declare wars against, Indian tribes. This is perhaps the case because nowhere in the Eleventh Amendment are sovereign nations precluded from filing suit. The amendment only applies to citizens. That means the Eleventh Amendment could not protect Texas from being sued by Mexico or Georgia from the Cherokee Nation. Thus, if Indian tribes were granted sovereign status the national and state government would be forced to relinquish some of their power. It is to the government's advantage to treat Indians and tribes as nonsovereigns.

Recall the protection granted to states under state sovereign immunity. In nearly every instance preference was given to the state. This is not the case with regard to tribal immunity, particularly when a state and an Indian tribe conflict, because states act to bring all actors under their authority. I do not support tribal sovereign immunity any more than I support other types of sovereign immunity. No person or entity should be immune from being held accountable for its actions. This separates me from many of the critics of the Court's decisions regarding tribal sovereign immunity. I use it only as an example of how the state monopolizes power to acquire the power of all nonstate actors. "Indian rights are losing the limited protection they had as the Court forsakes foundation principles and expands the ambit of control over Indian tribes to include not just congressional but also judicial power to redefine and restrict tribal sovereignty" (Kunesh 2009: 398). This point is widely held, as Fletcher writes, "federal and state courts tend to short change Indian tribes and tribal sovereignty . . . It is apparent that state and federal courts treat the sovereign immunity of the states and federal government with more deference than the immunity of tribes" (Fletcher 2005: 5).

The unequal treatment of Indian tribes is reflected in more than just cases of sovereign immunity. In asking questions of who is an indispensable party in suits, the courts have decided that a representative from an Indian tribe need not be represented in court even when a tribe is being sued or is enjoined in a case. Two cases, *Saratoga County Chamber of Commerce, Inc. v. Pataki*[33] and *Dairyland Greyhound Park, Inc. v. McCallum*[34] both decided that Indian gaming tribes were not indispensable parties in gaming compact cases. That means, when negotiating a gaming compact with a state, or when a case arises challenging a compact, the gaming tribe does not have to be party in the suit. In these cases it was decided that the public's interest in bringing about a resolution to the matter was more important than the tribe's interest in being represented or than the tribe's interest in remaining immune from suit. But, such is not the case when a state's interest is in question. In *Kickapoo Tribe of Indians v. Babbitt*[35] the absent party was a state. Though the situations were similar and the state made all the same arguments made by the tribes in *Saratoga County* and *Dairyland Greyhound*, the state's argument prevailed.

> The district court's opinion [in *Kickapoo* that decided the state does not have to be joined], in most respects, reads exactly like the state court decisions in *Saratoga County* and *Dairyland Greyhound* [that did not join the tribes] . . . . . The D.C. Circuit, in reversing the district court [in *Kickapoo*], rejected all of those arguments in favor of, essentially, on factor—the absent party in interest was a sovereign, immune from suit without its consent. (Fletcher 2005: 101–2)

There is little that can be more threatening to a tribe's sovereignty than denying that its presence is unnecessary. "The courts will dismiss actions that challenge the federal government's recognition of a tribe in the absence of the recognized tribe. Federal recognition creates and vests property and liberty interests in a particular group" (Fletcher 2005: 56). But when the recognition is denied, so too are property and liberty. This is central to a discussion of political recognition. First, it shows the importance of recognition. Second, it shows the problem of recognition in that one must be recognized by the government to be considered valuable enough to have rights. Recognition is lost in this juridical model.

To extend this discussion briefly, the case of sovereign immunity and representation are not isolated cases. The Court decided in 1978 that Indian tribes do not have the inherent power to exercise criminal jurisdiction over non-Indians on Indian land because tribes—remember they were once thought of and treated as nations—have submitted "to the overriding sovereignty of the United States."[36] Even in matters of civil jurisdiction the Court has decided that Indian tribes have almost no civil jurisdiction over nonmembers and nonmember owned land within reservations because granting that power to tribes would be "inconsistent with the dependent status of tribes."[37] Just to drive the point home as to the superiority of state officials, the Court decided that state officials are immune from tribal jurisdiction in civil matters.[38]

This is simply a trend that began with the ratification of the Constitution.

> Treaty and other diplomatic negotiations between colonies and Indians indicate that each regarded the other as distinct political formations, but unified sovereign states in the modern sense did not exist on the continent. Among other things, the founding of the U.S. began the process of creating such a modern unified sovereign state, a process that spelled disaster for the Indians. (Young 2000b: 244)

Both the limiting of tribal immunity and the amplification of state sovereign immunity is what we should expect from a government that has misunderstood federalism. Our understanding of federalism has developed in such a way that limits the people's ability to protect itself against government action.

An examination of how Indian tribes have been stripped of their sovereign immunity protections reinforces the claim that the modern conception of the state is distinct from the traditional idea of community. The modern conception of the state argues that anything outside of the state must be brought under state control. If one refers back to Althusius and Aristotle one will recognize that government control is a product of modernity given that the ancient conception did not allow for either civil life or political life to control the other but encouraged cooperation between each.

The point here, to state again, is not that tribal immunity should be strengthened, but to show that sovereign immunity is a malleable judicial concept that can be used to strengthen the nation-state. The concept of sovereign immunity stands in contrast to a system of government that grants its citizens sovereignty and thus stands in contrast to federalism. If an actor is granted sovereign immunity, and that actor defines the bounds of its sovereign immunity, those boundaries will increase.[39]

By examining the Native American conflict with the U.S. national government I not only emphasize the importance of equipping the constituent parts in a federal system with the proper mechanisms to defend their zone of authority, but it allows us to resituate our understanding of what federalism can be. That is, federalism does not have to be a state-centered solution to the problem of centralization. In fact, by offering only state-centered solutions, one is reinforcing the Hobbesian perspective that has bestowed legitimacy upon the tendency toward centralization. This case study serves two additional purposes: (1) it allows for an elaboration of the argument that federalism should not end with a discussion of state vs. national government but must go to a smaller and more local level, and (2) it shows that courts, especially those who are part of the central structure, cannot be the final arbiters of matters of federalism nor the mechanisms which are designed to preserve federalism.

Locke's Rejection of Sovereign Immunity

Should one remain unconvinced by the criticism of sovereign immunity as practiced, I shall offer one more criticism on normative grounds. What I have attempted to convince the reader of is that state sovereign immunity is inimical to federalism in that it enhances the power of the state at the expense of nonstate actors. Not only do the outcomes associated with state sovereign immunity undermine federalism but the theory of sovereign immunity itself undercuts one of the primary components of federalism: the citizen's sovereignty.

In order to show how sovereign immunity runs counter to one strand of liberal political theory I will go to John Locke. Locke's political theory is an objection to sovereign immunity. Where Locke says that all persons living within civil society must have a common judge to appeal to, sovereign immunity takes the common judge away and puts the government in its place. Thus, if we apply Locke's argument, sovereign immunity reduces civil society to a state of nature for when sovereign immunity is used by the state to shield itself from the citizens there ceases to be a common judge.

It is enough for now to state that for Locke, civil society provides three features that are absent in the state of nature, and it is the presence of these three features that distinguishes civil society from the state of nature and makes it preferable to the state of nature. The three features include a known and indifferent judge, known and fixed law, and known and common executioner of law.

> [S]ince 'tis easily to be imagined, that he who was so unjust as to do his Brother an Injury, will scarce be so just as to condemn himself for it: But I shall desire those who make this Objection, to remember that Absolute Monarchs are but Men, and if government is to be the Remedy of those Evils, which necessarily follow from Men being Judges in their own Cases, and the State of Nature is therefore not to be endured, I desire to know what kind of Government that is, and how much better it is that the State of Nature, where one Man commanding a multitude, has the Liberty to be Judge in his own Case, and may do to all his Subjects whatever he pleases, without the least liberty to any one to question . . . (§13[40])

L. T. Hobhouse echoes the sentiment when he writes, "the first condition of free government is government not by the arbitrary determination of the ruler, but by fixed rules of law, to which the ruler himself is subject" (Hobhouse 1964: 17).

When sovereign immunity is practiced, at least two of the three distinguishing features disappears since the judge is not unbiased—as it is the state deciding for itself what should be done—and the law that citizens are subject to is not extended to the government. If Citizen A sues Government B for wrongdoing, and an Agent of

Government B is left to decide the matter we may not conclude that the Agent is an unbiased judge since the Agent has a vested interest in the case. Moreover, if the Agent decides that Citizen A cannot file suit against Government B because the law does not afford him this right when it would afford him this right against another citizen, then Government B cannot be said to be subject to the same law as the citizens.[41] However, the second of these is less pertinent than the first in the matter at hand since we are dealing with judging under a known law—primarily the Eleventh Amendment—which was approved by the people. The question is whether the first of these—the known and indifferent judge—is vacated with the practice of sovereign immunity.[42] I argue that because an agent of the government is deciding a case in which the government is a party that the judge is not indifferent. Even when state sovereign immunity was abrogated, it was done so in such a way that the power of the national government was strengthened. This argument is supported by my above discussion, but the point is made more salient when looking at cases of judicial immunity specifically.

One of the problems with the state of nature, according to Locke, is that when there was a grievance between two parties, the two parties had to decide for themselves how to settle the matter and decide who was at fault. And because men tend to be biased in their own cases, conflict would result. Therefore, when a dispute arises between two citizens in a civil society, the government can step in and be the common judge. "Those who are united into one Body, and have a common establish'd Law and Judicature to appeal to, with Authority to decide Controversies between them, and punish Offenders, are in Civil Society one with another." But in civil society, when there is a dispute between citizen and government, one of the parties remains the judge, and that party is superior to the citizen because it can execute the law and has the authority to judge, thus making it equivalent to the state of nature. "[B]ut those who have no such common Appeal, I mean on Earth are still in the state of Nature, each being, where there is no other, Judge for himself, and Executioner; which is as I have before shew'd it, the perfect state of Nature" (§87).

Locke's objection to monarchy in the *Second Treatise* is based upon the premise that a single individual with the power to make and execute laws, and make judgments about those laws, will remain in the state of nature with his subjects because there is no recourse for the subjects should the monarch act contrary to their interests. This is very much the case with sovereign immunity. Although there is a division of power within government, the powers are all vested within government, and when there is need for appeal on behalf of the citizens, there is no where to go but to the entity who is thought to be at fault.

[N]ow whenever his Property is invaded by the Will and Order of his Monarch, he has not only no Appeal, as those in Society ought to have, but as if he were degraded from the common state of Rational Creatures, is denied a liberty to judge of, or to defend his Right, and so is exposed to all the Misery and Inconveniencies that a Man can fear from one, who being in the unrestrained state of Nature, is yet corrupted with Flattery, and armed with Power . . . For if it be asked, what Security, what Fence is there in such a State, against the Violence and Oppression of this Absolute Ruler? (§§ 91and 93)

And to this last question we must answer none.

In civil society there is no recourse beyond the government or its agents that the citizen may go to for relief. Therefore, should the court system decide—particularly at the Supreme Court level in the United States—that the citizen may not bring suit, then the citizen may not go to an arbiter other than the government. But, if the government cannot be indifferent then "there is no common superior on Earth to appeal to for relief," which then defines the situation as "the State of War" (§19). When a suit is being decided between the government and a citizen there is no common superior for the government is the superior and the government is party to the suit. The problem arises when we recognize that the judge between government and citizen is not common, and that there is no appeal except to the government. This means that if a citizen is wronged by the government, the entity being accused gets to decide if it has done wrong. If that entity decides against the citizen, the citizen has no other outlet. If this is the case, then it is hard to see how a government with sovereign immunity is not in a state of nature with its citizens.

No individual would enter, or should enter, into a society where she has no recourse against the government should the government act against her interests just so she can escape the state of nature.

Betwixt Subject and Subject, they will grant, there must be Measure, Laws, and Judges, for their mutual Peace and Security . . . As if when Men quitting the State of Nature entered into Society, they agreed that all of them but one, should be under restraint of Laws, but that he should still retain all the Liberty of the State of Nature, increased with Power, and made licentious by Impunity. This is to think that men are so foolish that they take care to avoid what Mischiefs may be done them by Pole-Cats, or Foxes, but are content, nay think it Safety, to be devoured by Lions. (§93)

This is to say that the concept of sovereign immunity, as understood in the United States by the U.S. Supreme Court, was an irrational act on behalf of the citizens. While it may be that the citizens acted against their own self-interest, it is equally likely that the Supreme Court has distorted the meaning of the Eleventh Amendment to run counter to the interests of the citizens. This last conclusion is not unexpected for someone who has read Locke, for there is no common judge on earth when a citizen sues the government.

Locke's rejection of sovereign immunity rests, primarily, on the argument that people should not be judges in their own cases because people will always be biased in their own favor. No instance of sovereign immunity makes this claim more salient than judicial immunity. Because it is a quintessential repeat-player in federal litigation, the federal government exerts a powerful influence on federal courts and the development of legal doctrine. (Sisk, 2006).

Bivens v. Six Unknown Named Agents,[43] and the cases which hold it as the controlling precedent, recognize that most government employees receive only qualified immunity, but judges have given themselves what seems to be absolute immunity. For instance, a mother of three criminal defendants wrote objectionable letters to the judge hearing her children's case and the judge found her in contempt and sentenced the mother to 30 days in jail. She sued on the basis that state law prohibited the judge from punishing out of court contempt. In *Adams v. McIhany*[44] the Fifth Circuit decided against the mother despite the fact that the judge acted contrary to a state statute. The decision in *Malina v. Gonzales*[45] protected a judge who illegally tried to pull a car over in a fit of road rage. Malina, not knowing it was a judge in the car with a flashing red light did not pull over. Three hours later the judge sent a police officer to his house to bring Malina in to the judge's chambers. The judge charged him with six criminal acts. It was decided by the Fifth Circuit that the judge's actions on the freeway were not immune, but sending Malina to jail was an immune act. In *Stump v. Sparkman*,[46] a long standing precedent was supported which stated that

> a general principle of the highest importance to the proper administration of justice that a judicial officer, in exercising the authority vested in him, [should] be free to act upon his own convictions, without apprehension of personal consequences of himself. . . . The scope of the judge's jurisdiction must be construed broadly where the issue is the immunity of the judge . . . A judge is absolutely immune from liability for his judicial acts even if his exercise of authority is flawed by the commission of grave procedural error . . . Despite the unfairness to litigants that sometimes results, the doctrine of judicial immunity is thought to be in the best interests . . .[47, 48]

Perhaps the idea behind sovereign immunity as originally constructed was not as mischievous as its later practice, but granting such protection to the agents who decide how far the protection will extend will expectedly result in an expansion. What Locke shows is that the presence of sovereign immunity violates the principles which legitimate government is founded upon. In this instance, practice follows theory. I would not go so far as to say that the national and state governments have entered into a state of war with the citizens even though Locke might, but it could be said that the use of sovereign immunity is an abuse of power that should undermine the legitimacy of the government. Because the judiciary is the central institution in the perpetuation of state and federal sovereign immunity the analysis of the issue raises another interesting suggestion: the judiciary should not be relied on as a protector of rights, particularly minority rights. In order for a federal system to prevail, the capacity for judicial review should be minimized for the judiciary, particularly the national judiciary, will look to consolidate power at the national level.

Judicial Review

To accept NVS, particularly nullification and veto, one must undergo a shift in paradigm from thinking that the government needs, at all times, to provide us with a final word on the matters it considers. One needs to function under the paradigm that government policy is a way we improve our conditions, but in no way does the government get it right each time it tries and therefore it is only through revision, challenge, and iteration that it has any hope of attaining the good. For some reason, in the United States—and it is a model that is gaining popularity in other countries—the judiciary has the authority to define and redefine the law. In a quasi-federal structure like the the United States, the problem with judicial review is not only a problem of reconciling practice with theory, but that the power of judicial review in the hands of the national government unbalances the federal structure. "To save such interpretative matters to the federal judiciary is thus 'tantamount to inviting any other form of federal political control over the states'" (Kahn 2002: 37). There are still those who think that "State legislatures, or *ad hoc* conventions, reflecting and beholden to the popular temper of the moment, are improper tribunals to decide matters that affect the entire federation" (Kahn 2002: 37). But what this criticism fails to recognize is that the federation is not a monolith, and unless every constituent part is consulted through democratic—preferably deliberatively democratic—means independent of its national-level representatives, it loses its federal nature. Moreover, there is no reason why the national structure's interests should be given preference to those of the constituent members. The will of the constituent members should not be overwhelmed by the will of the national government.

This chapter has attempted to show that the judiciary should not be relied upon as an unbiased arbiter of the law. In its place we should put a more deliberative framework. But it is not a call for deliberative democracy as currently understood in the literature. As argued in Chapter 1, my version of federalism goes beyond standard versions of deliberative democracy in that it incorporates a theory of scale and a reconceived notion of liberty. To further distinguish my deliberative framework from what is typically encouraged by deliberative democrats—and to provide a contribution to democratic theory more generally—I will consider the place of judicial review in a democratic society.

A discussion of judicial review in a book on federalism may seem out of place. For the following reason it is not. Federalism runs counter to the state-centered focus of modern democratic theory of which judicial review is apart. Modern democratic theory tends to place an emphasis on state-generated solutions. This has caused some to excuse the undemocratic nature of the judiciary in their search for a government that will protect minority rights and the majority's right to rule. Aside from an electorally independent judiciary with the power of judicial review there appear to be few alternatives to checking the will of the majority in order to preserve constitutionally protected rights. The only manner by which most researchers see to correct the misdeeds of the majority is through judicial review (Lemieux and

Watkins 2009: 40). Some have tried to say that judicial review can be placed in the hands of other agencies and thus be termed constitutional review (Zurn 2007), but this does little more than shift the focus away from the central issue of whether it is necessary and proper to have unelected oversight of popularly chosen policies. The argument for a heightened status of judicial review in constitutional democracies begs for an insurrection. Judicial review is neither democratic nor deliberative, and failure to accept this seems more like justification for the way things are rather than a defense of what ought to be. Surely we must not be willing to sacrifice the good for a pursuit of the perfect, but we need not heap more praise upon the "is" by calling it good simply because it is what has been achieved. Federalism, as constructed throughout this book, offers a viable alternative that breaks from the existing paradigm of institutional theorizing.

The debate over judicial review in democratic theory has created a dichotomy in which one side argues that it is democratic because it can help preserve democratic values and the other argues that it is undemocratic because its outcomes are not popularly controlled. The first group argues that the ends associated with a particular decision, the substantive outcome, is what should be used to define whether something is democratic. "Democratic rule is not exclusively majority rule. Democracy entails a set of ideals and principles beyond the mechanism of majority rule" (Lemieux and Watkins 2009: 39). The second group argues that the means for making decisions, or the procedures of democracy, are the defining characteristic of democracy. A proceduralist would say that a U.S. Supreme Court decision overturning a law that was passed democratically, but limits the right of political participation to a certain minority population is undemocratic because the decision to discriminate was made through democratic procedures and thus consistent with the will of the majority. A substantivist would argue that a court decision to overturn a discriminatory practice is democratic as there are certain values that must be preserved in order for something to be considered democratic. To put it rather crudely, proceduralists argue that the ends do not justify the means and substantivists argue that the means do not justify the ends. Of course, the nuances of the debate are considered by the participants to be much more sophisticated than what I have outlined, but when the façade is stripped away this is what is left.

There are those, like Corey Brettschneider, who have taken an original look at this problem and therefore deserve some consideration apart from the general debate. Brettschneider develops, while borrowing heavily from John Rawls, a value theory of democracy in which equality of interests, political autonomy, and reciprocity are the three core values of democracy (Brettschneider 2006: 261). These values implicate both democratic procedures and substantive rights. They allow, though it is less than ideal he admits, for a nondemocratic procedure to step in without the act being undemocratic because he has set up a theory in which procedures and outcomes are linked. However, it seems to me that while his attempt pushes us forward, it still falls into the camp of substantive arguments without fully addressing how we can side step the procedural constraints of democracy and still be considered democratic. For instance, equality of interests requires "that all reasonable interests of citizens must be respected as having equal weight. No one person should have his interests counted as more than any other person by virtue of his social position or class" (Brettschneider 2006: 271). Even though each party to a case presented in court is represented, certain groups have advantages over others. For instance, in front of the Supreme Court, repeat players, which are typically the well-heeled, have far more success than those without the resources and experience.

As for his second core value, political autonomy "[b]roadly, entails the treatment of citizens as individual rulers in a society characterized by collective self-rule. Part of the requirement of political autonomy is a role for citizens in deciding through democratic procedures how policy should be formulated" (Brettschneider 2006: 271). It is tough to see how judicial review, or the courts in general, meets this standard. Judges, particularly in appellate courts with discretionary dockets, take the ability to self-rule away from the citizenry. This power is placed into the hands of attorneys and judges. It is not a matter of right that wins, but a matter of skill and resources at the attorney's disposal or the political bias of judges. But aside from the practical, constitutional courts are generally designed to be isolated from citizen influence, therefore by definition, self-rule, and thus political autonomy, is violated by the courts. Perhaps it is my inability to take what I know of judicial decision making out of the discussion that makes accepting Brettschneider's theory so difficult. Judges should not be given deference on matters of justice. Because the courts can error in their determination as often as the majority can, how are we justified in turning to an undemocratic institution that is not proven to be any more proficient than the majority? That is, if the courts were always correct then the argument on behalf of the substantivists has merit, but the courts do not meet this rigorous requirement.

Finally, reciprocity provides the most difficult sticking point for Brettschneider's theory on theoretical and practical grounds.

> Reciprocity is the notion that policies governing citizens' treatment must be defensible by appeal to arguments that reasonable citizens can accept . . . citizens who engage in mutual justification seek to justify particular public policies and the coercion these policies entail by appealing to the core values of equality and autonomy. (Brettschneider 2006: 272)

Embedded in this definition is the presumption that people will choose to play by the rules of democracy, and the primary rule is that the majority will rule. The unhappy person or group who appeals to the courts is abandoning the rules of the game in favor of an outside arbiter in hopes of getting a more favorable decision. If someone is dissatisfied with the policy, and they appeal to the courts, are they then not violating the value of reciprocity as set forth by Brettschneider? According to his definition, all one needs to do is make their claim "defensible by appeal to arguments that reasonable people can accept." Nothing says that the majority must acquiesce to objections or that a defensible argument is still not objectionable from the minority's position. But by preserving judicial review as a democratic procedure, Brettschneider is saying that the majority must appease the minority in all of its decisions or risk having those decisions overturned in court. It seems to me that to appeal a majority decision to the court would violate the value of reciprocity as Brettschneider has defined it as all that he requires of the value is that a position is defensible and appeals to the other two core values. From a democratic perspective, the decision of what is defensible and what appeals to core democratic values should occur among the citizens and the elected officials, to do otherwise would be to violate the rules of the game and thus reciprocity. Going to the courts is essentially giving up on democratic procedures in the hope of getting a more favorable decision. This concept then runs counter to an idea of reciprocity that requires one to respect the rules of the game.

Aside from these critiques, Brettschneider ends one of his articles with a thought provoking sentence. "While democratic procedures provide for rule by the people, substantive rights ensure that these procedures function for the people" (Brettschneider 2006: 273). What Brettschneider fails to explain is how procedures other than democratic ones can consistently provide government for the people. The primary shortcoming I see in Brettschneider's work is that it fails to confront what we know of politics and judicial decision making. The most consistent protector of the people is the people. This may not, as Brettschneider assumes it must, take the form of a centralized democratic government.

In addition to the above theoretical and practical critiques of the substantivists' position, it should also be recognized that courts often lack the capacity to be unbiased arbiters. Seen as a protector of minority rights, courts are put forth by advocates of judicial review as the only means by which majority tyranny can be thwarted. But as seen in my discussion of sovereign immunity and references to the literature on judicial decision making, this is hardly the case. But, aside from the practical and theoretical objections already put forth, it should be remembered that courts are not particularly good at protecting minority rights, largely due to the fact that courts lack implementation authority which means that if the view of a court is not supported by a majority in government, or in the population, there will be little acceptance of its opinion. Current scholarship recognizes that "A practice of judicial review cannot do anything for the rights of the minority if there is no support at all in the society for minority rights" (Lemieux and Watkins 2009: 47).

Look for instance at *Brown v. Board of Education* (1954). While most people are aware of specific instances of retaliation against the decision, more impressive is the general trend of inaction for the decade that followed the landmark decision. Gerald Rosenberg in *Hollow Hope* points out that desegregation in schools did not occur until Congress took action in 1964. He shows that until 1964, fewer than 7 percent of all Black school children went to school with White school children. Not only does the increase in desegregation correspond to legislative action, but also to the increased level of Black voter registration in Southern states. In 1956, only 2 years after *Brown*, registration level was at 25 percent, the same as in 1958. Then, in 1962, 29.4 percent of southern Blacks were registered to vote, by 1970 that number increased to 66.9 percent.

A concern about the inability of courts to promote social change only supplements my primary argument that courts do not provide an unbiased arbiter between competing interests. As I have argued, it is only through deliberative institutions that legitimacy can be conferred upon decisions consistently and enduringly.

So the reader does not think I adopt than the standard procedural argument as my own, I offer a critique of a proceduralist account that is far more sophisticated than any that have preceded it. Josiah Ober, providing that sophisticated account, argues that democracy has both instrumental and intrinsic values. Democracy produces good policy, thus giving it an instrumental value, but being involved in public decisions is also "a good-in-itself that is both inherently happiness-producing and necessary to our full happiness. It is necessary to our complete happiness because . . . the capacity to associate ourselves in decisions through the medium of speech is constitutive of our distinctive kind of being" (Ober 2007: 62). His assessment of democracy is grounded in a self-termed, "liberal-leaning Aristotelianism." Ober simply states that engaging in dialogue and taking part in decisions as part of a community has an ancillary benefit to humans as doing so is part of human nature. And since democracy allows us to do what is already in our nature to do, it makes us happy to do these things, even separate from the policies it produces. Ober makes four claims regarding democracy that have a direct bearing on my treatment of federalism.

(1) "Certain natural capacities are necessary for the happiness of that distinctive kind of being." And since democracy engages a human's natural capacity to engage with other humans it produces happiness. But, what Ober does not discuss is the political arrangements and institutional designs that must be present to allow citizens to engage in that capacity, for citizens will disengage from politics if they do not feel their engagement does not have an influence on government actions. Federalism, designed in the way I lay out, will increase citizen engagement and therefore allow human nature to partake in what is natural to it, thus potentially making people happier. Without the proper institutional design and incentives to produce citizen dialogue and engagement, democracy fails to deliver on Ober's first point.

(2) "Actions that are best construed as the happiness-producing expression of natural capacities, capacities that are in turn constitutive of an unconstrained and healthy adult actor's distinctive kind of being, ought to be promoted." Democracy, as it functions in the United States, does not promote these types of expressions of one's natural capacity. Democracy does not fulfill this requirement if left on its own, particularly in large-scale governing units, as people will lose interest and disengage from politics. Federalism, because it compensates for the largeness of most governing units, has the ability to promote these expressions.

(3) "Among human beings, associating in decisions is a natural capacity; the occasional exercise of that capacity, especially through public speech, is among the

characteristic behaviors of healthy adult humans in a state of nature and is constitutive of the human kind of being." This follows what I said with regard to point (2) above. When one looks beyond Ober to research on voter turnout one finds that there is a link between happiness, scale, and function in democracies. For instance, "the greater the extent of participation, the greater degree of happiness reported. This relationship . . . emerges from the fact that positive feelings are directly correlated with social participation . . ." (Phillips 1967: 479). Similarly, as Barreto, Segura, and Woods (2004) found, when voters are empowered, they are more likely to turn out to vote. Voters must feel as though their vote matters in determining who gets elected and in what gets done by those who are elected. Finding the proper scale of a governing unit can help increase the sense of efficacy among voters (Oliver 2000).

(4) "Participatory democracy is a particularly robust form of association in decision making." This point simply builds on the earlier two. It says that participating in democracy—through discussing policy with neighbors, signing petitions, voting for candidates or referenda, attending town hall meetings, running for office, volunteering for a campaign—will have a positive effect on the individual because it is what he or she is naturally inclined to do. But, Ober does not discuss what institutions need to be in place to encourage, or even allow, for this sort of behavior to occur. In fact, Ober recognizes that people will not stay engaged in political discourse or become involved on their own, for it is natural that they get side-tracked by events that happen at work, or with friends and family. Another drawback he admits is that "it might be the case that, due to problems of scale, robust participation would fail to produce policy in a timely manner" (Ober 2007: 69). Because of this he recognizes the need to abandon democracy as it is not suitable for all circumstances. I think Ober has conceded too easily. With regard to the objection he formulates based on scale, federalism solves this problem if implemented properly. That is, federalism will provide the relevant framework for democracy to achieve the instrumental benefits associated with it, which will then allow democracy to maintain its intrinsic value. Federalism is a facilitator of democracy.[49]

Judicial review raises serious doubts about its compatibility with democracy on purely procedural grounds given that it limits participation. But that critique does not address the substantivists, or those who have tried to bridge the divide. For those groups I argue that participation is a substantive and procedural right— or as Ober would say, it has both intrinsic and instrumental value. This point is in agreement with Lemieux and Watkins who observe that "[d]emocracy is a concept infused with both normative meaning and empirical assumptions and claims, and it is both difficult and unwise for democratic theorists to attempt to avoid serious consideration of either dimension of democracy in favor of the other" (Lemieux and Watkins 2009: 41). But Lemieux and Watkins, like others in favor of judicial review, fail to take notice of the fact that judicial review is not the only manner in which we can protect the normative meaning of democracy against a threatening majority, nor have they considered that participation does not operate on a single-value dimension. Participation has both a procedural and substantive dimension, which makes it distinctive. Most democratic theorists agree that the ability to participate in the political process is fundamental for democracy. For those of the substantivist bent this may not be persuasive. For substantivists, the characteristics of a democracy are values like liberty and equality, values that are consistent with democratic procedures, but are put in danger by a majority that does not respect the minority's claim to those values. Thus, for substantivists, the only reason why democratic procedures are good is for the good that they produce. Once they begin violating the values substantivists are for, democratic procedures lose their value. But, it is not just the ends produced by democratic procedures that are valuable as democratic procedures themselves are a desirable end for facilitating an integral component of human nature. Therefore, judicial review proves to be anti-democratic for both substantive and procedural reasons. Unfortunately, what Ober's understanding of democracy lacks—as does the understanding of other proceduralists—is an acknowledgement of the majority's willingness and ability to treat the minority unjustly. While he invokes powerful evidence of democracy's benefits he does not propose a solution for those instances in which the majority has become tyrannical. Thus, while his objection to the substantivists is philosophically convincing, his practical objection carries less weight. Federalism offers an alternative to the proceduralist-substantivist debate by allowing us to stop focusing on judicial review as the only option for keeping majority tyranny at bay.

Before federalism can be seen as a viable alternative to judicial review, it is important to look at another argument in favor of judicial review. Judicial review has been adopted by those who favor deliberative democracy as a way of enhancing deliberation (Zurn 2007).

Christopher Zurn has put forth a creative and daring attempt to justify the judiciary in a democracy. Zurn appropriately recognizes that the reasoning usually given for judicial review's compatibility with democracy is *ad hoc* in the sense that it takes the most prominent systems, typically the United States., and tries to make theoretical arguments for democracy and judicial review consistent with observation. But arguments dealing with first principles should be developed first, then used to measure the goodness of a system in practice (Zurn 2007: 9 and 13). Unfortunately, Zurn does not convincingly escape this trap.

One of the primary reasons democratic theory has taken this *ad hoc* approach, Zurn argues, is that the democratic theorizing is done against the backdrop of the United States. Since the United States has a strong judiciary with the power of judicial review and is also the world's leading democracy, it forces those in the discipline to justify judicial review as consistent, or necessary for, democratic practice. This is problematic in that the model of democracy employed (namely the United States may not be democratic. But democratic theorists implicitly deny this possibility. None of the leading theorists who use the United States as a backdrop consider that just because the United States has a strong judiciary and is a relevant example of democracy does not mean we must justify judicial review as democratic as it may in fact be a weakness of the U.S. model.

However, this does not stop Zurn from encouraging a deliberative model that utilizes a judiciary, or a judiciary-type institution. Zurn clearly sees the problem but his solution does not go far enough. The deliberation which he says is encouraged in his model is indirect and more of policy iteration than deliberative democracy. We must take Zurn's assessment of the problem seriously, but must be willing to go further in reforming the institutions from which the problems are derived.

Conclusion

To avoid the inequity that exists within a regime that is not subject to its own laws or subject to the decisions of an indifferent judge, groups and individuals must be able to retain their ability to look out for themselves. Over the next three chapters I will show how federalism can be so constructed as to achieve this end.

Over the next three chapters I will provide a working model of how a federal system can be constructed so that civil society is energized, respect for the minority is shown, deliberation is the basis for decisions, identity is constructed naturally, and recognition based upon that identity is granted. The next three chapters show how nullification, veto, and secession (NVS) act as federalism enhancing mechanisms which lead to those desired ends listed above.

Notes

1. Federalism entails a question of sovereignty in that each level of government is sovereign to a given degree within its geographic borders and over its designated responsibilities. Politics is a power struggle, and sovereignty is a grantor of power, thus if sovereignty can be manipulated then so too can the balance of power. The winner in such a power struggle maintains its sovereignty, assumes its competitor's and the loser then moves under the control of the winner.
2. "The social groups composing civil society, like the individuals within them, can effectively seek their own ends." But while associations at the local level have "an intrinsic knowledge of one's own proximate needs, [and] the ability to manage quotidian details. No group or individual, however, is self-sufficient. All have natural incapacities and thus must rely on assistance from higher groups to realize their own ends" (Duncan 2006: 67).
3. "The value of associations derives, in significant part, from the extent to which associations stand in tension with the individual on one side and the state on the other. In other words, associations are important relationally, as their relationship with the individuals and the state equips them to fulfill a mediating role. This role allows associations to serve as bridges between the individual and the surrounding, impersonal society, but it also injects tension into the association's relationships with the individual and the state" (Vishcer 2004: 951–2).

4. Within subsidiarity there is a "principled tendency toward solving problems at the local level and empowering individuals, families and voluntary associations to act more efficaciously in their own lives" (Vischer 2001: 116).

5. *New York v. United States*, 505 U.S. 144, 181–182 (1992).

6. If we take James Madison at his word in *Federalist #46*, we find some support for O'Connor's view. "The State governments will, in all possible contingencies, afford complete security against invasions of the public liberty by the national authority." Madison's sentiment is admirable, but he misses the point that states can turn against their citizens as well. Moreover, the Constitution, we have found, does not provide the necessary provisions for protecting national encroachment on state authority.

7. In the next three chapters I will show how centralized planning in certain areas increases the likelihood of conflict by either redrawing historical borders or politicizing certain cultural characteristics that had henceforth not been a source of conflict.

8. Feeley and Rubin seem to be going against mainstream opinion in that most commentators mock the inconsistencies within—or at least criticize the unsettled nature of—Eleventh Amendment jurisprudence (Doernberg 2005; Shortell 2008). McGinnis and Somin write, "The lack of a compelling structural rationale for state sovereign immunity under the Eleventh Amendment parallels the lack of strong textual support for this doctrine" (McGinnis and Somin 2004: 120).

9. *Seminole Tribe of Florida v. Florida*, 517 U.S. 44 (1996). The Court also stated in *Kimel v. Florida Borad of Regents*, 528 U.S. 62 (2000) at 78 that "Even where the Constitution vests in Congress complete lawmaking authority over an area, the Eleventh Amendment prevents congressional authority of suits by private parties against unconsenting states."

10. *Central Virginia Community College v. Katz*, 126 U.S. 990 (2006).

11. Fruehwald (2008) mentions, but does not consider it as evidence of a previous reversal in the manner *Central VA. C.C.* is a reversal of *Seminole Tribe*, that the Court reversed course in *Seminole Tribe* overturned *Pennsylvania v. Union Gas Co.* 491U.S. 1 (1989), which held that Congress could abrogate state sovereign immunity under the Interstate Commerce Clause.

12. 2 U.S. (2 Dall.) 419.

13. 517 U.S. at 54.

14. According to the Court, the founding generation supported an expansive application of sovereign immunity because "it was well established in English law the Crown could not be sued without consent in its own courts" (*Alden*, 527 U.S. at 715).

15. *Seminole Tribe*, 517 U.S. at 95 (Justice Stevens dissenting).

16. Scott (2007, 2009).

17. "It is part of our history, that, at the adoption of the constitution, all the States were greatly indebted; and the apprehension that these debts might be prosecuted in federal Courts formed a very serious objection to that instrument. Suits were instituted; and the Court maintained its jurisdiction. The alarm was general; and, to quiet the apprehensions that we so extensively entertained this amendment was proposed in Congress, and adopted by the State legislatures. That its motive was not to maintain the sovereignty of the State from the degradation supposed to attend a compulsory appearance before the tribunal of the nation may be inferred from the terms of the amendment" (*Cohens v. Virginia*, 19 U.S. 264 [1821] at 406).

18. "Where Congress has created a remedial scheme for the enforcement of a particular right, we have, in suits against federal officers, refused to supplement that scheme with one created by the judiciary" (*Seminole Tribe*, 517 U.S. at 74).

19. *Federal Maritime Commission v. South Carolina State Ports Authority*, 535 U.S. 743 (2002) at 751.

20. According to Akhil Amar, "each state's ratifying convention was superior to its ordinary legislature, for the convention was in theory the virtual embodiment of the people of that state" (Amar 1987: 1459).

21. *Alden v. Maine*, 527 U.S. 706 (1999) at 714.

22. 465 U.S. 89 (1984).

23. *Atascadero State Hospital v. Scanlon*, 473 U.S. 234 (1985) and *Dellmuth v. Muth*, 491 U.S. 223 (1989).

24. See comment below about Chief Justice Marshall's rejection of this reading of the Eleventh Amendment in 1821, 69 years before the *Hans* decision.

25. 2 U.S. (2 Dall.) 419 at 457, 455 (1789).

26. 480 U.S. 202 (1987).

27. 25 U.S.C. PP 2701(5).

28. 497 F3d. 491. (5th Cir. 2007).

29. 192 F.3d 951 (10th Cir. 1999).

30. 139 F.3d 1397 (9th Cir. 1998).

31. 192 F.3d 951, 960 (10th Cir. 1999).

32. 131 F.3d 1379 (10th Cir. 1997).

33. 798 N.E. 2d 1047 (N.Y 2003) cert. denied, 124 S. Ct. 570 (2003).

34. 655 N.W. 2d 474 (Wis. Ct. App. 2002) review denied, 655 N.W. 2d 129 (Wis. 2002).

35. 43 F.3d 1491 (D.C. Cir. 1995).

36. *Oliphant v. Squamish*, 435 U.S. 191, 210 (1978).

37. *Montana v. U.S.*, 450 U.S. 544, 564 (1981).

38. *Nevada v. Hicks*, 533 U.S. 353, 360 (2002).

39. Section 25 of the Judiciary Act of 1789 makes the U.S. judiciary paramount to that of the individual states. I am not arguing that sovereign immunity is unconstitutional, only that maintaining federalism in a system such as the United States is impossible without giving the states power and authority equal to that of the national government. Moreover, the states themselves should not be the sovereign, but sovereignty must reside with the people. An enunciation of this point will be argued through John Locke in the next section.

40. All references are to the *Second Treatise*, MacPherson edition.

41. "But Freedom of Men under Government, is, to have a standing Rule to live by, common to every one of that Society, and made by the Legislative Power erected in it; A Liberty to follow my own Will in all things, where the Rule prescribes not; and not be to be subject to the inconstant, uncertain, unknown, Arbitrary Will of another Man" (§22).

42. "For where there is an Authority, a Power on Earth, from which relief can be had by appeal, there the continuance of the State of war is excluded, and the Controversy is decided by that Power" (§21).

43. 403 U.S. 388 (1971).

44. 764 F. 2d 294 (5th Cir. 1986).

45. 994 F.2d 1121 (5th Cir. 1993).

46. 435 U.S. 349 (1978).

47. *Stump* quoting *Bradley v Fisher*, 80 U.S. (13 Wall.) 335, 347 (1872).
48. *Stump* 435 U.S. 349.
49. It is instructive to contrast Ober with Tocqueville. Tocqueville argues that once both governmental and administrative procedures are centralized the result will be tyranny. (*DIA* I.2.8). Tocqueville appropriately assesses the psychological impact the centralization of government has on citizens. Tocqueville argues that it is only when government and administration are centralized that "habituates men to make a complete and continual abstraction from their will . . . it also captures them through their habits; it isolates them and afterwards fastens them one by one onto the common mass" (*DIA* I.1.5). But what we see from Ober is that these two forms do not need to both be centralized to have a deleterious effect on human nature as Tocqueville argues. By centralizing only one, it is abstracted from the individual because centralizing decreases the relevance of, and influence of, the individual in the making of decisions and the administration of policy.

CHAPTER 4

Nullification

As shown in the first three chapters, federalism is not a new concept, nor has its benefits and faults been hidden from scholarly and popular scrutiny. Federalism promises to provide a system of government in which the governed are in close physical proximity to the governing. This closeness is supposed to enhance the responsiveness of government to the people and endear the people to their government. There exists a familiarity between those who can see and talk to one another that otherwise would be absent. This familiarity should allow the government to do its job better, and confer legitimacy upon its decisions.

As Will Kymlicka defines it, "[f]ederalism refers to a political system which includes a constitutionally entrenched division of powers between a central government and two or more subunits, defined on a territorial basis, such that each level of government has *sovereign authority* over certain issues" (Kymlicka 1998: 119). It is possible for there to be shared authority over certain issues but for the most part Kymlicka's definition works. Federalism allows individuals to look at the community as the primary governing body and therefore they tend to focus on themselves and their neighbors when making decisions. However, unless the subnational governing units maintain their authority this will not occur. In a federal system in which the subnational governing units have authority and autonomy the national government is not the most important entity and citizens can shift their focus from the national to the local level. When the focus shifts to the local, it will also shift away from a single-minded focus on government and shift to personal connections with fellow citizens. This shift will be formal and informal and politics will undoubtedly enter the conversation. Civic engagement will increase as a result, as will a concept many have thought was lost and never to be found again: civil society. This characterization of the affects of federalism is not that different from certain aspects of communitarianism in that the community is seen as an integral part of the individual's life, but a community can only do so positively if it is of the proper scale. As Christopher Lasch writes, communitarianism

> proposes a general strategy of devolution or decentralization, designed to end the dominance of large organizations and to remodel our institutions on a human scale. It attacks bureaucracy and large-scale organizations, however, not in the name of individual freedom or the free market but in the name of continuity and tradition. (Lasch 1988: 174)

There will also be a move to meaningful democratic participation that reinforces the objectives and methods of deliberative democracy. While the final role of the citizen may still only take the form of voting, the vote cast, and the dialogue that has informed that vote, will have been based on more than a heuristic. And while the vote can only be read as "for" or "against" a particular individual or policy, thus leaving the possibility that elected officials will misinterpret the results as a mandate the voters never intended, the close proximity of the voter to the elected can reduce the tendency to misinterpret.

If the elected official lives in a small district, she or he will be more aware of the sentiments of those living in that district compared to a representative from a much larger district. Moreover, the political positions of a small district's population will be easier to know as the variation in that district will be less than in a larger district. Certainly a district's views will not be homogeneous, but differences will be less dramatic, in most cases, and the differences that do exist will be overcome with much more ease due to the interpersonal relationships between voters and elected officials.

Chapters 1and 3 have argued that we should not adopt a state-centered view of federalism, for doing so undermines its theoretical structure and prevents its practice. However, formal governing institutions are a necessary component of federalism and the proper institutions must be in place for federalism to operate effectively. The challenge is to create institutions that incorporate and protect non-state actors. The next three chapters will show how nullification, veto, and secession (NVS) are integral for the practice of federalism as they protect subnational governing units from the centralizing tendency of national policies and equally important, NVS—as I craft them—create an environment in which the people remain sovereign.[1]

While federalism has been studied with the utmost scrutiny, nullification does not receive any attention from mainstream political science which is startling considering that the act of nullification can strengthen the position of the subnational levels which will then reinforce the benefits of federalism as described previously. Nullification is an act by a constituent governing body—one that is at a more local level than the central government such as a state, province, county, city, or water district—in which it declares an act null within its political borders. The town of Charlotte, Vermont, would be able to say that a law passed by state legislators in Montpelier would not apply to them. Or Texas could say a law passed by the national government in Washington, DC, would not apply to it.

What this chapter shows is that nullification is a mechanism missing from most mature federal systems, and because of its absence, federalism lacks the ability to fulfill its potential. The idea is grounded in Alexis de Tocqueville's understanding of dual powers, one administrative and one governmental. In order to avoid tyranny, both powers should never be placed into the hands of a centralized governing authority. In order to keep the national government in check, "it must rely for the execution of its commandment on agents who often do not depend on it, and whom it cannot

direct in each instant" (*DIA* 1.2.8). Because, "municipal bodies and the administrative counties form so many hidden shoals that delay or divide the popular will.
Were the law oppressive, freedom would still find shelter in the manner in which
the law was executed" (*DIA* 1.2.8). But this cannot be realized without giving the
constituent authorities the ability to defend themselves against the centralizing
tendency of the national government. We can preserve the benefits of federalism,
as Tocqueville and others envision it, by legitimizing nullification. Central authorities have the tendency and ability to circumvent the authority and autonomy of
the constituent levels. In order for the constituent levels to maintain their authority
and autonomy they must have the tools to protect themselves. This chapter will
show how nullification can improve federalism and how the virtues of deliberative
democracy can be replicated in small-scale governing units within a larger nation
when recognition of competing claims is required.

In the next section a few historical examples of nullification will be provided.
Then, in the following section, I will provide an outline of how nullification might
be instituted. The third section will deal with the relationship between civil society,
deliberative democracy and federalism. In the final section of the chapter I will
revisit the role federalism plays in democratic theory and how nullification prevents
the acceptance of a contradictory arrangement.

Examples of Nullification

Despite its rarity, nullification is not a radical idea; in fact, it is employed in countries
as varied as Sweden and Ethiopia. Sweden offers its citizens both a consultative
and rejective option. The Swedish people are sometimes asked to consult on a law
that has already been passed by a parliamentary majority. Since 1979 the Swedish
constitution has allowed a rejective referendum on constitutional matters, which I
wish to extend to all matters that have been passed by a parliament or legislature
(Setala 1999: 111).

The concept is not foreign to the United States either, but because of its historical
relationship with the Antebellum South it carries a negative connotation and as a
result has not received the attention it deserves from political scientists in the United
States.[2] Nullification was used, most notably, by South Carolina to nullify a national
law. In 1828, some 30 years after James Madison and Thomas Jefferson argued for
the legitimacy of nullification in their Virginia and Kentucky Resolutions respectively, a tariff was passed by the national government which the Southern states
regarded as the Tariff of Abominations. The agrarian South saw the tariff as a way
for the North to gain benefits for its industrially based economy by placing a tariff
on imported goods, but would ultimately harm the South's ability to export its
cotton across the Atlantic due to a retaliatory tariff imposed by England on Southern
cotton. John C. Calhoun, serving as the vice president under Andrew Jackson,
published the *South Carolina Exposition and Protest* (1828) in which he laid out a
justification for nullifying the Tariff of Abominations. After Congress passed yet

another tariff that would injure the South's economic interests, Calhoun resigned his post and became a U.S. senator representing South Carolina and moved to nullify the tariff. Seeing the nullification of a state law as treasonous, Jackson urged Congress to pass a revenue collection bill that would authorize the president to use force against South Carolina. Not wishing to see violence, Henry Clay, in his usual capacity of compromiser, produced a bill that would gradually reduce the level of the tariff to its 1816 level. This led South Carolina to rescind its ordinance of nullification.

> The compromise tariff of 1833 put forth by Henry Clay was in direct response to South Carolina's nullification of the previous set of tariffs. Had South Carolina not used its power of nullification there might not have been a repeal of the tariff. Like Calhoun anticipated, the use of nullification forced compromise. (Read 2009: 7)

This episode provides preliminary evidence that nullification does work to subvert the affects of damaging national legislation by forcing compromise with a numerical majority that would have otherwise not been willing to compromise. Although the nation was on the brink of violence due to the executive's unwillingness to compromise, it was a member of the legislative branch, someone representing a smaller constituency than the president, who was unwilling to use violence as a means of ending debate.

While South Carolina openly and directly nullified a national law, Vermont only in spirit nullified the Fugitive Slave Law, a law making it mandatory for citizens of both free states and slave states to return slaves, within its borders, when it passed the Habeas Corpus Law on November 13, 1850, in an effort to make enforcement of the Fugitive Slave Law impossible within its borders. Vermont's actions prompted President Millard Fillmore and his cabinet to issue a statement saying he would use military force to implement the law in Vermont. While John C. Calhoun is seen—wrongly—as only being interested in protecting slavery, Vermont's use of nullification is an instance in which states' rights were promoted in order to oppose slavery. Oddly, Vermont's action has gone largely unnoticed. "That state's courageous pursuit of racial justice and human freedom emphatically deserves rescue from historical oblivion" (Houston 2004: 254).

Fortunately, Millard Fillmore did not follow up on his threat even as the Fugitive Slave Law went unenforced in Vermont and most of New England. But the actions of Vermont sparked a firestorm of debate in the South and the North. The South's position took Vermont to be violating the Compromise of 1850 and therefore a direct attack on the South's right to hold slaves, whereas abolitionists in the North defended the actions of Vermont. But no one, unfortunately, engaged in the broader debate of states' rights separate from the slavery question. Perhaps it would be impossible to do so, but the unwillingness of the executive branch (both Jackson and Fillmore) to refrain from threats of violence did not help, and the rantings of newspapers that were not interested in sparking debate but only outrage, made sure that a legitimate debate was never held. Unfortunately the constitutionality of nullification, and the issue of states' rights, was left undecided, and it was not to be settled until 1865 with the North's military victory over the South.

If the question over nullification had been settled independently of the slavery issue, then the issue of slavery would not have been attached to it and a more meaningful dialogue on the issue of slavery could have been had as it would not have been clouded by another issue. Moreover, the threats of violence could have been avoided as well. The need for legitimizing nullification before a conflict arises is reflected in these two episodes. Once nullification is used to refute a controversial law, and the question of nullification has not been settled, then it becomes difficult—if not impossible—to separate the two issues: the first being the legitimacy of nullification, and second the law being nullified. But, nullification should not be given up even when it goes unsettled as it is still a necessary component of federalism as it allows for states, provinces, and other subnational governing units to protect themselves against unjust action. Remember, states' rights, in so far as they press federalism, are intrinsically and instrumentally useful and therefore must be preserved. There is value in communities that mimic the natural order of individuals as it allows humans to act in their most natural capacity. The instrumental value, of course, is that there is a more humane understanding of individuals, their needs, and relationships between individuals within a community, thus producing policy that is consistent with the needs of the individual and the community at large.

A Possible Framework

Nullification makes federalism workable in a large republic by allowing the constituent levels to protect themselves against the tendency of power consolidation, and thus increases the likelihood of realizing the virtues of federalism, all the while avoiding the risk of minority tyranny. But, nullification will not produce positive results unless it is instituted responsibly.

For simplicity's sake I will use United States as my example of how this procedure might work. In what follows I provide a three-stage process. The first of which is a referendum, followed by town hall meetings, and finally the legislature votes on the measure with the vote being certified by the citizens.

Step One: Referendum

When dealing with a state's nullification of a national law there will need to be a three-stage process beginning with a statewide referendum on the question. The referendum can be proposed in one of two ways: First, a citizen, or group of citizens, may file a request for a referendum with the state legislature once that citizen or group has collected the number of signatures necessary for filing a request. The state will decide the necessary number of signatures. Once filed, the state legislature must implement a statewide referendum.[3]

The second way the nullification process can begin is if a majority in either house of the state legislature passes a resolution requesting a statewide referendum.

A referendum is implemented in the first stage for three reasons. (1) Referenda give elected officials an accurate reading of where the public stands on the issue in question.

> Proponents [of referendums] maintained these participatory devices not only would produce statutes and ordinances more in line with popular opinion but also would improve the quality of legislative bodies by making service in them more appealing to persons of high moral standards who would not be corrupted by the evil forces associated with such bodies in the past. (Zimmerman 2001: 234)

(2) Referenda involve the public and promote discourse among the citizenry in a manner consistent with the democratic ideal.

> The general initiative and its associated referendum encourage citizens to play a greater role in the governance process since opportunities for such participation are readily available on a part-time and as-needed basis . . . Campaigns waged for and against initiated ballot propositions inform the citizenry of the nature of public problems and possible solutions . . . most initiative campaigns generate considerable public debate that not only educates potential voters but also allows candidates for elective office to appeal to voters by stating their respective position on the propositions on the ballot. . . . protest referendum campaigns stimulate discussion and debate on important policy issues, thereby leading to the education of the public. (Zimmerman 2001: 234, 235, 244)

Advisory referendums, like the one I propose, "would tend to increase public participation in important issues and to improve communication between legislators and the electorate" (Goldman 1950: 303). Referenda resemble the democratic ideal.

> Advocates of the referendum device believe that one of its greater virtues is the belief of most ordinary people that decisions they make themselves are more legitimate than those made by public officials: decisions by referendums produce more unambiguous mandates than candidate elections; they are more likely than acts of legislatures to promote the public interest over special interests; and ordinary citizens are less subject than public officials to bribery, intimidations, and other forms of pressure . . . "The citizen is more likely to feel entitled to flout a law promoted by an elite . . . than one that is seen to reflect the free and informed consent of the majority of citizens." (Butler and Ranney 1994b: 14)

(3) Referenda on their own can be a politically powerful instrument in overcoming objectionable policy and leadership. "The protest referendum, where available, is a natural extension of the principle of checks and balances inherent in the existing

system of governance" (Zimmerman 2001: 244). For example, the referendum in Chile on October 5, 1988 brought an end to the 15-year dictatorship of Augusto Pinochet. In 1980 there was a referendum issued by Pinochet and the military that sought authorization of a new constitution, but in the referendum was a call for a second referendum in 8 years to either endorse Pinochet or hold a new election. Since the 1980 referendum passed there was another referendum in 1988 in which Pinochet sought popular endorsement. He was soundly defeated as he underestimated the organizational capacity of the opposition. While Pinochet remained in control of the military after his electoral defeat in 1988, power had peacefully changed hands from a dictator to a popularly elected Patricio Aylwin. This episode displays the capacity of referendums to validate popular opposition to government policy or discontent. Even with control of the military, Pinochet could not hold power when opposed by a well-organized and energetic opposition. If it works for military dictatorships, certainly referendums can be instrumental in other areas of policy reform or rejection. In the case of nullification, in which voters are asked to reject a law and not an entire regime, referenda bestow legitimacy upon the voice of the opposition by granting it an institutional outlet for reform within the government structure (Butler and Ranney 1994c: 7).

The case of Chile is not isolated. Beginning in 1989 with the rise of President F.W. de Klerk there was a push for constitutional reform in South Africa that would put a formal end to apartheid in that country.[4] But in the general election of 1989 and the by-election in 1992 the Conservative party, which opposed the end of apartheid, gained strength. President de Klerk knew he would have to go to the people if he wanted to bring a formal end to apartheid in light of the results of these elections. In President de Klerk's appeal to the people through referendum, 69 percent of the (white) population, with a turnout of over 85 percent, voted for de Klerk's position on ending apartheid. So while the Conservative party had won in 1989 and 1992, the people's position on apartheid was not consistent with that of the ruling party which demonstrates the need to return to the people from time to time through referendum as a vote for a party or candidate may send a mixed message. The Conservative party could have easily made the argument, as they did, that since apartheid was a salient and prominent issue that the people's vote indicated support for their position on the issue, but when the people were asked about that issue, they opposed the Conservative party's position.

> Therefore, in a system based on the principles of popular sovereignty, political equality, popular consultation, and majority rule, direct popular decisions made by referendums have a legitimacy that indirect decisions by elected representatives cannot match ... when a representative democracy wishes a particular decision to be made with maximum legitimacy, it would do well to make that decision by referendum. (Butler and Ranney 1994c: 15)

In other words, when a law is passed through a parliamentary or congressional majority, the will of the people may not be represented. In such instances the possibility for nullifying that law, with one component of the nullification process being a referendum, should exist. (Butler and Ranney 1994b: 9–10)

One of the primary goals of incorporating a referendum is to produce a deliberative environment. I rely on the Swiss example for further support of how a referendum may work to achieve this end. Gregory Fossedal explains the deliberative nature of direct democracy as practiced through referenda in Switzerland.

> The first is that the process itself has become deliberative. The effort by political leaders to secure arrangements for a central bank, or funding for desired projects, became an ongoing conversation. Political leaders first press one way, and then, finding there is insufficient support for a particular conception, they lead in another. The Swiss have seen this process in recent years regarding the debate over entry into the European Union: Proponents have had to rethink their arguments and their premises, and adjust their proposals and policies, in order to persuade the voters. In this, they naturally confer and deliberate among themselves, too, though with the people constantly in mind. Thus the process of establishing a national bank became a forty-year dialogue, and the value-added tax, one of almost twenty-five years. (Fossedal 2002: 105)

Contrary to what some might expect about popular rule, "direct democracy turns out to be significantly deliberative" (Fossedal 2002: 105).

Given the ethnic diversity in Switzerland, the Swiss model addresses the objection that ethnic tensions will only be exacerbated by federalism. Switzerland has been a federation since 1848. Rather than homogenize the diverse cultures that are found in the 26 cantons and 3,000 communes, Switzerland used federalism to integrate the various cultures and traditions. Even Napoleon, who successfully brought modernity and centralization to neighboring France, found it impossible to govern Switzerland through a centralized system, so after his 1798 invasion he gave up and renewed the cantonal system (Stauffer, Topperwien, and Thalmann-Torres 2005: 343).

> Stewardson viewed the protest referendum in Switzerland as a safety valve and explained that the device "serves to disengage the political atmosphere of the electricity with which for the moment it happens to be charged. By giving the people the last word it takes the sting out of parliamentary defeat and affords the minority a chance of explaining and defending its position before the public at large." (Zimmerman 2001: 244)

Additionally, the Swiss model allows a country to check the will of the majority without resorting to nondemocratic procedures.

One of the most recognizable features of Swiss federalism is direct democracy. Statutes and constitutional amendments are subject to a popular referendum according to Articles 140–142 of the Swiss constitution. For ordinary legislation the referendum is optional, but for constitutional measures it is mandatory (Stauffer,

Topperwien, and Thalmann-Torres 2005: 347). In the case of a mandatory referendum a double-majority is required in that a majority of the cantons must approve as well as a majority of the voters.

One potential roadblock to the referendum process in Switzerland is the diversity. Switzerland has no language of its own. Rather, its citizens speak a variety of languages. Somehow, the direct democracy approach works despite such a roadblock to deliberation. The Swiss example holds promise for somewhere like Ethiopia—a country to be discussed in a later chapter—where there are a multitude of languages spoken. One need not force a national language on the people as long as there are provisions made for translation and communication delays.

The protest referendum, in Switzerland, extends representation to those groups and individuals who would otherwise go unrepresented.

> In political practice, the democratic instruments are often used by groups that are not directly represented in the national parliament . . . or that have a weak parliamentary position. Thus, direct democratic rights serve as a political instrument for parties in opposition, but also for other kinds of minorities. (Biaggini 2004: 217)

But in protecting the minority they protect all people as the power is granted to the people and not the state or parliament.

> Whereas the British and American systems produce winners, the Swiss prefer to protect the losers . . . All political machinery in Switzerland has a provisional quality because the 'the people,' is really sovereign and may exercise its power to change this or that instrument of its will. (Biaggini 2004: 218)

The Swiss referendum process, and particularly the protest referendum, confers legitimacy upon controversial government decisions.

> The power to bring a strongly felt proposal on to the national agenda, and have it debated in the press and voted on by the people, is an important one, and one the Swiss cherish. It defuses passions, and gives the angry and the enthusiastic an outlet for their energies . . . A movement that has its measure rejected by Congress or vetoed by the President is likely to feel they were thwarted unfairly, that the will of the people was twisted by lobbyists and slick communicators. The Swiss whose initiative does not pass may feel some of this anger, but knows that his case has been judged directly by the people. (Fossedal 2002: 101)

This point explains how referendum can be a consensus-building mechanism. I use consensus not to mean unanimity, but rather as the term is used by George Silberbauer. "Consensus is neither unanimity nor majority will; it is consent to the judgment of those who make it" (Silberbauer 1991: 20). When discussing small-scale societies Silberbauer writes of consensus,

> [i]t was sometimes the case that the wishes of a single member prevailed against all others, who agreed to the will of a minority-of-one because they could tolerate adjustment to the dissenter's position and she or he could not move to theirs. A requirement of consensus is that all are bound by the eventual decision and that all have access to a common pool of information, including the rules, subject, reason and foreseen consequences of making the decision. (Silberbauer 1991: 21)

And aside from the direct impact the Swiss referendum has on policy, it also has the indirect effect of conditioning the behavior of elected officials.

> Referendums have also influenced allegiances within the Swiss Parliament . . . MPs of the governing parties have rarely remained united on important issues, mainly because of the splintering effect of direct democracy. If a coalition of parties stands a minimal chance of sticking together from referendum to referendum, there is little point in maintaining a tight allegiance in Parliament. In much the same way that referendums encourage individual voters to break from their preferred party, they also encourage parties to break from parliamentary alliances. (Kobach 1994: 133)

Additionally, referenda create an interesting game between politicians and the populace similar to the one that exists between the U.S. president and Congress. If politicians in Switzerland think their law will not hold up to a facultative referendum they will modify it or table it. Some politicians will even vote against a policy they support if they think the people they represent will vote to overturn it. Moreover, a politician who senses that a referendum will take place on a particular issue may push for a similar law to be passed in parliament before the referendum process can take place in order to show his constituents that he represents their preferences (Fossedal 2002: 102). "Thus the mere presence of institutions allowing for referendums affects policies adopted in parliaments" (Hug 2004: 322). The Swiss process of direct democracy has four desirable characteristics that I would like to replicate: (1) it creates a deliberative environment, (2) it confers legitimacy on government decisions, (3) it protects minority interests through democratic procedures, and (4) it relieves tensions and diminishes polarization.

Step Two: Town Hall Meetings

If a referendum in support of nullification passes by a simple majority there is a temporary hold on the national law that suspends its application in the state until the final two stages of the process are complete. The suspension serves three purposes. First, a national law that takes effect immediately may have immediate and irreversible affects. Second, it will allow a state to observe the affects of the new law in other states. Third, the delay will allow for a compromise to be made between competing sides before the law is nullified. This temporary hold procedure is derived from a similar feature in the Belgian parliament. At the parliament level in Belgium there is an alarm bell procedure that is triggered when 25 percent of the MPs in any language group consider a proposal harmful to their group. If triggered, debate on the procedure is suspended for 60 days at the end of which time a solution is proposed. The presence of the procedure has been enough to increase the willingness of both sides to work together as the procedure has never been used; only its threat is necessary in order to force negotiation and compromise.

If the citizens approve nullification through referendum the question is sent to the state legislature. The results of the referendum will be made available at the district level so that each legislator will know his or her constituent's desires. In addition, each legislator is required to hold one town hall-style meeting in his or her district before casting his or her vote in the legislature. This means that each district will have, with the exception of those in Nebraska, two meetings, one for the upper-house representative and one for the lower-house representative. The town hall meetings have three benefits:

(1) Town hall meetings institutionalize delay in an effort to stymie reactionary or alarmist sentiments from stopping what might be a good national policy. Furthermore, since the national measure will have taken effect in some states, the legislators and citizens will have empirical evidence to draw upon when discussing the policy and making their decision at this stage.

(2) By closing the physical proximity between the elected and the electors, the elected get a better understanding of what their constituents want and need, the electors have an increased feeling of efficacy and importance in the political sphere and the electors are more familiar with the actions of the elected and therefore become more informed citizens and voters. Efforts by politicians to make contact with potential voters will also increase the likelihood that they turnout to vote (Niven 2004).

(3) Town hall meetings serve to educate the public about the policy and the values of democracy. Tocqueville wrote, "Town meetings are to liberty what primary schools are to science: they bring it within the people's reach, they teach men how to use and how to enjoy it." Simply turning policy decisions over to the people in a manner similar to direct democracy requires that the people know something about the policy but equally important, they must appreciate the values of democracy. Imparting this knowledge on the people can only be done when the people are involved. John Rawls makes a similar point when he wrote about deliberative democracy. "Deliberative democracy also recognizes that without widespread education in the basic aspects of constitutional democratic government for all citizens, and without a public informed about pressing problems, crucial political and social

decisions simply cannot be made" (Rawls 1999: 580). Therefore, one criticism of the proposed process might be that the people who show up will not know what to do or how to do it. Town hall meetings must have moderators for fear that those who show up will have little or no experience. Plus, the environment will not be deliberative if one group or person is allowed to dominate the others. In their research of Porto Alegre, Fung and Wright (2003) show that measures can be taken to eliminate these problems. Fung (2004) shows the same in Chicago. By having trained facilitators and moderators present, the meetings can be productive and deliberative. It appears that once people have practice the moderators become less important. Also, the people who take part in these meetings take the lessons they learn about how to relate to individuals of different views, as well as the relationships they develop in these meetings, beyond the meeting hall which then works toward producing an invigorated civil society.

> Interviews showed that as persons became deeply involved in negotiations and became acquainted with other persons in the district involved in similar problems, they established lasting bonds with activists of other parts of their district and developed solidarities. This collective learning lies at the root of the transformations in civil society in Porto Alegre. (Baiocchi 2003: 57)

It would seem that if such a system can flourish in Porto Alegre, given its history of corruption and disenfranchisement, then a system of deliberative democracy can work in other places provided that the correct structural provisions are put in place. "[T]he success of the Porto Alegre experiment comes from its legitimacy-enhancing aspects rather than from 'exceptional features' of the city's history" (Baiocchi 2003: 66). Democracy demands a certain level of political skill and efficacy on behalf of the citizens, but these attributes can be improved through practice and thus provide psychological and educative benefits for participants (Fung 2004; Pateman 1970). Initially citizens may not know what they are doing, but over time their skills will improve.

A second criticism of the town hall meeting is that no one will show up. In communities where civic participation is already high this will not be a problem. But, in areas where there is not a culture of civic participation this is a concern. Take participatory city budgeting in Porto Alegre, Brazil, as an example. After years of corruption and misappropriation of funds, the Workers' party gained control of the municipal government. "Their most substantial reform measure, called 'Participatory Budgeting' (PB), attempts to transform clientelistic, vote-for-money budgeting arrangements into a publicly accountable, bottom-up, deliberative system driven by the expressed needs of city residents" (Fung and Wright 2003: 11). The system is designed so that there are budget meetings twice a year to settle budgetary matters within each region. Residents of the region have full voting rights at the meetings but in 1996 only 8 percent of the voting population attended the meetings. This is not unexpected given that the citizens lack trust of the political process and there are indications that turn out is not the most important factor. Between 1997 and 1998 some 300,000 volunteers (roughly 25 percent of the inhabitants) from the neighborhoods of Porto Alegre, Brazil, took part in training sessions to better equip the towns with the capacity for deliberative government.

However, the result of participatory democracy in Porto Alegre has been better public budgeting that more accurately reflects the stated needs of the inhabitants of the municipality. What the story of Porto Alegre teaches, when it comes to participation, is that the quality of participation can be more important than turn out levels. If those who turn out clearly articulate the needs of the community in such a way that decision makers can institute policies to reflect those needs, then the participation has been effective despite the modest numbers.

Step Three: The Legislature Must Vote and the Citizens Must Approve

Once town hall meetings are held, and legislators have returned to the statehouses to cast their votes, the decision to nullify must be supported by a majority in each house. The vote of each legislator will be made public. Then, the measure goes back to the citizens for final approval to certify the legislature's vote. The measure only requires a simple majority to nullify the national law. This step will help protect against interest group influence over legislative voting behavior, help ensure that there is enough sustained interest among the citizens to warrant action, and allow citizen deliberation to overcome the effects of elite framing (Druckman and Nelson 2003; Gerber 1999). "Neutralization of the undue influence of special interest groups is a recurring theme advanced by initiative supporters who are convinced the device forces legislators to monitor more closely and reflect more adequately popular opinion on major issues" (Zimmerman 2001: 234).

The process I have outlined will give the voters time to construct an informed and rational opinion on the issue. The entire system is built around delay and deliberation. The benefits of deliberation are elaborated upon elsewhere in this book, but the delay component deserves immediate attention. The idea for delay comes from Madison's *Federalist* #10. While I disagree that by "expanding the sphere" we increase the likelihood of finding virtue, I do agree that if enough hurdles are put into place, then an idea must have a sustaining resonance with the citizenry for it to become a law. What Madison takes for granted is that citizens will remain engaged, and that factions will lose interest when the going gets tough. But, what political scientists have found is that when the going gets tough, the factions go underground until people stop paying attention and push their measure through when no one is looking. The process I have outlined will require sustained engagement from the citizenry, the type of engagement Madison takes for granted.

There is no doubt that this system is susceptible to manipulation. All systems are. We cannot rely on paper barriers. But what this system has in place are mechanisms that require citizen engagement, and force it, if decisions are to be made. No decision can be made without a sustained and meaningful involvement from the citizenry. Such involvement is not taken for granted.

Civil Society, Deliberative Democracy, and Federalism

The importance of making nullification work in this way can only become clear if we take a step back and look at why it is important for citizens to be engaged in the governing process. In a representative democracy the citizen is not a formal part of policy formation, but rather it is the elected representative.[6] Thus, the realm in which the citizens operate has become known as civil society. Civil society is a persistent topic in political science that has some import into my conception of federalism, particularly the deliberative aspect that is generated through the method of nullification I have proposed.

One goal of federalism is to get citizens more involved in the decision-making process in such a way that encourages reasoned debate. If citizens withdraw from the political process, or become lazy in their engagement, then the potential is there for popularly ruled societies to deteriorate for the same reason Edward Gibbon gives for the deterioration of Athens.

> In the end, more than they wanted freedom, they wanted security. They wanted a comfortable life and they lost it all—security, comfort and freedom . . . When the Athenians finally wanted not to give to society but for society to give to them, when the freedom they wished for most was freedom from responsibility, then Athens ceased to be free. (quoted by O'Connell 1999: 40)

But it is not just to prevent negative outcomes that citizens need to take an active role, for as Aristotle states, "If liberty and equality, as it is thought by some, are chiefly to be found in democracy, they will be attained when all persons alike share in the government to the utmost." To some degree this reflects Michael Sandel's assessment of civic republicanism. "The central idea of that tradition [civic republicanism] is that liberty depends on self-government, and that self-government requires citizens capable of deliberating about the common good, capable of sharing meaningfully in self-government, and self-rule" (Sandel 1996: 67).

In addition to good policy, "a fortunate by-product is that when citizens become involved their morale improves." When decision making is centralized, and the people have little connection with those who deliberate, and decide, on policy, "'We, the People' feel a long way from the centers of decision. It doesn't seem like our venture anymore. Anything that repairs the sense of connection will help repair the mood" (Gardner, John W. "Foreword" in the O'Connell 1999: xiii). Therefore, in a government with a decentralized power structure that leaves avenues open for citizens to engage in an active and meaningful way, the potential is there for a renewed sense of civic pride and obligation. This objective is consistent with the

Athenian Code. "We will ever strive for the ideals and sacred things of the city, both alone and with many: we will transmit this city not less, but greater, better and more beautiful than it was transmitted to us."

The growing attention civil society has garnered has shifted our focus away from the real problem, which is society and government have become divided. There is no need for a separate space for public deliberation if the government allows for public deliberation. There is no need for surrogates if the government includes the people in the decision-making process. It is not a rejuvenation of civil society that is needed, what is needed is a redefinition of the relationship between government and society that more closely approximates the ancient model so that the rulers and the ruled do not occupy divided realms. Theorists have been unwilling, some unable, to make this necessary step for several reasons, but one of the most important is the size, scope, and structure of modern nation-states. Civil society theorists have taken the size, scope, and structure of the modern nation-state as a given. Redefining the proper spheres of government and society has been dictated by the structure of the modern nation-state. So, if we open the question of whether the modern nation-state is how it should be, new solutions present themselves. Federalism rightly understood reverses the standard formulation by making the structure of the modern nation-state dependent upon the definition of the spheres of government and society. In reformulating the question, it is possible to answer "the cosmopolitan challenge to traditional ideas of democracy" which "is based on the recognition that in complex societies there is a disjunction between the political administrative sphere, where decisions are taken, and the public sphere . . . where opinions are formed and debated" (Bellamy and Castiglione 2005: 299). In governments of proper scale, which federalism makes possible, there need not be this disjunction.

"Perhaps because it is so fashionable, the idea of civil society is increasingly ambiguous today" (Cohen and Arato 1992: 421). Because of this it is necessary to assess civil society in order to show how federalism can improve the theoretical development of the concept. Civil society can trace its heritage back to the Greek, *politike koinonia*, or political community. This conception of civil society developed from an understanding of human nature as being essentially political, and that it was natural—indeed, it was their *telos*—for people to engage in political activity. Thus, in the Aristotelian formulation there was no distinction between the state and society. The lack of a distinction was made possible because of two things: (1) the independence of each household, and (2) the absence of a distinction between society and community. The lack of economic dependence of the household meant that the only interaction between households was in the *polis*. (Polanyi 1968).

The rise of the modern liberal state demanded that there be a distinction between the state and society/community. The state was charged with protecting rights and its citizens. This meant, above all, that the state and society were set in opposition to one another: the rulers were on one side and the ruled on the other. A secondary result of this new distinction was a weakening of community bonds as individuals began relying on the state.

And in this very modern movement we find the irony of individuals set free from every association to which they are naturally attached—and at the same time bound with bands of iron to the strongest and most comprehensive regimes in history, not coincidentally regimes involved almost continually in wars and the preparation for war on a scale never before seen. (Conyers 2008: xii–xiii)

This may not be the result of Thomas Hobbes, but it is a move he certainly advocated.

Hobbes would argue that the only means by which a stable and peaceful existence could occur is by the presence of an all-powerful state that would serve the purpose of bonding individuals. Neither society nor community was needed as the state would accept that role. "Hobbes's theory, the social contract creates a state, not society. The fusion of society is accomplished only by the power of the state" (Cohen and Arato 1992: 87). Because of Hobbes's legal positivism, or perhaps this is where his legal positivism was derived from, Hobbes could not allow for a community to exist as there could not be moralized law, but only law that was commanded from the state. Cohen and Arato are even more forceful when they write, "[a]s any reader of Hobbes knows, the road to statism is prepared by the identification of society outside the state with egoistic competition and conflict" (Cohen and Arato 1992: 97).

After Hobbes there was a recognition that the citizens were outside of the government and therefore the government could not be the sole protector as the government was itself capable of tyranny. For Hobbes the threat was from social disorder, whereas for some who followed Hobbes, the threat was from the state. This shift was seen in the United States and in France. The revolutions that occurred saw declarations of rights and constitutions that made citizens the source of legitimate authority and gave people the ability to check and control their government. This only reinforced the distinction between the people and the government and thus took us further away from the Aristotelian conception of politics. In most instances, the interests of the government were pitted against the interests of the individual. The proponents of constitutional ratification in the United States epitomized the modern conception of politics.

The theory of government that the Americans clarified in their reading and discussion possessed a compelling simplicity: politics was nothing more than a perpetual battle between the passions of the rulers, whether one or a few, and the united interests of the people—an opposition that was both inevitable and proportional. (Wood 1998: 18)

Disagreement is inevitable in politics, but it does not have to be adversarial or quarrelsome. Disagreement can be positive as John Stuart Mill makes clear as it was he who advocated free and open debate as a way to allow competing ideas to arrive, through iteration, at the truth.

The shift in authority that occurred after Hobbes did not mean positive law was abandoned, but rather, the community was abandoned for society since the government remained the institution to which one took one's problems for resolution. Seeing the government as a threat to rights did not mean that it was seen as lacking legitimacy. Rather, the government was where one would go to see that one's interests were protected. Communities were sacrificed as a result.

Political thought does not occur in a linear path, and even if it did, it would still not be monolithic. Between Aristotle and Hobbes, but still in the middle of those who were trying to make the state the supreme authority—such as Jean Bodin and Machiavelli—was Johannes Althusius. Althusius sees the need for maintaining the traditional conception of society, community, and state. While he does not mirror Aristotle's thought he brings us closer to its realization than anyone has since. For Althusius, as discussed earlier, relationships between individuals begin with the family and extend outward until one has formed a nation. At each point, though, the former authority gives up some of its power to a new authority, but in no way does the former authority relinquish the ability to govern the former relationship. In other words, a mother does not cease being a mother because she now lives in a city. One always possesses multiple ways of identifying himself or herself. One's identity is not defined by the nation in which one lives, but rather, it is one of many identities.

There are parallels between civil society and deliberative democracy. In discussing civil society, Cohen and Arato make statements that also lend support to deliberative democracy.

> The laws they enact are to be considered legitimate only if the procedures of public deliberation are rigorously followed. Since Hegel insists on genuine and unconstrained discussion and deliberation, he emphatically rejects the *imperative mandate*, the principle of the traditional *Standestaat*. The assembly must be "a living body in which all members deliberate in common and reciprocally instruct and convince one another" . . . Under modern parliamentarianism, instead of direct pressure of constituencies or any form of bound or mandated representation, public opinion is supposed to "influence" the parliamentary public only through argumentation and persuasion that presupposes rather than suspends the independence of representatives. (Cohen and Arato 1992: 110–11, 202)

This is close to Schmitt's conception of public discussion and deliberation, which is

> an exchange of opinion that is governed by the purpose of persuading one's opponent of the truth or justice of something, or allowing oneself to be persuaded of something as true and just . . . To discussion belong shared convictions and premises, the willingness to be persuaded. (Cohen and Arato 1992: 201–2)

Deliberative democracy, like all systems of representative government, needs a space for citizens to partake in a reasoned dialogue. The modern state looks to civil society for this space, but federalism can forge a space within government for this debate so that the distinction between government and society disappears without the government impinging on the private lives of individuals or the realm of the community.

One of the common criticisms of deliberative democracy is that it cannot be implemented. "The challenge facing deliberative democrats is thus to find some way of adapting their deliberative ideals to any remotely large-scale society, where it is simply infeasible to arrange face-to-face discussions across the entire community" (Goodin 2003: 55). Goodin is correct if states had to remain large in size or in function. Large states can take on characteristics of small states if they are federal. But federalism has to allow the smaller constituent parts to have authority on par with the central government and mechanisms must be put in place to preserve that authority and to create opportunities for face-to-face interaction. The above description of how nullification can work in the United States answers Goodin's criticism by allowing for a large state to take on the characteristics of a small state.

The implementation of referendum and town hall meetings are a further response to critics of deliberative democracy. Deliberative democracy is a worthy goal, and through the use of referendum and town hall meetings the level of deliberation will increase which then heightens voter awareness and knowledge.

> Although the protest referendum focuses attention on a single important issue, in so doing it encourages citizens to analyze other important policy issue and legislative bills addressing them. Every time the mechanism is employed on a recently enacted statute on a different subject, a new group of voters with a special interest in the subject matter will become more active politically. (Zimmerman 2001: 245)

Moreover, this process will decrease apathy, alienation, and disenfranchisement among the citizenry.

> The protest referendum . . . reduces citizen alienation because voters know they are empowered to secure political justice overturning most decisions of legislators without removing them from office. In consequence, citizens pay closer attention to the activities and decisions of their state and/or local legislative bodies and a larger percentage of the registered voters cast ballots in elections. (Zimmerman 2001: 245)

Overcoming the Proceduralist vs. Substantivist Debate in Democratic Theory

A majority-rule system, even one with a strong civil society and deliberative procedures, presents a serious problem: majority tyranny. When there is a majority there will be a minority—saving for unanimity of course—which means that the majority, if given the authority to do so, can trample on the minority. The most popular response to this predicament is to develop a nonelected body to review decisions made in accordance with democratic procedures. This usually takes the form of judicial review.

There is a tension between judicial review and democracy due to the fact that judges are unelected in most systems. Advocates of judicial review are categorized as substantivists as they argue that the substance of the outcome is more important than the process from which it is derived. Therefore, if we have to abandon democratic procedures, temporarily, to end apartheid through judicial review, so be it. On the other side are the proceduralists who argue that democratic procedures should be adhered to as that it is the only way the rule of law can be preserved. A temporary set back is worth risking for a stable democracy, for in the long run, democracy will produce the most desirable results.

As shown in Chapter 3, substantivists lack a convincing response to the criticism that their philosophy justifies all action that leads to a desirable outcome. As for the proceduralists, I consider them to have failed to win the debate for two reasons. With only a few exceptions, proceduralists do not consider the multidimensionality of democratic procedures. Second, they do not offer a viable check against majority tyranny, but are merely content to throw stones at institutions such as judicial review.[7]

Judicial review has been set up as the only viable option for protecting minority rights in a majority-rule system. Substantivists and proceduralists have failed to present another option. However, the incorporation of nullification into a theory of federalism offers a relief in the tension between substantivists and proceduralists by showing that institutional arrangements exist that can satisfy both. The discussion is still relevant, but when it comes to such questions as judicial review it should not be the central focus for democratic theorists, as it takes their attention away from more important, and potentially more fruitful, paths.

Federalism can thwart majority tyranny and promote values consistent with democracy by adhering to democratic procedures, thus it renders the proceduralist versus substantivist debate irrelevant as it relates to judicial review. Certainly debates over judicial review would still exist, but they become less important from a theoretical perspective. Thus, federalism allows us to go beyond the current paradigm through which we see the problem of democratic values and democratic procedures. Scholars have often overlooked federalism as a viable option for expanding the sphere of involvement to disenfranchised groups and interests as well as a mechanism capable of checking majority tyranny in a manner consistent with both the procedures and values of democratic theory.

Nullification provides an adequate check on the will of the majority in a way that is consistent with both the procedures and values of democracy. There is no countermajoritarian difficulty and the power to protect oneself against a tyrannical government is maintained. Certainly some people will remain dissatisfied with government decisions as I have not argued that such a system will promote unanimity, but dissatisfaction is far superior to unjust treatment or constitutional crisis. For instance, my dissatisfaction with the government's choice to spend money building a bridge rather than renovating the sewer system is acceptable and does not mean my rights have been violated. But, if my tax dollars are contributing to the construction of a bridge that goes nowhere in an area that I have never been to and never will go, and those tax dollars are derived from a new tax that adversely affects my equality or liberty, then I may band together with others in my governing unit to try and put an end to the new tax through nullification. This will not prevent the bridge from being built, but it will stop me from suffering an injustice for its construction. This is far different than going to the courts for relief as my claim must be seen as legitimate by a large enough group to nullify the law which then means my action conforms to democratic principles: both substantive and procedural.

Conclusion

I anticipate that federalism-sustaining mechanisms such as nullification will produce result similar to those seen in Belgium and Switzerland. When a federalism-sustaining mechanism is legitimated it does not mean that it will be used with reckless abandon. Rather, it will produce an environment of deliberation and compromise as neither side will want to see the mechanism employed except as a last resort. A subnational governing unit that recklessly threatens to nullify every national law that comes to the table will no longer be taken seriously and a subnational unit that nullifies every national law that passes will be shown to be an unnecessary partner at the national level. If South Dakota nullified every appropriations bill that passed through Congress, the national government would function just fine and South Dakota would no longer be seen as a state that needed to be recognized in national debates. Moreover, it would be against South Dakota's interest to nullify a national law, for it would run the risk of receiving any of the positive benefits of the law. A subnational unit is better off having its interests represented in legislation rather than withdrawing from the process. Nullification will only be used when a subnational unit's interests are threatened and there is no chance of representation or compromise.

In the one instance in which nullification was used in the United States, the nullifying state would have rather had the legislation changed, or negotiated another deal in which its interests would be represented rather than nullifying the legislation. South Carolina's hand was forced because nullification was not seen as a valid option by other parts of the country. Had nullification been a recognized option, South Carolina may not have had to use it, for the mere threat may have been enough to halt the legislation. Thus, the lack of a nullification procedure in a federal government's constitution sets up an antagonistic environment, whereas the inclusion of such a procedure would create a more deliberative relationship.

"Nullification makes a law inapplicable within its realm of sovereignty" (Buchanan 1991: 38). This definition fits with most ideas of nullification, but I would like to expand it just a bit. Buchanan has in mind states or provinces; I would like to grant even lower levels and nongeographically defined groups the right to nullify a law as well. But, the power to nullify is only over those laws or ordinances that come from the level directly above. For instance, a county in the United States could not nullify a national law the way a state could, but only a state law. A homeowners association could not nullify a state law. The fragmentation and atomism this would cause otherwise would make the system unworkable. Of course, the system of nullification I have outlined would have to be adapted to varying circumstances.

I extend the ability to nullify to other entities because the size of states, and of many cities, are such that even they exceed the scale envisioned by Aristotle and Althusius as being proper. Since my understanding of federalism is so firmly entrenched in scale, I must extend nullification to the smallest elected level. It is necessary to go local if one wants to get the positive attributes of federalism. Federalism, as it is often understood, stops at the state level. However, federalism, the kind that provides what the proponents of federalism argue it can provide, must get closer to the community.

It will be difficult to set up clear lines of authority and responsibility, but such difficulties yield to potentially cooperative solutions. When the power to nullify is legitimized, it can create deliberation, by forcing the actors to the table.

Notes

1. To incorporate the economic terminology adopted by McGinnis and Somin we could say that in a federal system the people are the principals and the state and national officials are their agents. While there is much I agree with in their work, I disagree with McGinnis and Somin that the people cannot be trusted to make decisions that protect federalism. "Because of their rational ignorance of public policy, citizens will not consistently protect federalism, particularly because it is a complex issue of governmental structure that lacks political salience compared to the pressing public policy issues of the day" (McGinnis and Somin 2004: 90). Because nations tend to be large enough to allow free riders, there is a collective action problem when it comes to people becoming politically engaged. People know that their single vote will not decide an election, or that someone else will be able to pick up there slack, so they choose to remain ignorant of politics and stay focused on their everyday lives. The larger nations grow the more this problem is exacerbated. The challenge is not to abandon the people as McGinnis and Somin suggest, but to create a system in which collective action problems are solved through attention to scale. If a system was in place that endeared people to it, federalism would not be an issue of policy debate, but rather something permanent that the people act through to influence policy decisions. If policies go through a process that I outline in this chapter and the next two, federalism will protect itself and the people. The protection of federalism will be a by-product of policy debates, without focusing on the question of federalism.

2. Perhaps this is one reason why federalism, or especially states rights, has declined. Federalism has lacked a public relations expert who can save it from this bad publicity.

3. Tsebelis (2002) recognizes the importance of who initiates the referendum as a key determinate in the interests represented. In this instance the veto gives power to those

who initiate the referendum since the process is asymmetrical when it comes to agenda-setting since those who do not want nullification cannot take action until after the petition has been filed or the referendum passed. Therefore, those who favor nullification gain an initial advantage. But, as will be seen, the delay mechanisms that are instituted throughout will weaken this advantage. It could also be argued that the advantage of the opposition is counterweighed by the fact that the law has already passed and therefore the agenda has been set, to some degree, in the advantage of those who favor the law.

4. "In South Africa and in Chile, they [referenda] opened the door to a transformation of the regimes' basic characters" (Butler and Ranney 1994d: 259).

5. According to Fung, in Chicago,

> Deliberation-reinforcing interventions utilized three methods. In all three cases, facilitators imposed procedures of structured deliberation to improve the depth and quality of deliberations . . . external agents also sought to mobilize those who would have been underrepresented in these processes . . . external facilitators also helped to equalize differences of power and status between local factions, and to increase the respect of each for the others. (Fung 2004: 218)

6. With the exception of direct democracy, citizens do not have a direct hand in policy formation. While voting is a signal to policy makers, and there are consequences of not following one's constituency, citizens do not have a formal say in the development and implementation of policy.

7. See Tushnet (1999), Kramer (2003), Waldron (1999), and Sunstein (1996).

CHAPTER 5

Veto

Between nullification and secession is the power of veto. "Group veto" is, as Buchanan writes, "the right to block national legislative proposals" (Buchanan 1991: 38).[1] Granting a veto is not a radical concept, for as Wayne Norman discusses,

> Long before the idea of "deliberative democracy" charmed the community of political theorists in the 1990s, the more progressive federal and divided societies instituted procedures and forms of enhanced representation for minorities in parliaments to protect them from intended or unintended tyranny of the majority. (Norman 2006: 145)

While veto rights may be seen as undemocratic because they give the minority a hold over the majority, "they can also be seen as clever mechanisms for promoting cross-group deliberation by equalizing blocking power. They force majorities to seek consensus policies" (Norman 2006: 146). A group with a veto right is given a greater voice and a more powerful bargaining position. The majority cannot avoid recognizing the concerns of the minority, nor can they trample the rights of the minority for without the minority's acquiescence or support there can be no law passed. To persuade the minority to vote for, or at least withhold its veto, the majority will have to engage in reason giving. The veto will create a deliberative environment in which the majority will have to justify its position in a way that makes sense to the minority.

The veto power may seem redundant when the nullification power is granted, but there are some instances in which nullification will not get the job done. For instance, if a bill is proposed that will create a national religion, a subnational governing unit may nullify it to allow the practice of other religions within its borders. But, if that bill contains a funding measure for schools that stipulates a subnational governing unit must abide by the new religion law in order to get school funding, the nullification will be damaging to that subnational governing unit that wants to protect religious freedom. The governing unit can take the stand that it does not want funding if it means the repression of religion, but it need not make this choice if there is a veto. The veto can be used to strip the funding measure from the bill, so that the bill can still pass, but then allow the subnational governing unit to nullify the religious restrictions without financial repercussions. Or, the bill may be vetoed in its entirety depending on the circumstances. All this point illustrates is how the veto and the nullification can work together and how the presence of nullification does not render the veto a redundant measure. The remainder of this chapter provides a more detailed defense of the veto.

To show how the veto can enhance federalism[2] this chapter will unfold in four parts. First, it will define and discuss veto and how it can enhance deliberation and minority representation. Second, it will give an example of how the veto might be constructed. Third, it will show how the use of the veto can help settle religious disputes in the United States in a more equitable manner than the court system. In the final section the chapter will demonstrate how a veto could have been employed in Sri Lanka that could have helped that country avoid decades of brutal civil war.

Defending and Defining Veto

Veto is the power to unilaterally stop something from becoming enforced law. In most instances, absent the veto, the will of the majority will determine policy without hindrance. Minorities lack representation in purely majority-rule systems. When the will of the majority dictates what gets done and how, the voice of the minority can be ignored and the needs and interests of a particular minority can be ignored. The veto gives a voice to those in the minority and forces recognition of their needs. The veto is needed to stop repressive policy from taking effect. The presence of the veto will force compromise and limit the ability of one side from taking advantage of the other.

One objection to the veto is that it will induce gridlock. Veto authority does not mean gridlock. In the U.S. system the president can veto a bill passed by Congress. Thus, one who expects the veto power to create gridlock would expect greater gridlock when the majority of Congress is comprised of a different party than the president—this is called divided government—for the two branches would then have different ideological dispositions and their positions would be more likely to diverge on a range of issues. But, as Charles Cameron shows, in times of divided government—that is when the president and the congressional majority are of opposite parties and tension is highest—the presidential veto does not stop legislative productivity. Congress and the president will still enact landmark legislation and routine legislation gets passed "like clockwork." But, divided government—because of the presidential veto—does produce different results than a united government—that is, when the majority of Congress and the president are of the same party. "During divided government, a few items are taken off the legislative table that would have found a place under unified government" (Cameron 2000: 176). The content of the bills also changes. "In most cases Congress and the president find their way to an agreement that reflects the preferences of both parties" (Cameron 2000: 176). In a divided government the veto does not stop governing, it only forces recognition of the other side so that the governing that is done does not ignore one side, or take advantage of one side. One reason gridlock is avoided is because the players in the veto game are strategic and can work to avoid a veto prior to proposing legislation.

A veto does not have to be used in order for it to be effective, because its presence as an option is often times enough to change behavior if the actor anticipates that the veto might be used. This is the second face of power that was seen in the discussion of the impact Switzerland's use of popular referendum has on its members of parliament. The second face of power,[3] as opposed to the first, which is compulsion, is when an actor anticipates the response of another actor and alters his or her behavior based upon that anticipated response. This happens with presidential veto when Congress thinks the president will veto a particular bill and alters its strategy or content of the bill in order to avoid a presidential veto. Kiewiet and McCubbins (1988) and Charles Cameron (2000) provide empirical support for this theoretical expectation. This does not mean vetoes do not occur, for information in these scenarios is imperfect and one side may miscalculate the reaction of the other side.

Veto threats work to avoid vetoes and lead both sides to negotiate toward a mutually satisfactory bargain.

> Most bargaining situations do not resemble a stickup in a dark alley. They are more akin to buying and selling a house. Here, the trick is "getting to yes" . . . cheap talk can help bargainers identify opportunities for mutual gain and avoid bad outcomes . . . a verbal expression of favorable interest at the beginning of negotiations . . . can help the partners realize there mutual gains to be had . . . An indication that a particular provision or demand is a deal breaker can keep negotiations on track. The insight of the coordination model is that veto threats . . . are a bargaining tactic essentially like those seen in other types of bargaining. The empirical evidence backs up the insight. (Cameron 2000: 195)

In the drafting stages of legislation, when a veto threat is present, each side will express what it cannot live with, thus making clear what will trigger the use of the veto at the beginning. This is where the bargaining begins. For the veto to work, both sides must have a similar goal in mind (e.g., peace, better schools, roads, medical care). When they do not have a similar goal in mind, which is when one side will only be satisfied with the extermination of the other side, the veto will not work. These circumstances are rare, but they do exist, and because they exist, the option outlined in the next chapter is necessary. But, barring actors who are unwilling to compromise, the veto can work to bring two sides together by prohibiting extreme preferences from being turned into official policy. If there are more than two sides, such as in some proportional representation systems where coalitions must be formed in order to form a majority in parliament, the veto continues to increase representation in that the competing parties must secure more than just a minimum winning coalition to pass legislation. The party looking to enact legislation must satisfy as many objectors as possible in order to avoid a veto. Thus, policy typically becomes more moderate as the number of veto players increases (Schmidt 2002).

A second, and perhaps the most powerful, objection to the veto is that it is undemocratic because it violates the ability of the majority to rule. In its purist form, the veto does fall prey to this objection. But, the veto can be crafted in such a way that it protects the rights of the minority while not violating the majority's right to rule. One way this can be done is through veto override. While the U.S. president may override congressional legislation, a two-thirds vote from each house can override the presidential veto. While this means that a majority of 50 percent + 1 does not have the right to do whatever it wants, it provides a supermajority with the power to put its preferences into action. The U.S. model may not be ideal, nor may it override the concerns of those who take the position that a veto is undemocratic, the point is that properly constructing the veto procedure can eliminate objections on these grounds. The objective the next section is to construct a veto consistent with democratic ideals, both procedural and substantive.

The veto, if properly constructed, can enhance representation by including all groups into the decision-making process. By setting up a system in which the majority and the minority are each given a voice in a deliberative environment, the outcome will be more moderate policy. Policy that is produced in this fashion will also have more legitimacy as no one will be willing to object on the ground that their voice was not heard or that they did not have the opportunity to influence or stop the decision. Legitimacy is difficult to gain in highly polarized settings, thus policy which lacks legitimacy is likely to produce more backlash. If a group perceives its rights and interests ignored by a particular policy then that policy will lack legitimacy and force recourse through nonapproved channels. Should this be systematic and continuous, then the system itself may begin to lack legitimacy for a particular group which will then force that group to explore other ways to press their claims. This is what happened in Sri Lanka, and will be explored in the final section of this chapter. If the veto is present, and each group has a veto, then the policies that make it through the system will have legitimacy as no group can make the claim that its voice was not heard as each group can express itself through veto. A policy can only become enforceable law if it has the approval, tacit or expressed, from each group.

Deliberation through Veto

As was done with nullification, I will use the federal structure of the United States to formulate an example of how the veto procedure may be constructed. As with nullification, I will include a direct-democracy component at the veto point. As discussed in the previous chapters, direct democracy has important theoretical and practical advantages. There are two advantages to direct democracy that should be repeated: First, outcomes more closely reflect the sentiments of the people and thus improve representation. Second, it helps educate the citizens on the values of democracy. Werner Pommerhene (1978) found that in those municipalities of Switzerland that used direct democracy as opposed to mediated democracy, the median voter was better represented on matters of government spending. On morally charged issues, the preferences of the median voter are also better represented through direct democracy (Gerber 1996; 1999). A veto point, particularly one that integrates direct democracy, enhances cooperation and deliberation. This may be what brings the policy closer to the preference of the median voter (Hug and Tsebelis 2002). Moreover, a direct democracy veto point moves the system from majoritarian model to a consensus model, thus more interests are considered when making policy. Such an effect is clearly seen in Switzerland.

> The basis for this particular way of policy-making [consensus-driven] lies in the institutions of direct democracy, particularly in the popular referendum. A federal policy with which a strong organized group does not agree is almost impossible to implement as a strong opposition may relatively easily block it by means of direct democracy . . . this system forces policy-makers to think their ideas over and has probably prevented Switzerland from many rash decisions. (Stauffer, Topperwein, and Thalman-Torres 2005: 349)

Of course there are critics who argue that the people are unqualified to make the necessary policy choices and that the choices on policy are only a small fraction of the available options as the agenda is set by those outside the public (Tsebelis 2002: 122). The first of these rebuttals is true if the people are not expected to be, nor given the opportunity to be, educated on the policy choices. This shortcoming can be remedied. That is, the criticism is an empirical claim and not a normative one. If citizens can become educated on the matters under consideration then the criticism vanishes. The second criticism is related to the first as it relates to knowledge of the policy agenda but is less damaging than it first appears given that agenda-setting, and being aware of the other issues off the agenda, is a problem for policy elites as well. There is little serious objection to the ideal of democracy as stated in Rousseau's formulation but there is substantial practical objection as we see that when put into practice, it does not always work out the way it is intended. To overcome this objection, at least partially, I allow for citizens to set the agenda by initiating a refer-endum. When this procedure is allowed, the resulting policy more closely represents the preference of the media voter (Hug and Tsebelis 2002).

Direct democracy will be achieved through referenda and town hall meetings. Direct democracy can be cumbersome of course, and there are examples of how direct democracy can fail to achieve its objectives and can be manipulated for political ends that have nothing to do with the will of the people. The problem is not with direct democracy, but rather with scale and procedure. As for scale, the idea is that democratic deliberation and participation work best in smaller, closer settings; so there is a democratic advantage to dividing a larger polity up into smaller subunits with decision making and administrative authority (Norman 2006: 144). A state the size of California is beyond the size appropriate for direct democracy, but direct democracy can be integrated more successfully if procedures are adapted, like those I advocate, that break the state up into smaller units in which direct democracy occurs.

But, even if there was not sufficient evidence to refute the claims made by opponents of direct democracy, the critics fail to appreciate and address the most sophisticated normative justification of direct democracy.

> Sovereignty cannot be represented for the same reason that it cannot be alienated; its essence is the general will, and that will must speak for itself, or it does not exist; it is either itself or not itself; there is no intermediate possibility. The deputies of the people, therefore, are not and cannot be their representatives; they can only be their commissioners, and as such they are not qualified to conclude anything definitively. No act of theirs can be law, unless it has been ratified by the people in person; and without that ratification nothing is a law. (Rousseau 1968: 141)

Sovereignty resides in the people as the people must consent to be governed. Lacking their consent, the government is tyrannical and the people are not governed but merely kept under control. To authorize a system of government that does not allow for direct democracy the people have their sovereignty stripped from them and thus whatever action that government takes cannot be legitimate as it does so without the consent of the people. The empirical evidence sides with Rousseau on this issue as well, as it clearly shows that people are better represented in systems of direct democracy.

Aside from Rousseau's claim, it is important to remember what was said earlier in the discussion of deliberative democracy. It is natural for humans to reason and to communicate, therefore combining these two elements into a system of government is consistent with human nature. Democracy, and particularly deliberative democracy, is the only system which integrates these aspects of human nature. Therefore, I do not rely solely on the pragmatic argument put forth by some democratic theorists who state that the only reason for having democracy is to improve government output. While this may be so, I think it is more important to recognize the humanity behind the choice. The process allows for humans to do what is natural; it takes into account the human condition and allows it to flourish.

The three-step process I outline below will lack some of the detail that the plan for nullification had due to the fact that much of the nullification procedure is carried over and therefore there is no need to repeat what has already been written.

General Outline for Veto

The first step will be to hold a referendum on whether a national bill should be vetoed. If there is opposition to a national policy at the state level a referendum can be initiated. At the state level a referendum can be initiated by either the state legislature or the people. If a group gets the necessary number of signatures on a petition then a referendum can be initiated just as if the state legislature can generate enough votes to initiate a referendum. The referendum is designed to give an accurate representation of how the people feel on this particular issue so that their representatives know how they should proceed (Hug 2004).

If the referendum passes with a majority in the state then town hall meetings will be held in that state. Each member of the state legislature is required to hold one meeting in his or her district in order to discuss the matter with his or her constituents. In these meetings opponents and proponents will be allowed to voice their concerns. There should be officials in place who can keep the discussion constructive and keep it from turning into a yelling match. The state legislator will take from this meeting recommendations and a general sense of what his or her constituency demands. The reason and advantages of the meetings were discussed in the previous chapter.

Following the referendum and town hall meeting there will be an open and public vote in the state legislature on whether the state should veto the national bill. Once the state legislature has acted, the people will certify the legislature's decision by popular vote. If the people certify the vote then the next step is triggered, if the people do not certify the vote then the process ends.

A state that vetoes does not provide a simple 'up-or-down' vote, but rather their decision comes with a description of what it is it objects to and what can be changed in a bill for them to accept it. If Congress chooses to act upon the recommendations of the state and revise accordingly, then it is recommended that a conference be held with representatives from each state and members of Congress to see if any of the new changes will provoke a veto in another state. If no compromise can be reached then the bill remains vetoed, if a compromise is reached then the bill is resubmitted to Congress for its vote and presidential approval. This new bill, if passed, is not exempt from being vetoed which is why the conference is recommended so that at this point a passed bill will become law.

There is also a veto override procedure. If a state vetoes a bill, each of the other 49 states may vote in their state legislature to override that state's veto. In order to facilitate deliberation, each state considering a veto-override vote will have to meet with the vetoing state to discuss the action. The views expressed will be documented and certified—the certification procedure is to show that both sides agree on what the other side's position is and what recommendations were made so as to eliminate communication error—by the two sides at the end of the meeting and submitted to their state's legislature and people for viewing. It will be up to each state if it wishes to add a direct-democracy component to the veto override. If a majority of the states vote for an override, then the bill goes back to Congress, which must pass it with a two-thirds majority in each house for it to become law. I include a supermajority component at this point since a supermajority has been found to better protect minority rights, maximize the protection of individual rights, and economic efficiency (Guinier 1994; Buchanan and Tullock 1962).[4]

Because of the veto override it is important that there is a deliberative component in order to ensure legitimacy. When given the ability to deliberate, and given the opportunity to directly influence policy and the opinions of others, a state on the losing side might more easily accept the legitimacy of a loss. This does not mean the loser will be satisfied or unwilling to continue efforts to overturn the policy, only that the loser is less likely to think it did not have a legitimate role in the process or that the process excluded, or did not give proper recognition of, its concerns.

It is also possible to formulate a procedure that ignores state boundaries. The procedure I have outlined assumes that states will be the primary sources of objection, but this might not be the case. For instance, if a country was divided into states but the people identified most strongly with their religion, and no state was identified with a particular religion, then veto could be granted to religious groups. For instance, if the national population consisted of 23 percent Muslims, 27 percent Buddhists, 44 percent Catholics, 6 percent Jews, and each of the 12 states in that country had those exact proportions, then granting states the veto would do little to protect a religious minority. In such a nation, Muslims, Buddhists, and Jews could form a majority coalition, or Buddhists and Catholics could as well, at the national level or within any state. The veto procedure would depend upon the federal structure of that nation, but the components of deliberation and direct democracy would need to be included in such a way that each group is given a voice and opportunity to veto.

On Religious Freedom in the United States: The Insufficiency of the Courts

Federalism, as Kymlicka argues in his reading of the *Federalist Papers*, prevents factions and their tendency to threaten the rights of other groups (Kymlicka 1998: 125). But the presence of a multilayered government system is not enough if the subnational governing units are not given the ability to protect themselves. Moreover, if a purely majoritarian system is in place, even in a federal scheme, rights can be threatened. For this reason there is a need for countermajoritarian institutions, such as courts, to prevent the violation of minority rights. But as shown in previous chapters, the courts are not the answer. This present section will further show how and why the courts, particularly in the United States, are insufficient avenues for protecting minority interests. What should be used instead is a system of deliberative decision making that is triggered through a veto.

In defending her idea of deliberative democracy, Iris Marion Young provides some support for my view of how the veto can enhance representation:

> Where there are real group-based positional differences that give to some people greater power, material and cultural resources, and authoritative voice, social norms that appear impartial are often biased . . . A common consequence of social privilege is the ability of a group to convert its perspective on some issues into authoritative knowledge without being challenged by those who have reason to see things differently. As long as such unequal circumstances persist, a politics that aims to do justice through public discussion and decision making must

theorize and aim to practice a third alternative to both a private interest competition and one that denies the reality of difference in public discussions of the
common good. This third way consists in a process of public discussion and decision making that includes and affirms all particular social group perspectives
in the society and draws on their situated knowledge as a resource for enlarging
the understanding of everyone and moving them beyond their own parochial
interests. (Young 1997: 399)

Young provides a strong argument for deliberative democracy, and an even stronger
argument for why all groups should be given a voice. But, in order to have a voice,
each group must be empowered. Should a group not have institutionalized self-
defense mechanisms, their voice will be quickly drowned out by those who are better
positioned to use a majority-rule system to their advantage. Young emphasizes the
importance of maintaining group identity, and in a federal structure that grants a
veto right, groups can maintain their identity as they are given the opportunity to
express and protect their identity in an institutionalized capacity. This gives legitimacy to their interests and the ability to have their voices heard, as well as control
policy, in a way that a centralized democratic regime does not allow. A system based
on concurrent majority, or something analogous, does better to protect identity, and
give an equal voice to all groups, than does a majority-based system.
    Religion is an issue, which is the source of violence and tension the world over.
In the United States, where the freedom of religion is codified in the Bill of Rights,
one might think that the establishment of a religion or government preference for
a religious sect would be forbidden and unlikely to occur. But, the U.S. Supreme
Court has granted unequal protection to religions. Just as important, the Supreme
Court undermines an important component of individual and communal identity
by controlling what religion can be practiced and how. Because religious groups are
not equally dispersed—that is, there can be high concentrations of members from
one group in a region or city and nearly none of that group in another region or
city—and because religion can play a central role in constructing one's identity and
system of morality, the decision on how religion is practiced should be left to local
entities. This is not to say, that if a community dominated by Baptists passes a law
saying all Methodists have to give a donation to the Baptist church because it is the
one and only true church, that some governing body above that community cannot
step in. But it is to say that if in that community liquor sales are restricted to certain
times, days, and stores because the consumption of alcohol is objected to by the
dominant group it should be allowed to do so and the Supreme Court should not
decide in favor of a universal standard for liquor sales on Twenty-first Amendment
grounds.
    In *Wisconsin v. Yoder* (1972) the U.S. Supreme Court was asked to decide whether
Wisconsin's law forcing Amish parents to send their children to public school beyond
grade school was a violation of the First Amendment's protection of freedom of
religion as the Amish argued that the public high schools taught values inimical to

their own. The Supreme Court decided for Yoder, and against Wisconsin. The problem might be seen as one in which an unelected branch of the government decided for a state what should be done within its geographical and political borders. Had the Amish been mistreated by Wisconsin when the state made their children go to public school, perhaps there would have been more of a case, but it is antithetical to a representative system of government and a federal system of government for an unelected branch of the national government to interfere in a state matter such as this on the grounds that there was no alleged abuse or misuse. The Amish had not been denied the right to practice their religion nor denied an education, but instead were forced to send their children to public school. The first problem with this decision is that it denied the opportunity for a deliberative resolution. Had the Amish a veto on the school board there could have been some revision of the curriculum that could have satisfied both sides. Could no such revision be made, then perhaps the state of Wisconsin would have come to let the Amish not attend school on two possible grounds. First, the Amish might have persuaded the state that it meant no malice toward the state but it preferred an alternate system of education that would still produce educated citizens. Second, the Amish could have used its veto to override any measure passed by the school board. Thus, the school board would have eventually acquiesced if it wanted to get anything done. This may seem anti-democratic, but in fact, the underlying decision is whether the majority would rather have no measure passed or let the Amish educate their own. This second option could have then led to a negotiated withdrawal in which the state was granted some oversight of the Amish curriculum though the Amish would not have to attend public schools.

The second problem with this decision, as it relates to federalism, is that it forces the Court to decide which religions are deserving of special exemptions rather than the community. Whether to grant an exemption should be decided on grounds of how disruptive the behavior is and how threatening the behavior is to the other norms and customs of the community. It should be left for the community to decide which religious practices are threatening and disruptive as it is the members of the community who have to live with the practitioners. If the citizens of a community object to the practices of a particular religion because it disrupts their daily life or produces and undue burden on nonpractitioners, there is no reliable way for a centralized nonrepresentative body to decide the matter. Moreover, the Court cannot properly balance whether the religion is truly a violation of community norms or if the community norms produce a repression of religious right for it does not know the community norms first-hand.

On the question of whether a member of the Native American Church ought to be granted an exemption from state drug laws is an instance of when the Court was forced to delineate which religious practices were worthy of exemption from state laws. In *Oregon v. Smith* (1990), Alfred Smith was fired from his state job when he tested positive for peyote. Since peyote use was part of his religion, he appealed his firing as being a violation of the Free Exercise Clause of the First Amendment.

The Court decided against Smith and for Oregon's ability to restrict the use of peyote as a religious practice even though the state Supreme Court of Oregon had decided that Oregon's restriction was unconstitutional. I do not object to banning peyote in the work place just as I do not support its use as a religious instrument, but I am calling into question the Court's wisdom on such matters. In deciding cases such as this the Court is forced to decide the question of what sort of religious practices, and thus religions if a defining part of a religion are its practices, are valid. This seems to be in direct conflict with the First Amendment's separation between church and state. But more important for the question at hand is that when *Smith* is compared to *Yoder*, it appears the Court is no better equipped to defend minority rights than majoritarian institutions as the Court has suppressed the rights of the minority to practice its religion in the case of *Smith*, but allows the practice of the Amish in *Yoder*. This seems to be the Court showing a preference for one religion over another. Imagine if this were not the United States, but perhaps Israel, and the high court decided that a sect of Judaism—just as the Amish are a Christian sect in so far as they read from the same religious text—was exempt from a state mandate but another religion—perhaps Islam—was not granted an exemption. This would be even more troubling, and threaten the legitimacy of the institution, if every member of the Court deciding the case were Jews, just as every Supreme Court Justice deciding *Smith* and *Yoder* was a Christian. Even if the Court was not showing a religious preference, in a nation divided along religious lines these two cases could serve as a flashpoint given the perception. There are situations in which the threats to a religious group, or the conflicts between religiously based interests, are far graver than what was presented in *Oregon v. Smith*. This is not to demean the importance of peyote use to certain religions, but in the cases of Palestinian-Israeli relations and religious conflicts in Sri Lanka, it is appropriate to say that there are more serious threats to liberty and justice. All *Oregon v. Smith* demonstrates is that the Court is ill-equipped to make such decisions for it cannot successfully decide matters that should be left to the community to decide.

In the cases of *Smith* and *Yoder*, the state and communities, through proper representative instruments, should be in charge of the matters in question. Proper representation means, in addition to what we typically think of, the opportunity for an affected group to repeal a government decision. In the case of *Smith* and *Yoder*, there is no reasonable chance for repeal. The Amish and the Native American Church should be given the opportunity to repeal the perceived discriminatory laws through representative institutions. If the repeal process was set up so as to allow deliberation and reason giving, then the democratic ideal would be more closely approximated, on both procedural and substantive grounds, than a Supreme Court ruling.

The Court can also make decisions restricting religion in which there has been no harm done by the religion or where the religion poses no immediate threat. In *Santa Fe ISD v. Doe* (2000) the U.S. Supreme Court held that it was a violation of the Establishment Clause of the First Amendment for the school district to allow student-initiated and student-led prayer at football games. The prayers were permitted but not required by the school district or the state. The school district allowed the students to vote on whether there would be a prayer before the football game, and if so, vote on which student would serve as spokesperson and deliver the prayer. The two individuals who objected did so on the grounds that it violated the Establishment Clause of the Constitution while claiming no harm. In the case of *Santa Fe ISD* there is no reliable evidence to suggest that a majority of the district opposed prayer, but it is known that a majority of students supported the prayer as the decision to have a prayer was voted on by the students. Because the majority of students in the district supported prayer, the Court acted only in the interest of the minority. Assuming the Court had the best interest of the nation in mind; it did not act in the best interest of each individual school district. It cannot, nor should it be expected to.

In addition to giving the minority the ability to dictate the actions of the majority in Santa Fe ISD, this decision exhibits how a national court can hold the *majority* will in one community hostage to the *minority* will of another community. For instance, if Minority X objects to a policy in Region Y, and the Court sides with Minority X, Region Q has to abide by the decision of the Court even if no one from Minority X resides in that region or objects to the policy. *Santa Fe ISD* ignores the possibility that there are other school districts where nobody objects to prayer at a school related event, but still forces that school district to abide by the decision. This decision might be useful for those areas where the majority of people do not want prayer, or in an area with so many different religions that implementing a policy for each religion to express itself publicly before a sporting event would be impractical, but it does a disservice to those areas where there is no conflict. It runs the risk of imposing a view of religion that is contrary to the will of a particular community. These sorts of decisions are best left to the local communities to decide for themselves. A national court should not inhibit a district's ability to look out for its own best interest. Instead, mechanisms should be put into place so that districts can resolve the issue for themselves. The Court, in each of these cases, has violated democratic and federal procedures and principles, and in so doing, the Court has increased the people's reliance on nondemocratic and national institutions while threatening the legitimacy of local institutions.

The Supreme Court, in making decisions that should be left in the hands of local communities, reverses the process and advantages of federalism discussed heretofore. One additional advantage of decentralized decision making that is particularly pertinent to religion is the connection between decentralization and civil society. Religious institutions are generally considered components of civil society and when politics is centralized civil society is diminished because the local level, which is where civil society is located, loses its importance and legitimacy. "[A]dministrative decentralization and subnational democratization (the creation of space for citizen participation in local government) provide incentives for social movements to shift their efforts from the center to local government" (Greaves

2007: 306–7). This also means that political efficacy and participation diminish in conjunction with weakened civic organizations and participation. The negative effects associated with diminished political participation and a dying civil society has been well documented. One must consider whether it is self-defeating for religious groups to appeal to a centralized court if the long-term effect will be that the organization will lose its importance in the lives of its members should litigating disputes become a trend.

Sri Lanka: Veto and Conflict Resolution

The failure to adopt a system that promotes equality, ethnic pluralism, and the sharing of power in this multiethnic country has led to decades of violence. The two primary groups in Sri Lanka are the Buddhist Sinhalese and the mainly Hindu Tamils. Both groups speak different languages and have different religions. Further complicating matters is the fact that within the Tamil-speaking community are Muslims and the Indian Tamils. While the Sinhalese constitute over 70 percent of the population, they perceive themselves as the minority due to the fact that their population and physical boundaries are shrinking and because of the close proximity of Sri Lanka to India, a country where they would be minorities. Additionally, the Sinhalese consider to have been at an economic and social disadvantage under British rule, and still feel the need to exert their authority over the Tamils for fear of returning to their preindependence condition. When the majority feels fearful and persecuted, cooperation and power sharing is nearly impossible due to the fact that the party in control has no incentive or inclination to do so. The Tamils live in the northern and eastern provinces where they constitute nearly 60 percent of the population in those regions, thus further fueling a sense of minority status among the more extreme Sinhalese. As a result, the Sinhala interests were "defined in opposition to the interests of ethnic and religious minorities" (Tirucelvam 2008: 199). This means that, in many instances, the Sinhalese did not consider a measure a political victory unless it promoted their own interests at the expense of others. Politics had become a zero-sum game.

A sense of minority status and a history of perceived colonial persecution is not all there is to the story. The Sinhalese have employed a form of symbolic-identity politics that has increased polarization between the two groups.[5] In 1948, as soon as political power was transferred from Britain to Sri Lanka, the Sinhalese used their majority position to pass discriminatory laws against the Tamils, but it was not until 1956 that the most aggressive measures were taken. In 1956, 8 years after British rule ended, the Sri Lanka Freedom party swept the general election, except in the northeast, which gave the Sinhalese a strong hold on the government. With their new found power, the Sinhala promoted their centralist motives that were founded on the idea that the land belonged to the Sinhalese for religious reasons. The Sinhalese effectively promoted ethno-nationalist sentiments, by focusing on religion and language, among the voters in an effort to effectively outbid their opponents (DeVotta 2004).

Of course, the election of 1956 would not have been the same without the passage of the Ceylon Citizenship Acts of 1948 and 1949. In these acts the Indian Tamils were stripped of their voting rights by the ruling Sinhalese party.[6] Not only did this limit the number of Tamils who could vote, but it splintered the Tamils into competing parties of which the most extreme began attracting the most support. Had there been a veto mechanism in Sri Lanka, perhaps the Acts of 1948 and 1949 would have never passed. But absent such a mechanism the stage was set for the 1956 elections in which the Sinhalese gained insurmountable authority.

In 1952, a splinter-Sinhala party referred to as the SLFP lost to the dominant-Sinhala UNP. To win the 1956 elections the SLFP sought to gain more votes by becoming extreme. One of the ways they promoted their agenda was to further politicize religion by pronouncing the need for increased ties between the state and Buddhism in addition to stronger economic nationalism. The SLFP reached out to rural villages and the economic disadvantaged with their message. They promoted the need for a stronger Sinhalese government with policies designed to keep from the Hindu Tamils what was rightfully intended for the Buddhist Sinhalese. The SLFP positioned themselves as the only hope for those disenfranchised and economically disadvantaged Sinhalese, by spreading the message that their plight was due to the fault of the Tamils. One of the first acts by the new government in 1956 was to pass the Sinhala-Only Act which meant the language used for government and business would be Sinhala. In addition to pro-Sinhalese economic policies and pro-Buddhist social policies, the Sinhala-Only Act forced the Tamils to respond with their own extremism. Given that there were no mechanisms, least of all a veto mechanism, that the minority could use, there was no manner by which the extreme policies could be tempered and the rights of the minorities protected.

This pattern was continued through 1972 when a new constitution was drafted to replace the 1948 constitution that had been introduced by the British. The 1972 constitution included articles giving Buddhism an even greater status and insured state patronage to Sinhalese youth. This move was in response to the JVP's campaign for political power that had attracted the youth and the economically disadvantaged. The SLFP feared that if they did not match the extremism of the JVP they would lose political power. But, in the 1977 elections the SLFP would go on to suffer huge defeats due to the economic burden its policies put on the system. Most of the population was suffering economically and the UNP secured 140 of the 225 seats.

Prior to the 1977 election, Tamil opposition reached a new high with the formation of the LTTE, which advocated for violent opposition to the Sinhalese and the establishment of a separate Tamil state. The LTTE saw no way around the institutionalized dominance and discrimination of the Sinhalese, which meant they had to use extreme measures to secure their rights. In this way, extremism begat extremism. The new government passed another constitution in 1978 in order to reconcile tensions, but the new UNP government could not abandon the more extreme Sinhalese, which meant the new constitution was still discriminatory. For instance, the new constitution went from giving Buddhism a preferred status to actively promoting Buddhism. In 1983 an amendment was added to the constitution that separatism was not allowed and that those expressing separatist sentiments would be punished.

The provisions of the 1978 constitution guaranteed that Hinduism, and thus the Tamils, would have an inferior status in Sri Lanka. Had the veto been given to the Tamils in 1948, 1949, 1956, 1972, 1978, or 1983 perhaps some of the violence, or at least the institutionalization of discrimination, could have been avoided. As important and useful of a mechanism the veto is, it cannot be effective unless the implementation of the veto does not reinforce the behavior that makes it necessary. One of the primary reasons the Sinahlese parties adopted extreme policies was because they thought it was the best way to win office. By making the Tamils the source of everything that went wrong with the Sinhalese, the answer was to promote Sinhalese interests at the expense of Tamil interests. There was some extremism among the voting masses, but the elites in Sri Lanka created an environment in which extremism spread to those who had previously adopted more moderate positions. The dominant parties were able to co-opt religious symbols and myths for their own political gain. In using myths and symbols, rather than reasoned argument, the dominant party became intolerant, fearful, and angry at the other (Imtiyaz and Stavis 2008). Thus, any attempt to resolve the ethnic conflict in Sri Lanka is dependent upon elite negotiations, tempering the most extreme members of each side, and making it politically disadvantageous to court and encourage extreme views. Had there been institutional mechanisms in place to delay policy adoption, force deliberation and encourage participatory democracy, then the polarization may have been tempered. I suggest that federalism and the veto could bring Sri Lanka closer to conflict resolution so long as they incorporate procedures that force deliberation and reward participation.

Like most of history, the path was not linear as there were attempts to pass more moderate measures. Reforms aimed at devolving power and relieving the ethnic tension began in 1977, but they were largely ineffective and the violence continued. The attempts to devolve power only increased political tensions because the heads of each province were appointed by the central government, thus they tended to reflect the policy positions of the central government. And while certain powers were devolved to the provinces, the Reserve List ensured that the center would still be the ultimate authority. "The majority in the *Thirteenth Amendment* case ([1987] 2 SLR 312) relied on this provision to hold that parliament would retain the authority to legislate on all subjects for any part of Sri Lanka and, therefore, the devolution scheme was within a unitary state" (Tirucelvam 2008: 201). The Reserve List in the Second Republic Constitution is but one factor. Article 2 of the Constitution defined Sri Lanka as a unitary state as interpreted by the judiciary and bureaucracy. Therefore, provincial authority is wholly dependent upon the center as made clear in a later article. "Article 154G provides that any law passed by parliament in respect of a subject in the Concurrent List shall prevail over any contrary provision in a statute made by a provincial council with regard to the subject" (Tirucelvam 2008: 201). Further attempts to resolve the ethnic conflict have often resulted to military confrontation, and the result has been a failure to produce any lasting solution. Even the intervention of outside mediators, such as India and Norway, has failed.

Beginning in 1995 there was a serious move toward decentralization in which five proposals were put forth: (1) the framework document prepared by a British firm and supported by the newly elected President Kumaratunga, (2) the Devolution Proposals of 1995, (3) the Legal Draft of January 1996, (4) the Draft Constitutional proposal of 1997, and (5) the Draft Constitution Bill of 2000, which sought to end the unitary state and bring about a federal structure in which the Tamils and Sinhalese would each be able to achieve self-determination. Each measure ultimately failed because the Sinhalese were fearful that this would lead to Tamil secession and the Tamil Tigers objected because they were not consulted during the drafting on any of the documents. But, the atmosphere was one in which federalism was put forth and, as a concept, accepted as a possible remedy to the years of violence. This is what made the 2002 breakthrough possible. With negotiations led by the Norwegians, the Tamils and the Sinhalese were able to reach some agreement about government restructuring on the principles of federalism. But the issue of whether Sri Lanka will be considered federal or unitary has been a major sticking point for a Sinhalese majority does not want to give ground to the Tamils. The point, however, is that federalism is a familiar concept and therefore attempts to implement a properly designed federal structure would not be a revolutionary proposal. Unfortunately, absent higher levels of trust, empathy, and perceived legitimacy, any reform will be doomed. Any reform proposal would need to gain legitimacy from the Tamils by including them in the reform process and each side would need to learn to trust and empathize with the other. The first component is institutionally straightforward, the last two are more difficult to manufacture institutionally.

Empirical evidence shows that empathy and trust can be manufactured through a close and controlled interaction of members from antagonistic groups. In Sri Lanka high school juniors and seniors were selected to participate in a peace workshop. The workshop was a controlled environment in which teenagers would meet and interact with teenagers from different ethnic backgrounds. The workshop lasted only four days, but 1 year after the workshop had ended it was found that those who participated still exhibited higher levels of trust and empathy for other ethnic groups than those who did not participate (Malhotra and Liyanage). Based on these results and others, it can be seen quite clearly why a veto decision ought to incorporate town hall–style meetings. These meetings, with the proper oversight and direction, can lead to a greater understanding and tolerance for competing arguments. Moreover, this study shows that increasing empathy and trust among citizens is not outside the purview of a constitution's powers. A constitution that requires the collaboration and deliberation from all sides is one that will temper extremism and discrimination.

The violent conflict between the Tamils and the Sinhalese was officially brought to an end on May 17, 2009, when nearly all of the LTTE leaders had been killed. However, it cannot be classified a resolution when one side is incapable of continuing a war because all of its leaders are dead. Given that only time and discontent are needed for another group to form or the LTTE to reorganize, a lasting peace seems unlikely since the same policies and extreme views that fostered the violence are still present. Just because the shooting has stopped for now does not mean we should stop looking for ways to relieve ethnic tension in Sri Lanka. My suggestion is to look for ways to increase intergroup deliberation and contact through a federal structure that would give the minority parties a veto over discriminatory policies.

Conclusion

The veto, like nullification, is vital for preserving federalism, for if the constituent parts are not equipped with the tools to protect themselves against the centralizing tendency of the national government federalism will be lost. However, this is only important if federalism is worth preserving in the first place. As I have tried to show in each chapter up to this point, and as the last two chapters will also try to show, federalism is the only means by which disparate groups living within the same nation will be able to produce solutions to the issues which divide them. But even in societies where there is not a risk of war or violence federalism is vital for preserving civil society, thereby humanizing politics. Through federalism, and mechanisms such as the veto, people are forced to deliberate in a manner consistent with the ideals set forth by those favoring deliberative decision making.

Notes

1. Here too I extend the right to veto to all constituent actors and follow similar constraints I laid out for nullification.
2. For empirical research that demonstrates American federalism provides opportunities, and perhaps encourages actors to be opportunistic and thus ignore federal constraints see Conlan (2006). For a formal theory arguing that federal structures are typically too weak to prevent opportunism see Bednar (2009).
3. Bachrach and Baratz, 1962.
4. Objections can be made that the supermajority procedure can be used against minority rights. If one looks at the success the filibuster in the U.S. Senate at preventing civil rights legislation one may say that the veto infringed upon minority rights. This all depends on how one constructs the minority. In this instance there were two minorities: blacks and senators in favor of discrimination. The second group used the filibuster to keep discriminatory policies in place that were directed at blacks. However, the power of the filibuster eventually gave way and allowed for civil rights legislation to be passed. There are three lessons from this episode: the filibuster did work, for a time, to protect the minority even though it was a different minority than we usually think of; second, when there is enough support for a policy, a supermajority can be formed; third, the super- majority is effective at maintaining the status quo. On this last point, minority rights will be exploited for a greater length of time in a supermajority system if that is the status quo as it was in the United States up to the 1960s. If the supermajority system is in place

from the beginning, and everyone has an equal right to participate, then discrimination will not be an institutionalized part of the system and thus the status quo is different from the outset, thus overturning the status quo in favor of discrimination would be much more difficult.

5. As Murray Edelman (1971) argues, symbols acquire certain values that a group identifies with and thus influences their political actions. Their identification with these symbols is emotional rather than rational, which can lead to a type of politics in which there can be no reasoned debate or discussion. Symbolic politics use myths to give "events and actions a particular meaning typically by defining enemies and heroes and tying ideas of right and wrong to people's identity" (Kaufman 2001: 28).

6. This is similar to the Nationality Law of 1952 in Israel, which denied Israeli nationality to displaced Arabs.

CHAPTER 6

Secession

One of the prevailing arguments of this book has been that countries are better off decentralizing. I have shown instances in which decentralization, accompanied with the appropriate federalism enhancing mechanisms, has been successful. But there is still a chance that federal societies may fail to create workable solutions to persistent problems. If this occurs then the right to secession ought to be respected. While I have demonstrated, as have others (Brancati 2006), that decentralization can decrease ethnic tension by bringing the government closer to the people, without the proper mechanisms in place a federal system may still allow for ethnic conflict and the suppression of minority rights (Bakke and Wibbels 2006; Hale 2004).[1] And while some worry that federalism may encourage secession, the most sophisticated research has shown that only in the short term does repression work to ensure unity whereas federal states show greater promise in maintaining a unified state without force (Lustick, Miodownik, and Eidelson 2004). Decentralization and ethno-federal structures do not encourage secession. In this chapter I will take the objectionable stance that even if secession were more likely to occur in federal systems, these types of systems should still not be avoided for disunity and secession are not in and of themselves bad. This chapter argues that secession is a right that ought to be protected for normative and pragmatic reasons.

As I have tried to demonstrate, particularly in Chapter 3, sovereignty ought to remain with the people. As A. J. Conyers so astutely observes, the rise of the nation-state has not only led to a greater nation-state—in terms of reach and authority—but it has atomized individuals.

> Over the next three centuries [from the seventeenth century on] the world saw a continuation of the trend toward larger and more comprehensive governments and of the tendency to identify peoples with large, powerful ruling centers, rather than with the variety of associations that had always made up complex human society. Even though in our time we have become accustomed to thinking almost exclusively in terms of nation-states with broad powers exercised over vast territories and diverse peoples, the rise of the nation-state brought about an astounding change in social arrangements. This change, furthermore, occasioned the isolation of the individual. People began to think of themselves not so much in terms of their social setting, or their families, or their churches, bust as autonomous free agents . . . Therefore, the identity of the individual was less and less to be found in his primary relationship in the community. (Conyers 2008: 5)

State-defined identity has contributed to the deprivation of popular sovereignty as the people become individuals and the individuals become dependent upon the state.

It is in Michael Walzer that we see what it is Conyers and others who are skeptical of the nation-state object to. Walzer writes,

> the nation-state is now the more likely regime of toleration: one group, dominant throughout the country, shaping public life and tolerating a national or religious minority—rather than two or three groups, each secure in its own place, tolerating one another. (Walzer 1997: 24)

Walzer paints an image in which the majority is "dominant" in "shaping" how the minority functions in the society. Walzer seems to show a preference for dyadic conflict, minority vs. majority, in which problems seem more easily observed than the messy conflicts that occur when there are multiple actors. But, it seems Walzer has confused suppression with toleration. A group that forces another to adopt its worldview is hardly being tolerant. It is through the nation-state that we have seen the greatest acts of intolerant behavior.

Walzer and Conyers agree on at least two points, but they disagree in their evaluation of those two points. Where Conyers sees the artificial identity created by the nation-state as a negative, Walzer praises the nation-state for being "a kind of cultural corporation [that] claims a monopoly on such arrangements within its borders" (Walzer 1997: 25). As will be seen in the following discussion of Ethiopia and the former Soviet Union, and contrasted with Belgium, artificially constructed identities, particularly ethnic identities, can prove counterproductive and force an identity and political crisis.

There does not seem to be much disputing Walzer's assessment of the nation-state, only its value. Clarissa Hayward, taking a similar worldview as Walzer, argues that "[S]tates play a critical role in constructing social identities and differences. They help define, institutionalize, and order the categories and the relations that produce and maintain identity/difference" (Hayward 2003: 501). Hayward understands that this can be problematic, but rather than abandon the state-centric vision, she seeks to restructure the method by which identity construction occurs in the state by democratizing the process. Hayward recommends that we acknowledge difference so that we may tolerate difference. The acknowledgment of social group differences must be "affirmative" and "public." Hayward suggests that by facilitating deliberation—which she provides no proscription of how this might be done—in a society that recognizes difference there can grow a greater appreciation for, and toleration of, those differences. What Hayward fails to note is that once differences become a part of the political system there is a political value to maintaining that difference. Identity does not have to be static or nation-state defined, but Hayward assumes that it is. If identity can change, then institutionalizing identity has the ability to make identity artificial if it provides a disincentive for changing one's identity. This is commonly seen when certain groups become entrenched within a political party even when that party stops serving their interests because the identification with that party gains an inertia that is hard to stop. Moreover, by institutionalizing differences we are left with no choice but to focus on our differences. If we are different through race and classified as such by the nation, then our politics will center on questions of race since it is that difference that has become institutionalized and by which we become recognized. There must be a respect for one's political identity, but it must not be incorporated into the political realm in such a way that prohibits fluidity.

A second aspect of the nation-state Walzer praises is that while the nation-state is "less tolerant of groups, it may well force groups to be more tolerant of individuals" (Walzer 1997: 27). There are few who dispute this point, but Conyers—and communitarians—would refute the claim that this is a positive feature of the nation-state. Encouraging atomization, and separation from the community, is one source of the decline of civil society and an increased dependence upon the state. As Althusius and Aristotle teach, the state should not be the primary association in the individual's life, for the types of relationships that the state fosters is not the kind that brings a person to his or her *telos*. Relationships, such as friendships and familial, ought to be the primary types of associations. The nation-state cannot let these associations continue to be the primary associations, as they were before the rise of the nation-state.

When the nation must be mobilized to meet a crisis, or when the state has assumed both the right and the duty to see that national life functions well, the kinds of distinctions that make up the fabric of a society tend to obstruct the efficiency needed for effective action. (Conyers 2008: 7)

Drawing on the work of Carl J. Friedrich, as McCoy and Baker do, I find appealing the notion that

It is important to view "federalism and federal relations in dynamic terms," as Friedrich reminds us. Rather than a static pattern or design, he explains, federalism is "primarily the process of federalizing a political community, that is to say, the process by which a number of separate political communities enter into arrangements for working out solutions, adopting joint policies, and making joint decisions on joint problems, and conversely also the process by which a unitary political community becomes differentiated into a federally organized whole. Federal relations are fluctuating relations in the very nature of things. Any federally organized community must therefore provide itself with instrumentalities for the recurrent revision of its pattern of design." (McCoy and Baker 1991: 13–14)

If we incorporate this view into the theoretical construction of federalism, then we must allow secession into our system as secession legitimizes the fluidity and revision that is integral for a healthy federal system. This view is unsettling for most people on the grounds that there is too much uncertainty and that too much uncertainty will lead to violent conflict. But, uncertainty and fluidity do not create the violence, it is the attempt to prevent the natural progression and reordering, in an attempt to make the situation more certain and manageable, that creates violent conflict. Seceding areas only use violence when they are violently opposed. If an area were allowed to secede there would be no violence. Consider the most prominent examples of secession. When the Southern states in the United States seceded from the Union it was the North that fired the first shot at Fort Sumter, when the Tamils sought a separate state it was the Sinhalese who opposed it by force, and when Eritrea tried to leave it was Ethiopia that used force to prevent separation. Secession is opposed to violence. Most secession movements occur because a group or region is trying to escape state-sanctioned violence.

On the most basic level, to accept secession is to accept the fact that humans cannot control their destiny through governments and institutions in the way the modern nation-state promises. To adopt secession is to adopt a dynamic view of society in which most of the moving parts cannot be controlled and must be allowed to run their natural—so long as it is a peaceful—course. The nation-state can avoid a modernist trap by constitutionalizing secession.

Opponents of constitutionalizing secession, such as Cass Sunstein, worry that one secession will lead to another and constitutionalizing secession will lead to more incidents of secession. As Wayne Norman points out, who at times appears to oppose secession, "he [Sunstein] is too quick to assume that secessionist politics is necessarily encouraged by a secession clause and discouraged by its absence" (Norman 2006: 204). Furthermore, this worry is unsubstantiated by the historical record. For instance, when Tennessee seceded from North Carolina, Kentucky from Virginia, or Maine from Massachusetts, there were no additional moves for secession. Similarly when Sweden seceded from Norway in 1905—with Norway's permission—there were no further secessions that followed. When Belgium seceded from the Dutch, there were no subsequent secessionist movements. If one would expect for a strong secessionist movement to be continued it would be in Belgium where there have been strong nationalist movements based on ethnicity. But, the federal structure has allowed for coexistence without secession or the suppression of secessionist movements. In Ethiopia, Eritrea was granted the right to secede in 1993, and to this point no other secessionist movement has occurred in Ethiopia or Eritrea. When the Soviet Union collapsed it did so because the former Soviet states seceded. More than one state seceded, but it was not a domino effect because the secessions occurred in a single wave. After the initial wave of secession was over, no others occurred (Kahn 2002: 35). Thus, the occurrence of secession does not encourage more secessionist movements.

If Percy Lehning has Kymlicka right, then it is Kymlicka's view that a federation is inherently unstable (Lehning 1998: 6). The instability results, in part, from the fact that "the option of secession will always be present. It is the baseline against which participation in the federation is measured" (Lehning 1998: 6). Kymlicka and I depart on secession in that he views federalism as a means of avoiding secession whereas I see secession as a necessary component of the federal constitution (Kymlicka 1998: 112). Kymlicka, like most proponents of federalism (Karmis and Norman 2005), sees it as a way of addressing multiethnic societies. But, this view of federalism misses the point in that federalism, and political tensions, go beyond questions of ethnicity and multiethnic societies.

"In dealing with secession inevitably questions arise pertaining to obligation, morality, authority, justice, and comparative assessments of political systems" (Buchanan 1991: 7). In doing so it allows us to better examine the metaphysical implications of these questions and our premises. Because of this, Sunstein deserves to be congratulated for taking the topic seriously and recognizing its importance to debates in moral philosophy and practical politics. But this is where my agreement with Sunstein ends on the issue. Sunstein argues that granting a constitutional right to secede defeats the purpose of constitutions, since the objective of constitutions is to preserve institutions. I dispute this view as I understand that constitutions are given value through their ability to protect life, liberty, and property; not by their ability to preserve institutions. Constitutions create institutions with the goal of preserving valuable ends, not the means by which those ends are to be sought. Should constitutions fail to preserve the designated ends, then they fail to achieve their goal, even if the institutions remain intact. There is no justification for an institution that allows for the systematic killing or deprivation of a particular group or geographic area, nor for the continuation of the constitution under which those institutions function. If a constitution is designed with this purpose in mind then it is illegitimate on moral grounds and therefore a move to secession is morally justified. Additionally, if a constitution that is designed to preserve life, liberty, and property cannot stop gross infractions to the contrary, then that constitution has already failed, regardless of how well the institutions are operating, and secession would thus not be the cause of its failure. In either case, secession would merely be a reaction to a poor constitution and its institutions. On this point I am in full agreement with Onora O'Neill (1994) who argues that nation-states are justified if, and only if, they are instrumental in the achievement of justice.

Sunstein's constitutional objective is too narrow in that its primary focus is on the preservation of institutions. This definition of the constitutional objective forces him to reach the conclusion that a constitutional right to secede is self-contradictory. But, this contradiction can be eliminated if we change the formulation to say that the goal of a constitution is to protect institutions so long as those institutions aid in the pursuit of life, liberty, and property. It is true that a constitution that fails to maintain union is seen as a failure, but there is a paradox here that disguises the nature of the constitution and meaning of failure. If a constitution is good only to the extent that it protects life, liberty, and property, and it can do it better by letting a region (or group) transition out of it in order to protect those things the constitution deems valuable, then it has succeeded in achieving its end. While the constitution has been dissolved, or at least one area or group no longer operates under the constitution, does not mean the constitution has failed. Failure would occur if the constitution was used as an instrument of coercion or injustice. "If a secession clause is an extension of existing federal rules, such a clause should not appear completely out of place within a modern, progressive, federal constitution" (Norman 2006: 119).

"Most scholars find it difficult to defend secession as a right of federal units" (Kahn 2002: 34). But, "the ultimate check against the power of the center is . . . to exit from the system" (Kahn 2002: 33). Kahn is not a defender of secession. Secession, according to Kahn, is the rule of the minority over the majority. But, because the minority is given the power of self-determination, or in some cases self-defense, secession can be used as a method of forcing deliberation, thereby enhancing democratic practice and subsequently further legitimizing the authority of the majority.

Sunstein suggests that secessionist politics will have a pernicious effect on democratic deliberation and stability (Sunstein 2001b: 96). I reach just the opposite conclusion because secession gives the minority a voice that will force the majority to recognize it and consult with it. Absent a mechanism to force recognition by the majority, the minority is only left with hope. Buchanan makes a similar claim when he writes, "if, as the theory prescribes, international law recognizes a unilateral right to secede as a remedy for serious and persisting injustices, states will have an incentive to act more justly" (Buchanan 2004: 370). Secession means that the majority must include the minority in the governing process.

I am in agreement with Sunstein when he argues that

a constitution should promote deliberative democracy, an idea that is meant to combine political accountability with a high degree of reflectiveness and a general commitment to reason-giving [while it creates structures] that will promote freedom in the formation of preferences and not simply implement whatever preferences people have. (Sunstein 2001b: 6–7, 8)

I advocate for the constitutional inclusion of secession because it will produce these results. When the minority has a check on the majority, the majority is forced to give reasons because it has no other way of progressing if it seeks to prevent secession. Moreover, secession allows the minority to hold the majority accountable. Surely I do not defend the view that secession should be done capriciously, but the presence of it as an option will force the majority to the negotiating table without the minority threatening to secede or seceding. Deliberation will not occur just because the constitution has a secession clause, but the procedure by which the decision to secede is made should adhere to mechanisms that force deliberation. But, without the presence of the option, there is no reason for the majority to consult with the minority or take the interests of the minority seriously.

By constitutionalizing secession we avoid conflating problems. If a nation does not recognize secession when a group advocates secession it will first have to argue for the legitimacy of secession at the same time it articulates the reason they would like to secede. Opposition to the group's claims may come from those who oppose their policy and those who oppose secession but might agree with their policy position. The United States provides an interesting case study for this phenomenon. Modern advocates of secession in the United States are seen as racists or slavery sympathizers because the U.S. Civil War determined that secession was illegitimate and done only for the preservation for slavery in the South. This conflation occurred at the time of the Civil War as well. There were those in the North who favored secession as a concept, but were forced to change their views on the issue, or were forced to be quiet about them in public, if they were to avoid being seen as Southern sympathizers or slavery supporters. It would be possible, at that time and now, for one to both support secession as a concept and oppose both the South and slavery. Prior to the Civil War the strongest secessionist sentiments were expressed in the North.

> Dissatisfaction ran high in New England, where concern about the disruption of its trade with Britain was intensified by dismay over the lack of military success [in the War of 1812]. Connecticut virtually declared its independence, and representatives of various New England states gathered at Hartford in 1814 to threaten a more general secession. (Feeley and Rubin 2008: 107)

It was fewer than 50 years before the Civil War when secessionist claims were being made in New England. But, because the issue of slavery was attached to secession at the time of the Civil War, Northern secessionists were forced to abandon their original position. Conflict resolution becomes more manageable when issues can be isolated and seen for what they are. Secession need not muddy the waters, and will not if it is given constitutional protection.

If we agree that a secession clause ought to be in a constitution, then the natural next step is to define when an act of secession is justified. "In international law secession is only permitted in the instance of extreme brutality" (Norman 2006: 172). Such a statement offers very little guidance in that "extreme brutality" is open to any number of interpretations. "The international recognition of the right to secede is far too limited and is indicative of the prevailing statist-unionist view" (Norman 2006: 172). One of the first philosophers to make secession philosophically legitimate was Allen Buchanan. He posits that secession is legitimate when there is a persistent violation of human rights, rectification of past unjust takings of territory, and discriminatory redistribution. There are others, such as Birch, who provide additional justifications such as continuous refusal on the part of a people to give consent to membership in a union, failure of the government to protect the basic rights of certain citizens, failure to safeguard political and economic interests of a region, and failure to keep a bargain made to preserve the interests of a region that would be outvoted nationally. There are even those such as Kip Wellman who do not argue that secession must be motivated by self-defense or the unequal distribution of goods and rights, but only that the seceding state must be able to sustain itself and leave the original state in a condition in which it can sustain itself. While all of these are defensible reasons for secession, none of them should be included in the constitution. The constitution, while providing a secession clause that outlines how secession is to take place, should not itemize the events that can trigger a move toward constitutional secession. There are too many possibilities to include. What if Yugoslavia's constitution had a secession provision but genocide was left out as a reason for secession? Should we say that ethnic Albanians should be forbidden the secession option? Moreover, if broad and general grounds for justifiable secession are given in the constitution (e.g., violation of human rights), there is room for interpretation as to what those grounds are and if they have been actualized. Because events are unforeseeable, and the justification for secession is open to interpretation and perversion, the only thing that should be provided by the constitution is the means by which secession is to be carried out. A people or region should be able to choose for itself the conditions under which they consider life unbearable. For this reason I employ John Locke because it is in Locke that I find a popular-sovereignty defense of secession.

Especially when there are provisions for veto and nullification, secession should be difficult. "The hope would be that the qualifications of secession would be such that minority-nationalist leaders could not expect to mobilize enough support to make secessionist threats credible in the absence of genuine oppression by the central government" (Norman 2006: 205–6).

This chapter will provide a justification for secession, which is grounded in Locke's account of popular sovereignty and move on to a discussion of secession in the former Soviet Union and Ethiopia. Belgium will be discussed next, and provide an example of how a multiethnic nation might be constructed so as to avoid secession. Finally, I will provide a general outline of what secession procedures might be implemented. In the course of doing so this chapter will demonstrate the importance of public deliberation, direct democracy, and political legitimacy. The people must be given the right of self-determination, and secession is the ultimate act of self-determination. When secession is an option and the nation stays together, it is by choice. When a nation does not allow secession, the nation stays together through compulsion.

Legitimizing Secession with Locke

For those who study federalism, John Locke is not necessarily viewed as an ally. It is not as though those who study federalism think of Locke as an opponent, only that they rarely rely on him for support. Generally, I tend to agree that Locke does not explicitly provide a defense of federalism. But, he does provide the foundation for one of the essential components of federal governance: secession. By leaving the people sovereign, Locke allows for self-determination in all forms, including secession. While I do not argue he has done so in order to enhance federalism, his theory of secession can be adapted to the needs of federalism. This section will work toward a Lockean theory of secession by discussing the reason and means through which government is formed, the defining characteristics of government, the ends of government, and the essential rights of individuals under government. By the end of this section I will not have given a comprehensive treatment of Lockean political theory, but rather an adaptation of his theory that supports secession within the context of my theory of federalism.

As seen in the previous discussion of Aristotle and Althusius—and as will be seen in the discussion of John C. Calhoun—Locke begins with a man that is social by nature. "God having made Man such a Creature, that in his own Judgment, it was not good for him to be alone, put him under strong Obligations of Necessity, Convenience, and Inclination to drive him into Society . . ." (§77). But, because man is also naturally inclined toward self-preservation, conflict will result since he will always choose to preserve himself over another when a choice between the two must be made. Thus, when two people's self-preservation comes into conflict—that is when I must choose between whether you or I will live—the individual will always choose himself (§6). For this reason Locke concludes, man cannot be judge in his own case.[2]

> That it is unreasonable for Men to be Judges in theory own Cases, that Self-Love will make men partial to themselves and their Friends. And on the other side, that Ill Nature, Passion and Revenge will carry them too far in punishing others. (§13)

In a state of nature man not only serves as judge in his own case but also the executioner of the decision. This means that when a man feels he has been wronged he can retaliate by taking another's life (§11). The state of nature is, at the very least, one which is uncertain and unsettled. There is some dispute over whether there is a true distinction between the state of war and the state of nature, or whether there is only a rhetorical divide, but without getting into the debate it is enough to say that the state of nature is not necessarily one of peace and does not exclude the possibility of being one of war.[3] Man, because of the unsettled nature of the state of nature, forms a government through compact (§§7, 21, 23). It is through unanimity that men agree to be governed, though the requirement of unanimity is no longer required once a government has been formed. Moreover, a government may take on any form so long as it provides the proper ends of government.

> Political Power then I take to be a Right of making Laws with Penalties of Death, and consequently all less Penalties, for the Regulating and Preserving of Property, and of employing the force of the Community, in the Execution of such Laws, and in the defence of the Common-wealth from Foreign Injury, and all this only for the Publick Good. (§3)

Political power is only legitimate, and thus deserving of the name, if it produces the requisite end. The requisite end of government is the preservation of life, liberty, and property.[4] Because their property is unsafe in the state of nature, men will be willing to turn over some of their natural authority to an agreed upon authority in order to preserve life, liberty, and property.

> Thus Mankind, notwithstanding all the Priviledges of the state of Nature, being but in an ill condition, while they remain in it, are quickly driven into society . . . the irregular and uncertain exercise of the Power every Man has of punishing . . . make them take Sanctuary under the establish's Laws of Government, and therein seek the preservation of Property . . . (§127)

In the course of defining political power, Locke includes a description of those things government provides that the state of nature lacks. Government provides "established, settled, known law" (§124), "a known and indifferent judge" (§125), and the "Power to back and support the Sentence when right, and to give it due Execution" (§126). Men in the state of nature are governed only by the law of nature and serve as judge and executioner in their own cases. In government, the law of nature is replaced with a legislative law that seeks to replicate it and make it known to all, and men forfeit their power to judge and execute the law in almost all cases. Beyond §125, however, the power of judging rarely occurs in this context. In fact, when revisiting this discussion in Chapter XII, Locke drops the power of judging altogether and adds the federative power in its place. The seemingly mysterious, and all-important, power of judging is central to understanding Locke's political theory, but my reading of it must wait until a discussion of the proper ends of government has concluded. But, by way of preview, I think it is quite telling that at §§129–30 Locke states that when joining a civil society man conditionally forfeits his right to judge while unconditionally giving up his right to execute the law. However, the power to execute the law will return to him when he has judged the government to have acted against its ends.

Political power is similar to parental power in that both gain their legitimacy from their capacity to provide the proper ends. The power of the parent only extends to the degree to which the parent works toward the best interest of the child. (§§67, 74). "The Power of the Father doth not reach at all to the Property of the Child, which is only in his own disposing" (§170). When the parent no longer leads the child to the attainment of reason, the authority of the parent is lost. So too it is with political power. With regard to legislative power,

> It is not, nor can possibly be absolutely Arbitrary over the Lives and Fortunes of the People . . . cannot assume to itself a power to Rule by extemporary Arbitrary Decrees, but is bound to dispense Justice, and decide the Rights of the Subject by promulgated standing Laws, and known Authoris'd Judges. (§§135, 136)

It does not matter whether it is a father or a government, when force is used without right, or when actions are taken that run contrary to the proper ends, authority is lost and a state of war has begun (§§16, 17, 205, 232, 235). "Allegiance being nothing but an Obedience according to Law, which when he violates, he has no right to Obedience" (§151).[5]

Locke's theory to this point proves straightforward and difficult to dispute: Men, seeking a better life, turn over some of their power to an agreed upon authority in order to produce a better life. When that agreed upon authority does not provide that better life, it ceases to be an authority. At this point Locke seems to have very little to do with federalism or secession. But, when one recognizes that government does not have absolute authority, one sees how a justification for secession is just around the corner. In order to justify secession—or civil disobedience or rebellion— one must properly understand the power of judging.

Locke never forgets that the same individuals who made the state of nature unsafe fill the ranks of government in the new society—and their character has not changed—which is why he leaves the power of judging in the hands of the people, although at times the power may lay dormant. If one recalls, man's inescapable tendency toward self-preservation is partly what made the state of nature unsettled, but this tendency cannot be given up for it would be against nature to do so. At no point can man consent to his own destruction, nor would he ever knowingly consent to something which would injure him (§93). One need not even refer to the text further—although I will—to reach the conclusion that one can never relinquish the power of judging if one only assumes that Locke understands the implications of his statements. That is, if one understands Locke to mean that man has a natural tendency toward self-preservation that he can never willingly and knowingly quit, then one must also understand Locke to mean that man will never turnover his power to judge for doing so would be to give up his power of self-preservation. In order to act in accord with one's self-preservation one must be able to judge which actions run counter to self-preservation and which are in harmony with self-preservation. If one does not have the power, or capacity, to judge, then one will not be able to choose between acts with reference to self-preservation. Instead, one will be left only with the ability to act arbitrarily. Without the capacity to judge, one lacks the capacity to choose. In making a choice between Option A and Option B, the Lockean man would have to judge which option would lead to self-preservation. If we take out self-preservation as a reference point (which we would effectively do if we took away an individual's ability to judge), then there is no relevant distinction between Options A and B. Assume Option A is a bad tasting drink full of nutritious vitamins and Option B is a good tasting drink laced with hemlock. Which one should a person choose? A person with the power to judge relative to self-preservation would choose Option A. A person who has relinquished the power to judge must go with what his or her taste buds preferred or whatever option is offered and would have no grounds for objection. The person who lacks the ability to judge may not even be able to choose based upon taste, for she or he would not be able to judge what tastes good or what tastes bad. And for Locke, a person who has the ability to judge can no more choose not to preserve himself any more than a person with taste buds can refuse to distinguish between what is tasty and what is not.

Locke does not leave us to draw our own conclusions on this matter, however.

> And where the Body of the People, or any single Man, is deprived of their Rights, or is under the Exercise of power without rights, and have not Appeal on Earth, there they have a liberty to appeal to Heaven, whenever they judge the Cause of sufficient moment . . . they have, by a Law antecedent and paramount to all positive Laws of men, reserv'd that ultimate Determination to themselves, which belongs to all Mankind . . . And this Judgment they cannot part with , it being out of a Man's power so to submit himself to another, as to give him a liberty to destroy him; God and Nature never allowing a Man so to abandon himself . . . (§168)

To judge when a government is unfit to rule always remains with the people, a mere majority, may determine when this is the case. And when a government is deemed unfit to rule, the people can choose another one.

Locke gives insight into his position early in the text. In Chapter IV, *Of Slavery*, Locke states that no man can put himself into a station of slavery—which is "the State of War continued" (§24)—nor can any man justly put someone into such a station. Without the power to judge one is incapable of resisting being put into slavery. Furthermore, relinquishing the power to judge is putting oneself into slavery because one will not act for one's self-preservation without the power to judge, so too in a state of slavery one cannot act for one's self-preservation. "This Freedom from Absolute, Arbitrary Power, is so necessary to, and closely joined with a Man's Preservation, that he cannot part with it, but by what forfeits his Preservation and Life together" (§23). This argument can be extended to any argument relating to political power. The political power cannot act arbitrarily, and a person cannot turn over the ability to judge to the political power, for then the political power would be free to act against a person's self-preservation.

The people are always in possession of the power to judge, but they must suspend their execution of the power when under government until such time arises that they can suspend no longer. So long as the government acts in accordance with the proper ends, the power of judging is only needed to the degree to which the people must confirm that government actions are in accord with the proper ends. When the people have judged the government's actions acceptable, the government is free to go about its business of making and enforcing laws. It is only, "after a long train of abuses," that the people may judge the government unfit to rule and dissolve it.

> [T]here can be but one Supream Power, which is the Legislative, to which all the rest are and must be subordinate, yet the Legislative being only a Fiduciary Power to act for certain ends, there remains still in the People a Supream Power to

remove or alter the Legislative, when they find the Legislative act contrary to the trust reposed in them . . . And thus the Community perpetually retains a Supream Power of saving themselves from the attempts and designs of any Body . . . whenever they shall be so foolish, or so wicked, as to lay and carry on designs against the Liberties and Properties of the Subject . . . whenever anyone shall go about to bring them into such a slavish condition, they will always have a right to preserve what they have not a Power to part with; and to rid themselves of those who invade this Fundamental, Sacred, and unalterable Law of Self-Preservation. (§149)

So it is that the people have the right to rebel against unjust rule, and when it is asked who shall be the judge when the question is raised as to whether a government has gone astray, Locke answers, "[t]he People shall be Judge" (§240). When a government has entered into a state of war with the people—which occurs when the government uses force without right—

[E]very Man is Judge for himself, as in all other Cases, so in this, whether another hath put himself into a State of War with him . . . in that State the injured Party must judge for himself, when he will think fit to make use of that Appeal, and put himself upon it. (§§241–2)[6]

The power to judge animates people, and when they are in a state of war, it allows them to rebel against that force that they are at war with. When placed into the context of political power, the people can rebel against a government that has entered into a state of war by using its power in a manner inconsistent with what is in the best interests of the people. Locke's rhetoric can be difficult to decipher on this point because he seems to suggest at certain points that man has no right to rebel against its government and at other points authorize the overthrow of a destructive power. To sort this out one must understand that a government is only a government if it acts in accord with the proper ends of government. A government that acts against the people enters into a state of war with the people, thereby nullifying the compact, which then leaves the people free to choose form a new government (§205). Locke only calls a government that which executes political power, and political power is that power which is aimed at the preservation of life, liberty, and property. Once a government uses power against life, liberty, or property it ceases to use political power and therefore is no longer a government. In that instant it has entered into a state of war with the people, thereby legitimizing a people's rejection of it. "I say using Force upon the People without Authority, and contrary to the Trust put in him, that does so, is a state of War with the People, who have a right to reinstate their Legislative in the Executive of their Power" (§155).[7]

The primary difference between Locke and Hobbes is that Hobbes did not grant people the power to question their government. The most absolute form of protection one can have, particularly within a federal scheme, against a gross usurpation of power, is secession. The unifying feature between Locke and my theory of federalism is that the people remain sovereign. If the people remain sovereign, there is no means by which to deny the legitimacy of secession.[8]

The task remains to settle the matter of whether the right to resist tyranny grants the right to secession. Near the middle of the *Second Treatise* Locke suggests that an individual may leave the protection of government, or a group may leave a government and go to a land that has henceforth been unsettled and start a new government (§121). One may reject this as an argument for secession since secession entails taking land away from one state in order to create another. But this objection does not recognize Locke's definition of political power or government. Using only the references to Locke's work already considered one can see that a person is free to take his or her property when he or she leaves if that property was made unsafe by the government. Man enters into a government to make his property safe. Thus, prior to government the individual owed the protection of his property to himself only. Once he joins government he owes the safety of his property, and therefore the enjoyment of it, to government, which is why he may not take it with him in a fit of rebellion. But, if the government fails to make his property safe he no longer owes the safety of his property to government—which then fails to retain its name as such in Lockean terms—and thus whatever property he has left he owes to himself and may then take it with him wherever he chooses. When a government turns tyrannical— as defined an unjustified use of power against life, liberty, property—it has entered into a state of war with the people it had been charged with protecting. When this occurs, the same rules that applied under the previous state of war/nature are reinstituted (§222). Thus, a group of individuals may reconstitute themselves on their land to form a new legislative since the old legislative no longer has dominion by the virtue of its own abuse (§§212–17). A people need only be obedient to the government in so far as it provides what is good. No obedience or reverence is necessary when the government turns to tyranny. It, like any other entity, is in a state of war when it uses force without right, and the measures that can be taken to guard against it are the same as well. The "union" the people formed may become disbanded at any time the legislative is altered or the government acts against the best interest of the people (§212). People, when they become unsecure, may make a new government for it was out of a similar situation that they created government in the first place.

> In these and the like Cases, when the Government is dissolved, the People are at liberty to provide for themselves, by erecting a new Legislative . . . For the Society can never, by the fault of another, lose the Native and Original Right it has to preserve itself. (§220)

Opponents of secession, particularly constitutionalizing secession, worry that it will lead to an unending series of secessions. Not only does history refute this point, but so too does Locke.

> People are not easily got out of their old Forms . . . This slowness and aversion in the People to quit their old Constitutions, has, in the many Revolutions which have

been seen in this Kingdom . . . still brought us back again to our old Legislative . . . Revolutions happen not upon every little mismanagement in publick affairs . . . But if a long train of Abuses, Pervarications, and Artifices, all tending the same way, make the design visible to the People, and they cannot but feel, what they lie under, and see, whither they are going; 'tis not to be wonder'd, that they should then rouze themselves, and endeavour to put the rule into such hands, which may secure to them the ends for which Government was at first erected . . . (§§223, 225)

Locke goes on to argue that people desire safety and happiness, not a continual overthrow of government (§§226–9). Revolution produces uneasiness and uncertainty, something people generally have an aversion to. In order for there to be a revolution the presiding government would have to create a worse condition than no government at all.

Locke's political theory rests upon consent, either tacit or explicit, and without the option of exit with property there can be no consent. If a nation-state tells an individual, "if you leave you must leave your property, but if you stay we will take your property through unjust property seizures," then there is no choice. The events in Sri Lanka illustrate this point perfectly and are therefore worth considering here. Some Tamils in Sri Lanka were stripped of their citizenship and denied the right to form their own state. The power of the government was continuously used to exploit the minority in favor of the majority, but still the Tamils were unable to form their own state. The Tamils could either live under a regime that took away their rights, their livelihood, and their property, or they could leave behind what remnants of a life they had in the hopes that another country would be more hospitable. Because the Sinhalese majority had no reason to consult the Tamil minority, they could use their power however they wished. We can see from Sri Lanka what happens when secession is constitutionally prohibited. The 1983 amendment to the 1978 constitution that prohibited separatism and established punishments for anyone who advocated separatism was a rearticulation and extension of the discriminatory practices begun in 1948. All civil rights were stripped from those Tamils who sought a separate state and the Tamil members of the parliament who failed to support the amendment were forcibly removed from office. Locke could not support a political arrangement such as this, and to avoid it, he leaves the people sovereign so as to be the final and ultimate check on government. Secession is but one way the people can assert their sovereignty and the minority can check the majority.

Examples of Secession: The Former Soviet Union, Ethiopia, Belgium

The Former Soviet Union

The break up of the former Soviet Union provides an example of how constitutional secession can occur. As odd as it may seem, the Soviet constitution contained a secession provision which required referenda. While the constitutionally mandated secession procedure was not always followed during the dissolution of the union, the constitution served as a general guide on how a state could secede and legitimized the action. The legitimating of secession through its inclusion in the constitution is nearly as important as the procedures outlined for secession. Secessionists were not treated as fringe groups as they are in Quebec or Texas because the process was legitimized through its inclusion in the constitution. Therefore, there was no debate on the legitimacy of secession but rather the focus was on whether the state should secede. By disentangling secession from the policy debate there could be a healthy debate over whether the state should secede.

In 1990, Mikhail Gorbachev faced growing opposition from the Boris Yeltsin led parliament and the union republics. In order to create stability, Gorbachev took the issue to the people in form of a referendum on March 17, 1991, with the All-Union referendum. The results of some of the referenda were in Gorbachev's favor, but in those areas where the referendum was most important, it was either boycotted, altered, or preempted.

Gorbachev's policies ignited separatist sentiment, and a push for independence, particularly in the Baltic States. In a deft political maneuver that would invite both sides to take part in the referendum, in fear that there would be a boycott by one side that would threaten the legitimacy of the results, Estonia, Lithuania, and Latvia each held a referendum before March 17 thus distancing their referenda from Gorbachev's. In each state over 70 percent of the vote was for independence from the Soviet Union. Gorbachev tried to stop other states from following suit by making an example of Lithuania through economic sanctions, but ultimately the sanctions proved to be an ineffective deterrent.

> This was the point of no return. If a Union republic could declare itself independent of the USSR and get away with it, then the future of the whole Union was open to question. The Baltic republics, with their memories of national independence, democracy, and civil society, were pioneers, and in 1988–1990 they played their hand . . . (Hosking 2001: 586)

Similarly, but for different reasons, the Central Asian Republics issued their own referendum separate from Gorbachev. They did so because the Communist party had control of the government and they feared that if the Gorbachev referendum was allowed the Communist party would lose control. Since the referendum seemed inevitable, despite their objections, the Communist party of each republic issued their own, but the plan backfired. Tajikistan and Turkmenistan offered an unaltered Gorbachev referendum, Kazakhstan did not participate, and Kirghizia and Uzbekistan issued altered referenda. Each republic that held a referendum supported independence by over 60 percent, with Uzbekistan approving independence by over 90 percent.

In Russia, Boris Yeltsin had a complicated strategic dilemma on his hands. He could not embrace reform and abandon the nationalists and communists who still had control, nor could he embrace the status quo against his preference for reform.[9] Yeltsin allowed the All-Union referendum but with the added question of whether there should be a popularly elected president. In June 1991, after the March referendum passed—with the added question of whether there should be a directly elected Russian president—Yeltsin was elected president of Russia. On December 8, 1991, Russia, Ukraine, and Belarus announced the formation of the Common-wealth of Independent States that was to replace the Soviet Union with a loose organization of independent nations. By December 21, eight other former Soviet republics would join.

In the Caucasus, Georgia boycotted the Gorbachev referendum and held its own instead. Over 99 percent of those who voted, with over a 90 percent turnout, voted for independence. A similar result occurred in Azerbaijan, which approved independence by more than 99 percent with a turnout of over 95 percent. Armenia rejected the All-Union referendum and opted to follow the April 1990 USSR law of secession, which consisted of several referenda with a two-thirds "yes" vote on the first one. Given that the center of the USSR was already failing, and the sentiment of independence had been certified in other republics, the vote in Armenia con-firmed what had already occurred elsewhere, and appeared to be only a formality. Even still, the decision to secede, through a democratic and nonviolent mechanism, was profound.

The issue in the Ukraine was more complex than in other states due to its diverse ethnic population. The Russian population, concentrated in the Eastern and Central regions, could be expected to vote for union. But the other regions, with Russian populations below 10 percent, could be expected to vote for independence. With the sentiment of break up in the air, there was a concern that various regions would break away if the vote did not go their way. The referendum put to the people contained both the All-Union question and a question for independence at the recommendation of the Communist chairman of the Supreme Soviet, Leonid Kravchuk. "In the Ukraine, we clearly see the ethnic cleavages that underlay the moves toward independence in many of the republics. We also see how cunningly devised compromise referendums such as the one on sovereignty could cut through this cleavage . . ." (Brady and Kaplan 1994: 201). On March 17, Ukraine favored sovereignty, and on December 1, with a second referendum occurring after the August coup, all of the Ukraine—even Crimea, favored independence. The vote for sovereignty in the Ukraine was not much of a surprise given that in July it had already claimed that Ukraine law was superior to Soviet law.

As the process of secession unfolded, it became clear that dissatisfaction with the Soviet Union had as much to do with its poor handling of ethnic relations as it did with its failed economic policies.

By March 1991, when a referendum on the future of the USSR was held, 76 actual or potential ethnoterritorial disputes were identified . . . Ethnicity could clearly not be wished away . . . The evidence now suggested that the policies adopted by successive governments had failed . . . The issue is extremely complex, and while the territorial adjustments had been attempted in the past, in the last years of the Soviet Union ancient resentments and animosities resurfaced in violent clashes . . . (Hill 2003: 199–200)

Part of the ethnic problem in the USSR was the result of central planning. Individuals and groups were subjected to haphazardly drawn boundaries that lacked a respect for culture, history, or heritage. The USSR did resemble a federal system when established in 1922.

> Its structure was based on the allocation of territory to specific national groups, on a hierarchical basis, in which major groups on territory contiguous with an external border were granted the status of union republic . . . significant and relatively compact nationalities within such units were accorded the states of autonomous republics . . . and other nationalities or groups were allocated an autonomous region or autonomous area. (Hill 2003: 208)

Of course, territorial lines could be redrawn and republics abolished if the central authority deemed it necessary. One instance occurred after World War II when the autonomous republic of Moldavian was abolished and the new Moldavian union republic was established, thereby impacting the ethnic distribution in the Ukraine just as when the Crimea was taken from Russia and given as a gift to the Ukraine in 1954. The drawing and redrawing of boundaries, and the relocation of ethnic groups demonstrates "the essential limitations of its [nationalities policy] rational application" (Hill 2003: 209). There are limits to what a central planning committee can do. Federalism must follow natural boundaries, which means, boundaries may shift and change. Belgium would be a better model in this regard than the Soviet Union.

> While the mechanisms of federalism [in the Soviet constitution] permitted a measure of cultural autonomy, the central state authorities used the communist party structures and certain organizational principles to prevent fragmentation, and deployed the state education system, a unified system of military training, and other measures, to encourage integration, harmonization and eventual assimilation. (Hill 2003: 208)

The solution to the problem created by drawing arbitrary borders and implementing policies that did not reflect the various cultural demands was a push for homogenization. The Soviet program was designed for integration so there would be a single Soviet population. The program underestimated the people's attachment to those factors that contributed to their identity.

The Soviet experience does not suggest that all a state needs is a referendum to secede, for as the Russian and Ukrainian examples show, the situation must be handled in such a way that takes into account the complexity of the situation. The referendum must have legitimacy among the elites and the population.[10] The elites must respect the results so as not to engender conflict between the elites and voting population in case there are results unpopular among the elites. And the voting population must see the process as legitimate, for a boycott of a referendum could render the results questionable, particularly among those who boycott.

The dissolution of the Soviet Union did not immediately solve the violence between ethnic groups, but it did begin a process in which solutions could be pursued that did not include opposing violence with violence. That is, the new political landscape would allow for bargaining and negotiation rather than the quelling of ethnic conflict through military means.

In the span of 32 months 15 former states of the Soviet Union declared themselves sovereign states. The referendum was a powerful tool in legitimizing and bringing about secession (Kahn 2002: 102–3). Each situation was different, and the amount of opposition and success after secession varied, but the process of referendum allowed states to secede with less violence and opposition than there would have been otherwise.

The lessons learned from the Soviet break up have a direct bearing on how tensions might be diminished in the Israeli-Palestinian conflict and how Iraq can be reconstituted to take into account disparate ethnic factions. The Soviet experience does not offer a direct parallel, and situations in each country and conflict are different, yet even still, relevant lessons can be learned. The central problem with Soviet federalism and post-Soviet transformation was the diverse ethnic groups and the geographical distribution of those groups. Similar, but not identical, problems exist in Israel/Palestine and Iraq. This is important to keep in mind as we will address these two nations in the final chapter.

Ethiopia

Ethiopia provides an interesting case study in centralized-decentralization. This means that decentralization, and a derivation of federalism, was implemented from the top-down in Ethiopia. The method of decentralization used by Ethiopia disrupted natural ordering. In a critique of modern nation-state building that is applicable to Ethiopia, Conyers writes:

> Spontaneous society, or natural society, is made up of myriad interlocking and overlapping groups. The groups are constituted of families, friendships, voluntary associations . . . Each of these social aggregates performs the function of passing on obligations, intervening in disputes, distributing knowledge, enforcing rules, and providing a culture for the mutual expression of love and loyalty . . . A society that develops along lines of a strong central authority, however, finds itself in partial competition with these smaller and more local authorities. (Conyers 2008: 61)

While Ethiopia was trying to move away from a strong central authority in 1991 it did so through centralized mechanisms.[11] This has compounded some of the ethnic problems in Ethiopia. But with its adoption of Article 39, which legitimizes secession, Ethiopia has shown the ability to adapt to its problems and the humility necessary to learn from its mistakes. Because of this, I hold out hope for Ethiopia.

Decentralization began in late 1991 and early 1992 after the revolution against communist-military rule.[12] The intention was to create 12 regions based on ethnic identities and two urban regions that were too diverse to be subdivided along ethnic lines.[13] The regions were further subdivided into zones and districts, but this subdivision created difficulty particularly in those districts bordering other regions where the ethnic division could not be clearly made. The constitution had provisions to address border disputes, but they were insufficient, and in part created by the constitution's method of division. As suggested by Harold G. Marcus, "[c]ultural and political autonomy must be respected as a matter of right. Otherwise, the state will split apart as the minorities compete for power" (Marcus 1994: 219). The Ethiopian constitution admits this much, but it pursued recognition in a counterproductive way.

In Ethiopia ethnic groups have been traditionally distinguished by language. Therefore, geopolitical borders were drawn based upon the distribution of languages with no regard for identity.

> The delineation of geopolitical units was, to a large extent, based on the per-ceptions of language and ethnicity that the centre had developed over several centuries, as opposed to accurate reflections of the distribution of local languages and the realities of ethnic identity. (Cohen 2006: 172)

What the central government failed to recognize was that most people had already adopted Amharic, with the Eritreans being an exception, and did not desire for their local language to be their defining characteristic. The central government failed to take into account what mattered to people. Contrast this with the development of federalism in the West as seen by Will Kymlicka and one begins to see the potential problem Ethiopia created for itself.

> Multination federalism in the West emerged as a response to specific, actually existing cases of minority nationalist mobilization . . . The institutionalization of ethno-national identities is not, in and of itself, either good or bad. What matters is that this process of institutionalization is done in a peaceful and democratic way, consistent with human rights and liberal freedoms . . . The evolution of federal and quasi-federal autonomies [in the West] has been in response to peaceful democratic mobilization, creating new political arrangements that better reflect the actual identities and aspirations of citizens. (Kymlicka 2006: 56 and 58)

By not understanding what mattered to the people, or consulting the people to find out what mattered to them and how they identified themselves, the Ethiopian government ignored lessons from successful federal states in the West.

Ethiopia's error has caused some to be concerned with ethnically derived borders in federal states in general.

> The assumption that ethnic formulations of federalism provide a cure for the problems created by the existence of ethnicity is nevertheless flawed ... By forcing individuals [Ethiopians] to examine their own ethnicity more closely and to align themselves more explicitly within formulations of ethnicity established by the federal system, the policy of ethnic representation may encourage ethnic conflict ... Language issues have become increasingly politicized [in Ethiopia]. (Cohen 2006: 169–70, 171)

Cohen's point is accurate, but not for the target at which he aims. Federalism did not fail to resolve ethnic conflict, nor exacerbate the problem, centrally managed federalism did. There was not a push for ethnically divided states among the competing ethnic groups; the government implemented the method poorly.

For instance, the Ethiopian government consulted language maps published over a decade before to draw the divisions. Not only did the central government not recognize that language was not the defining characteristic of its people, it utilized a poor resource to do draw maps of language distribution. The Soviet Union made a similar mistake beginning in 1922 that contributed to the upheaval after the break up in 1991. Shockingly, the method of categorization after 1991 was the same method that had been adopted by the Derg, which was what the new Ethiopian government was trying to replace. It seems central governments cannot help but oversimplify local differences and identities.

Take the relations between the Oromo and the Gurage as an illustration of the problem. Prior to the language laws there were no real, lasting political conflicts between the Oromo and Gurage. The two groups live in villages scattered and mixed among the countryside and therefore one cannot draw a line around either group. But, the central government tried to draw a geopolitical border around each group based on language, which neither group thought of as a defining characteristic. As a result, there are now border disputes between the Oromo and Gurage. The dispute is grounded in language, as each group now thinks of its language in political terms. Language in Ethiopia has become politicized, but not because of the people.

> The increase importance of language and ethnicity, therefore, encourages trivial local conflicts, the consequences of which have no profound result for the bulk of the people living in the affected areas ... Rather, the inclusion of geopolitical units within particular areas gained political significance for local elites and could be used to create a political constituency. (Cohen 2006: 174)

This process has played out violently in Yugoslavia as well.

> Yugoslavia did not collapse because it was a multiethnic society of mutually antagonistic groups or because it was organized in a federal way, but because it was not a genuinely democratic federal state. The power elite of socialist Yugoslavia used decentralization as a means of avoiding democratization and liberalization . . . By giving more power to the party elites of individual republics instead of to its citizens, the Communist Party preserved its monopoly within the political system. (Malesevic 2006: 149)

We must worry about whether this will be replicated in Ethiopia. The potential for replication is there if the government and the people do not recognize the artificial nature of the language conflict produced by the nature in which federalism was instituted.

If a country wants to draw ethnically defined geopolitical borders it must be at the behest of those groups. A language program may be appropriate for some countries, such as Belgium or Canada, but it was not appropriate for Ethiopia. The government must know its people; the centralized Ethiopian government did not.

But even where language and ethnic boundaries are real, and the people are allowed to define for themselves what they are, we should still show some restraint in encouraging ethnically drawn boundaries because of what has been observed in Ethiopia.

> [E]thnic federalism in Ethiopia has served to essentialize ethnic identities, to privilege and reinforce these identities over other non-ethnic identities, to sharpen feelings of difference between groups, and thereby to increase tension about cultural and geographical boundaries between groups. Ethnic identities that used to be weak, contextual and overlapping are being restructured as primary and sharply bounded. (Kymlicka 2006: 57)

Federalism need not focus on ethnic groups as the basis for division, and if it does it need not necessarily lead to conflict—particularly if it is done through non-centralized means—but to put the focus on ethnic identities entirely is to put a focus on the differences between people rather than shared identities. Therefore, in trying to achieve a politics of recognition, the Ethiopian government forced an identity crisis in which recognition was granted in a manner consistent with the government's vision rather than the true identification of the people. Because of the government's actions, the people were required to identify themselves on language and ethnic grounds in order to gain recognition under the new government.

There were language problems even before 1991 however, but for the most part it was relegated to Eritrea. Though there were problems other than language that defined the relationship between Eritrea and Ethiopia, the language problem became a central concern. "The Eritrean intelligentsia regarded imposition of Amharic as a sinister impediment to building a successful career. Besides English, Eritreans now had to learn another foreign language to succeed in government schools and to gain access to the university in Addis Abeba" (Marcus 1994: 175). The relationship between Eritrea and Ethiopia appears to have always been quarrelsome, a fact exacerbated by involvement from the West. Seeking an accessible route for imperialistic ambition into the contested Ethiopia, Italy entered into a lease with Ethiopia giving it access to the Port of Aseb in Eritrea. Italy hoped that an open trade route would allow it greater access to inner Ethiopia. The lease agreement failed to give Italy its desired penetration, but it did provide Ethiopia a foothold in Eritrea. A protracted war over the matter ensued between Italy and Ethiopia. It was only at the end of World War II that the Italo-Ethiopian War was brought to a conclusive end. At the end of World War II, Ethiopia reached a deal with the United States that would give it control of Eritrea which had been under British military administration after the defeat of Mussolini's Italy. The advantage for the United States was that they would receive an important military ally and a strategic communications position. Factions in Eritrea wanted full integration with Ethiopia, but Muslin and Christian factions proved resistant. The United States decided, with the backing of the United Nations, that Eritrean history was different enough to disallow full integration into Ethiopia but Eritrea lacked the capacity to become a self-sustaining state. In 1952, Eritrea joined Ethiopia as a federated state through United Nations mandate. The solution was a federal one. The mistake was that an outside force unfamiliar with the intricacies of the region implemented the agreement.

The solution perpetuated by the West led to nearly unending civil strife that was exacerbated by unequal economic conditions and a language policy that required Eritreans to adopt the Ahramic language if they were to have any hope of securing a high-level government position. The centralizing tendency of Haile Selassie's regime was able to undermine the autonomy of Eritrea.

> Courts, schools, and social services had slowly become organs of the imperial regime; the freedoms enunciated in the Eritrean constitution had been eroded; political parties had been stifled and leading personalities sent into exile . . . in 1960, the designation of the Eritrean government had been changed to the Eritrean administration. (Marcus 1994: 172)

The developments should have only been a shock to people unfamiliar with the region's history and the nature of imperial regimes. The United States and the UN did not recognize the need for federation to develop organically in that the varied nature of past grievances and cultural complexity were not something which could be understood and adequately incorporated into a third-party imposed treaty. In addition, the constitution lacked federalism preserving mechanisms. The Eritrean government had no constitutional capacity to object to Haile Selassie or Ethiopian encroachment. It was only through rebellion and violence that the Eritreans could resist Haile Selassie's policies.

In 1974 Haile Selassie was forced out of power and the military regime that took over saw no reason to address the Eritrean problem through means other than military repression. It was in 1991 that the Ethiopian People's Revolutionary Democratic Front (EPRDF) took control of the country and rewrote the constitution and began devolving power from the central government. It was during this time of transition that Eritrea was given the ability, through Ethiopia's new constitution, to secede. The power to secede was a recognition of the fact that Eritreans needed the power of self-determination and that centralized efforts would never be able to create peace unless Eritreans were allowed self-determination.

Secession seems to be a natural extension of Ethiopia's new commitment to self-determination as outlined in its constitution. Self-determination is also a foundational principle of federalism,

> [s]elf-determination is the most important constitutional, legislative and policy instrument upon which Ethiopia has drawn to affect the positive development of federalism. The constitution includes the right to develop one's languages, promote one's culture and preserve one's history, and it gives the state the opportunity of leaving ... (Patz 2005: 141)

Had the right to secession been granted under the reign of Haile Selassie, his efforts to bring Eritrea under central control could have been thwarted through constitutional, rather than violent, means.

Article 39 in Ethiopia's 1994 constitution provides the secession provision. The procedure for secession requires a two-thirds majority vote by the council of the respective state and a majority vote in a referendum administered in that state by the national government. Even those who cannot be considered supporters of secession, but still open to the possibility, see Article 39 of the 1994 as a positive aspect of the Ethiopian constitution that has allowed it to produce peace among conflicting minority interests (Norman 2006: 176). The provisions of Article 39, which go beyond secession, were encouraged by nervous minorities as a condition of the acceptance of the document. (Griffiths and Nerenberg 2005; Norman 2006).

One of these nervous groups was the people of Eritrea, and under the new constitution the people acted. Eritrea was declared independent in April 27, 1993, after its citizens, through referendum, overwhelmingly approved of secession from Ethiopia.

> [E]ritrea declared independence from Ethiopia in April 1993, a year before the official ratification of the current constitution, after a UN-supervised vote with 99.81 per cent of Eritrean voters opting for secession. Nevertheless, it was through the process of Article 39(4) "that Eritrea gained *de jure* independence in May 1993." (Patz 2005: 193)

To date, Eritrea is the only part of Ethiopia that has successfully seceded. In fact, it is the only part of Ethiopia that has seriously tried to despite the legitimization of secession in Ethiopia through its constitutional inclusion of the practice.

Critics of secession may find it odd that during this time of transition and turmoil, Eritrea was the only region to secede, since it is the critics who oppose secession on the grounds that it will produce a domino effect. But history has not gone the way they expected. Federalism, with a built in mechanism for secession, has been one reason why Ethiopia has been able to transform itself from a militarily governed communist-leaning nation, to a nation which shows promise of a successful transition to a peaceable democracy. The work here is not done, but it is showing promise.

Federalism was a reaction to the centralized military rule and the exclusion of ethnic pluralism. After the fall of the Derg in 1991, federalism was seen as the best way of addressing the competing ethnic nationalities. The development of a federal state in Ethiopia—and the Ethiopia-Eritrean compact following World War II for that matter—exposes the difficulties of artificially imposing federalism and the need for the subnational levels of government to be equipped with the means to assert their authority and protect themselves against encroachment on their authority from the central state or other subnational levels.

The Ethiopian constitution reads as if someone attempted simply to deduce the appropriate structure of the federal state from a set of first principles, in conjunction with a census of ethno-linguistic groups. One result of this is that federal autonomy has been accorded to ethnic groups that had not in fact mobilized politically for it, and indeed may not have identified themselves as "nations" at all. (Kymlicka 2006: 55–6)

Ethiopia's constitution and experience shows that simply stating where the division between levels and actors is to be drawn, that unless each level is endowed with the powers to protect itself, there can arise disputes over the realm of authority each level has since a constitution can be interpreted differently by different groups. "However carefully the division of powers between two levels of government in a federation are delineated, disputes over the jurisdiction of power are bound to occur" (Fiseha 2006: 134). Ethiopia's federalism is flawed, but in Ethiopia we have at least one instance in which an instrument of federalism has been employed for the betterment of the nation. The employment of secession has strengthened Ethiopia. It will be difficult at first to accept how secession can strengthen a country, but one can more easily embrace the conclusion once one comes to grips with the reality that union does not always mean success.

Belgium

Belgium serves as a counter-example to the Soviet Union and Ethiopia. In many ways it is a country that has done things the right way. This does not mean it is without its faults, but as a country with a culturally diverse population it has done well to keep hostilities and tensions at an acceptable level. Even before Belgium became a federal state it did not have the violent conflict that exists in other culturally diverse nations. Part of Belgium's success goes beyond federalism and extends to the character of the people. Its size has also played an important role. But, Belgium is not an exceptional case and should therefore not have its success attributed entirely to factors that cannot be replicated by other nations. Not all nations who adopt a federal structure will have Belgium's success, but Belgium serves as one model nations can look toward in their development of a federal regime. Belgium serves a second purpose: It demonstrates that secession need not be utilized in order to relieve ethnic tension. Secession is not the only solution, and I would not want the reader to come away with that idea after reading my account of the Soviet break up and Ethiopia. Belgium is particularly pertinent in this function as it was a state born of secession.

Belgium was created in 1830. Its creation was the result of its secession from a short union with the Netherlands. The initial conflict in Belgium was language based. In a mid-nineteenth-century census, 57 percent of Belgians reported Dutch as the language they spoke most frequently with French coming in second (42 percent) and German third (less than 1 percent). Most of those who lived in Flanders spoke Dutch and less than one-quarter of those in Brussels spoke Dutch. French speakers held a majority in Wallonia with about 70 percent of the residents of Brussels speaking French. This trend held constant for the next century as well. Since the early 1960s, though, the linguistic conflicts have become much less divisive because Belgium took an active role in limiting the regional language boundaries by shifting some communes and its residents from Wallonia to Flanders and others from Flanders to Wallonia. This did not solve the Brussels problem, but by relieving tensions in other regions, tensions were lessened in the capital city. The improved language policy, and diminished tensions, coincides with that nation's shift toward federalism. Before federalism, the drawing of language boundaries and other policies taken to relieve ethnic tension were centralized and often led to an increase in tension and conflict.

Flemish nationalism began as a language grievance when in the nineteenth-century French became the national language. To show the Flemish they were not trying to take away its language, the government made Flanders an official bilingual community. This set up an asymmetrical bilingualism in which Flanders had to be bilingual and Wallonia and Brussels would remain all French. Thus, all one had to know is French, even in Flanders. This mistake was corrected though, in 1898, when Dutch was adopted as the second official language of Belgium. This revision shows an important aspect of Belgium politics that must be present for federalism to be adopted successfully: the willingness to admit mistakes and work to correct them.

But linguistic disputes did not end in the nineteenth century. In the 1930s Flanders and Wallonia became unilingual territories while Brussels became bilingual along with other disputed territories. But there was a socioeconomic component that the laws missed and consequently sparked concern among the Flemish. Because French was the predominant language among the upper class, there was fear that French would be perceived as the more attractive option and Dutch would be lost. What is peculiar about this worry, and comparable to the Sinhala in Sri Lanka, is that Dutch speakers held the numerical majority, and had since the mid-nineteenth century. But their concerns were justified as by 1960—with new territorial lines being drawn with each census based on what language the citizens of a particular territory predominantly spoke—the Flemish territory was consistently lost to Wallonia, particularly in areas around Brussels. These losses increased the sentiment of Flemish nationalism. In fact, Flemish local governments boycotted the 1960–1961 census which forced another round of language reforms. But these reforms, which have occurred as recently as 2001, have merely tried to refine the nineteenth-century strategy of classifying regions by language. The lesson seems to be that central planning can only prove a temporary fix to language-based ethnic conflict, and in some instances, central planning may even exacerbate the problem.

Language is not the only ethnic cleavage and the Flemish were not the only ones to view themselves as victims. Economics has played an important role in dividing Wallonia and Flanders, particularly after World War II when industries left Wallonia not to be replaced. But, the economic cleavages have an undeniable language dimension. Combined with the fact that they only held a minority of seats in the parliament, Wallonia felt it had a lot to fear from Flanders due to its unequal political and economic standing. With these factors in play it makes sense that the first push for devolution in Belgium came from Wallonia. While not much changed until the 1980s there was some financial and industrial decentralization that increased the sense that a push for federalism could be successful.

Like most successful reforms, the move toward federalism was gradual and required multiple waves. The first was the official recognition of the conflict and the inability of the unitary state to solve the problem in 1970.

> As a result of growing dissimilarities within the country and the waning of the national elite, a long process of constitutional reform began, to overcome the conflicts between Flemings and French-speakers . . . The resulting federalism is original. Other federal states were independent countries and became united in an increasing centralization process. Belgian federalism transformed a classic centralized state into a federal one. (Dubois 2008: 36)

Belgium's unique road to federalism reflects its historical willingness to try new things, admit error, and pursue solutions that do not necessarily maintain the current power configuration.

The second wave of reform in 1980 moved Belgium to regionalization, which created regions with more power than the central government on some issues and thus resulted in less cooperation between regions than existed before the reforms. The third wave of reform in 1989 recognized this problem and tried to strike a balance by moving toward a federal structure in which there were shared and concurrent powers. Finally, in 1993, Belgium became a federal state. In Belgium, federalism

> has enabled regions to tailor policies to their specific needs, allowing clear policy divergences to emerge in policies such as education and the environment . . . federalism has been more cost constraining when compared with some conflict-solving mechanisms that were used when all decisions were still centralised . . . [T]he transformation of Belgium into a federal state has not increased popular support for independence. Identity surveys demonstrate that Flemish and Walloon citizens often display complementary or dual identities. (Swenden and Jans 2009: 26–7)

One unique feature of the Belgium state is its willingness to adopt unconventional means of division and organization. Belgium is divided into three communities (Flemish, French, German) and three regions (Flanders, Wallonia, Brussels). The communities developed in 1970—with the German community following later in 1983—as a way of dealing with ethnic conflict and regionally based economic disparities that had an ethnic dimension. The institutions of the community have control over language, culture, and education. The communities, unlike the regions, are not territorially based. Article 4 of the constitution spells out the membership of a community with some reference to language regions.

The territorially based regions were a direct response to the Walloon concerns over the economic disparity that was developing. Flanders and Wallonia established institutions in 1980 with Brussels doing so in 1983. Regions focus primarily on economic matters, which do have some connection to ethnicity and culture given that in Wallonia, predominantly francophones felt as though they were losing economic power, and consequently since they were already the political minority, would become even more threatened politically. The inclusion of both territorially and culturally based divisions provides a unique way of addressing concerns from both sides. Too often the focus of federalism scholars is on how the territory should be divided up. Belgium shows that territory need not be such an encompassing problem. Perhaps if Ethiopia had looked to Belgium it might have avoided creating a conflict between the Oromo and Gurage when it tried to artificially construct territorial divisions.

In addition to the creation of regions and communities, the new reforms blend autonomy and cooperation through incentives. The resolution of the Flemish-Francophone conflict takes place at the national level so that they are forced to resolve their problems rather than merely ignore each other, and thus increase nationalist sentiment, as had occurred under regionalization. There are four primary areas of reform that aid in conflict resolution. First, the federal cabinet must be composed of an equal number of Flemish- and French-speaking members. This is important as it allows equal representation, but also because it does not ignore ethnic differences and allows one to identify with the group of one's choosing rather than forcing a citizen to assume a national identity. The second area is a reformed senate in which there is a mixture of direct election and appointment that reflects the ethnic composition of the country. Third, an improved bureaucracy that forces the national and subnational levels to work together. Fourth, the Court of Arbitration was established to hear cases dealing with the proper division of powers between levels of government and the constitutionality of national and subnational laws and decrees.

This fourth feature deserves a special note of hesitation. Belgium has always had an aversion to a powerful judiciary. But with devolution they have instituted a court to settle matters over jurisdiction. This is problematic in that part of the success of Belgium's system can be attributed to its lack of a litigious, or rights-oriented, society. While it is not accurate to say that Belgians did not care about rights before, it was that there was no sense that one had to press one's rights through a judicial structure. The concern is over whether Belgium will abandon the principles of compromise and reciprocity in lieu of a judicial arbiter.

What Belgium has been able to do better than Ethiopia, if not many other nations, is provide recognition to diverse groups in a way consistent with their naturally constructed identity. If we look at the components of identity and assume we can address each one individually we miss the interaction between the various components that go into creating identity and then do not adequately recognize a particular group. Such is what occurred in Ethiopia. With language comes a way of life that native speakers affiliate with that language. That language and way of life form a sense of community that is not entirely captured by language alone. Thus it would have been an error to consider Dutch speakers as autonomous individuals when they are Flemish.

> Identity is one of modernity's most contested concepts, not only on its own terms, but because it implicates our theories of the self. In fact, one definition of modernity is that it begins with Descartes' declaration that the isolated self is the starting point of knowledge. (Feeley and Rubin 2008: 7–8)

Modernity conceived thusly is in direct confrontation with my conception of federalism on the grounds that federalism incorporates the community into the political process, and not just the individual.

The modern emphasis on identity is quite separate from the federal emphasis on identity in that federalism takes identity—as grounded in tradition, education, family, religion, nationality, language, mores, and customs—to be a communal concept whereas modern identity becomes individualistic with its focus on individual rights or redistribution.[14] Identity does not have to become individualistic as one can recognize that his or her identity is intertwined with that of others. But, the modern state forces an emphasis on the individual and undermines a sense of community through its emphasis on rights, redistribution, and retribution, so that identity becomes individualistic and thus atomizing. As a result, a greater emphasis is placed upon the state for the individual comes to equate the benefits of identity as that which the state provides. Community and human relationships then become less important. The only manner through which this can be avoided is if the people are allowed to construct their own identities and the state respects this construction. Belgium has done so, and hopefully, Ethiopia is learning to do so.

When looking at Belgium one might become shocked that such a diverse nation in such a small geographical area would be able to avoid the type of violent conflict that has dominated the landscape in similar countries. Part of Belgium's success can be attributed to its ability to escape the centralizing tendency of modern nation-states and embrace a move toward federalism, or decentralization, as a way of dealing with ethnic conflict. Through its policies, Belgium has been able to keep nationalist sentiment among its competing ethnic groups at bay. Critics of federalism, and particularly those who oppose secession, must be surprised that Belgium has been able to remain unified despite a history of secession. Belgium, born of secession when in 1830 it left the Dutch kingdom because it opposed the linguistic and religious policies of King William I of Orange, has not known secession since. Belgium is still facing linguistic and cultural challenges, but instead of secession it has been able to remain unified through federal remedies to ethno-cultural conflict.

Secession: The Procedure

As will now be familiar to the readers who have read the previous two chapters, I will outline the procedures for secession within the structure of the U.S. federal system. Because the justification and evidence in support of the procedures I employ has been provided in the previous two chapters, in order to avoid redundancy, I will discuss only the procedures and leave the justification of those procedures to what has already been said.

When a group, region, or community remains the victim of unjust treatment despite having used all available legitimate methods to correct the treatment, the only option that remains available to that group may be secession. Secession serves as a substitute for violent rebellion or revolution. If the right to secession is constitutionalized there is no need for bloodshed. In addition to the other arguments I have made against those who attempt to discredit the constitutionalization of secession there remains one more reason.

> There is also a specifically theoretical quality to the debate on how constitutionalism can accommodate the politics of recognition, as symbolic recognition of the distinct identity of ethnic groups may be more important than the specifics of power sharing for an enduring resolution of the conflict. (Tirucelvam 2008: 198)

A group's identity is muted if it remains an unrecognized minority within a nation-state and therefore there will be a need to create a new state so that the minority can gain a sense of identity that is unique to nationhood. While power sharing may allow for political recognition in representative systems, the security and representation of that minority group will remain tenuous and unsecure. If the perception among the minority group is such, then they might be more likely to have nationalist feelings which can only be satiated through secession. As seen in Sri Lanka, nationalist feelings that are not given a release valve, particularly when the minority group is suppressed, will give way to violent acts. It is better to have secession than a civil war.

However, I will say little more about what conditions make for justifiable grounds for secession as circumstances are too varied to itemize such grounds. It need only be said that a people should be able to decide for itself when it is in a condition that is unlivable. As Locke wrote, people will be hesitant to revolt as preference is always for what is known unless the known is far worse than the unknown. When seceding from one country there is no guarantee that the newly created country will be any better than the previous. The risk in creating a new nation is high, which means the threat in the current state will have to be real, immediate and enduring if people will choose to create a new nation. Of course reactionary decisions are possible, which is one reason why the system I outline includes mechanisms for delay and deliberation. Like the two previous procedural outlines this is little more than a skeleton draft in which many particulars are glossed over. The point is to show that it can be done and what general procedures will be necessary to have in place if it is to be done responsibly and consistent with the principles I have set out as being desirable.

Step One: Town Hall Meetings

Because secession is so definitive it is necessary to have a step prior to a referendum on secession. The first step will be to hold meetings on the question of secession to itemize the list of grievances and to discuss what has already been done to address these concerns, why those measures proved insufficient, and what else can be done short of secession to address the concerns of the oppressed. The meeting will be called either by the people or a representative in the state legislature. The people, through petition, will call for a meeting. Or, a representative in a state legislature will make a motion for a meeting. If the move for a meeting on secession is denied, or in any way prevented by the opposition, a referendum will be triggered automatically. This will limit fraud and tampering. At the meeting will be those citizens who are interested and those representatives who are interested. There is no need for a quorum as this is simply an exploratory meeting. Should the concerns be inadequately addressed by the recommendations of the state legislators in attendance, there will be a call for a referendum. The decision must be made unanimously against referendum for a referendum to be blocked. Unanimity is required for two reasons: first, to protect minority rights, as those who are in attendance may not be an accurate representation of the people's true wishes for whatever reason, for example, lack of publicity for the meeting; second, opponents of those who called for the meeting may use illegitimate means to keep supporters of the meeting from attending. Intimidation, physical violence, or social ostracism could be used to keep some people who would like to attend from attending.

Step Two: Referendum

The referendum will be statewide with results made available at the district level. If a majority of the people votes for secession the measure will be sent to the state legislature with the clear signal that the people would like to leave the union. There is the possibility that a state is the perpetrator of the injustice which means local entities below a state should be granted the right to secede as well.[15] For instance, if a minority group resides in one particular urban center where it holds majority status, but in the rest of the state it is a minority, and the rest of that state is able to use the system to perpetrate injustices against the minority group, that urban center should be able to secede from the rest of the state. This is difficult to conceptualize geographically in that a map of Michigan with Detroit being its own state runs against what we are accustomed to. However, this would look no more peculiar than a map of South Africa in which Lesotho is completely surrounded by South Africa and Swaziland is a peninsula in which all but a small sliver is surrounded by South Africa. Of course, Lesotho has found it difficult to exist in this capacity but that is a risk the seceding locality will have to consider. The risk of being worse off is real for the seceding entity. But such a risk serves as a natural deterrent against a hasty secession.

For the purpose of clarity and simplicity it will be assumed from here on that it is only the state that is pressing for secession from the nation. Therefore, if the state legislature receives word from the citizens through referendum that they would like to secede, the legislature must hold an open vote within five calendar days with no parliamentary delay procedures allowed. Should the legislature fail to hold a vote the legislature will immediately be dissolved so as to force a reelection for every legislative seat. The election will be held one week after the dissolution. When the new legislature convenes it must vote on the referendum within five calendar days. Parliamentary dissolution is foreign to the American system but it is a common practice in other democracies.

If a referendum is held and fails to support a referendum the state legislature may still choose to vote on the measure. If the state legislature votes to secede, when the people did not, step three becomes even more important.

Step Three: Legislative Vote and Certification

Once the legislature votes, the citizens of the state, and the rest of the nation, will be made aware of the results and how each legislator voted. The vote is made public so that the elected officials can be held accountable by the voters in the next election.

When the legislature has voted it will become necessary for the citizenry to certify the vote as a way of making sure that the decision has not been reactionary or capricious. If the initial referendum was for secession, and the state legislature voted for secession, then the certification vote need only garner a majority for secession to be granted. If the public fails to certify the legislature's move then the legislature can override the voice of the people with a three-fourths vote in favor of secession.[16] If the initial referendum was for secession and the state legislature opposed secession, the citizenry may still vote for secession which would then force the legislature to hold another public vote, thus triggering a repeat of steps two and three indefinitely until the people certify the action of the legislature. If the referendum came out against secession and the legislature voted for secession, the certification of the legislature's vote by the people could come out either for or against the decision of the legislature. If it comes out against the legislature—which would be against secession—the legislature would be given the opportunity to override the people's objection. If the legislature fails to do so then secession fails.

If the legislature votes for secession, and that is what the referendum recommended, and the people certify the vote in favor of secession, the government will immediately call for a constitutional convention and begin creating a new nation. The new nation will be in charge of determining how this will be done, but the people still have the choice between exit, voice, and loyalty in their new country.

I have crafted the ideal scenario in which there is no ongoing war and the prevailing institutions and politicians will respect the constitutionalized procedures. The argument would be that in such an environment there probably would not be a need for secession. This is probably true in some circumstances, but I have only tried to give a general idea of what a secession procedure would look like. The conditions under which the decision to secede is made can be less civil, but constitutional secession can work as demonstrated in the examples of the Soviet Union and Ethiopia. The procedure I outline here, and in the previous two chapters, is a way of getting the reader to consider the possibilities in order to begin thinking about how NVS can work, and why they should be made legitimate options within federal regimes.

Conclusion

It is possible that there are problems that nullification and veto cannot solve. The problems that are left unresolved may in fact be irresolvable under the current governing regime. If that is the case, then secession needs to be preserved as an option in order to prevent the continuation of violent conflict, infringements on basic human rights, or some other grave injustice. This chapter has discussed the moral foundations of secession, why secession is not the nuclear option some have declared, and why secession will not promote instability within the existing world order. And to the last point, the transition of states, from one to another, without violence is more natural and consistent with human nature than the existing worldview.

Although I defend secession as an option, I do not think secession should be encouraged beyond the point at which it is necessary. Secession should not be taken lightly. Instead, I have tried to lay a theoretical foundation and defense for secession so that nations may consider it as a legitimate feature of their constitutional structure. In practical terms I have sought to move the debate from whether secession is a legitimate option, to one in which nations feel free to consider the option as but one of many.

Notes

1. Bakke and Wibbels (2006) and Hale (2004) make no mention of how a federal system can be constructed in order to avoid ethnic conflict or minority repression, rather they are content with their findings that ethno-federal systems may lead to increased ethnic conflict under certain circumstances. The previous two chapters, along with this one, will show how federal states can minimize these negative consequences.
2. See the previous discussion of Locke's rejection of sovereign immunity.
3. For my position on this matter, see Chapter 2 in my *The Price of Politics* (2009).
4. See §§123, 124, 131, 134, 135, 136, 149, 151, 155, 164, 166, 168, 205, 210, 229, 235, 240, 243 to name just a few.
5. See also §54 and §57. "[T]hat equal Right that every Man hath, to his Natural Freedom, without being subjected to the Will or Authority of any other Man . . . the end of Law is not to abolish or restrain, but to preserve and enlarge freedom: For in all the states of created being capable of Las, where theis is no Law, ther is no Freedom . . . But Freedom is not, as we are told, A liberty for every Man to do what he lists . . . But a Liberty to dispose, and order, as he lists, his Person, Actions, Possessions, and his whole Property, within the Allowance of those Laws under which he is; and therein not to be subject to the arbitrary Will of another, but freely follow his own."
6. "Whenever the Legislators endeavour to take away, and destroy the Property of the People, or to reduce them to Slavery under Arbitrary Power, they put themselves into a state of War with the People, who are thereupon absolved from any farther Obedience . . . By this breach of Trust they forfeit the Power, the People had put into their hands, for quite contrary ends, and it devolves to the People, who have a Right to resume their original liberty, and by the Establishment of a new Legislative such as they shall think fit" (§222).
7. "This is a power, which neither Nature gives, for it has made no such distinction between one Man and another; nor Compact can convey, for Man not having such an Arbitrary Power over his own Life, cannot give another Man such a Power over it; but it is the effect only of Forfeiture, which the Aggressor makes of his own Life, when he puts himself into the state of War with another" (§172). See also §§ 7–9, 222, 242.
8. There is a similarity between Althusius and Locke that when articulated will clarify a Lockean theory of secession. For both Althusius and Locke a theory of government builds from the original power of the family. In both Althusius and Locke the father (parent) gives up some of his or her parental authority to the state, but ultimately retains the ability to decide what is best for his or her family. The power reserved to the parent is not determined by the state but by the parent, as the parent retains the identity of such,

and the sovereignty inherent in such an identity, even in a state. That is, a parent does not cease being a parent when the family becomes part of a larger community. Inherent in this formulation is the ability for the parent to judge what is best for the family. So long as the government makes decisions consistent with the view of the parent about what is good for the family, the parent allows the government to make decisions that affect the family. For Locke and Althusius the family serves as one step on the path to creating a political society.

Like Althusius, there is an association that is not familial nor political which Locke calls civil society. Civil society exists when people come together to escape the state of nature, but it ultimately leads to the formation of a political society as the political society can create and enforce positive law. For Althusius there is greater attention given to civil society, for in Locke civil society more quickly gives way to political society. For Locke, rebellion and secession is a return to civil society, not the state of nature. When people break their political bonds they do not break the bonds they created which legitimate the creation of government. In Locke, people in the state of nature/war come together and through consent unanimously decided that they have the power to create a government. When they give themselves the power to govern they then decide on what type of government they will have. Thus, secession only overturns the type of government agreed upon, not the agreement that the people have the right to govern. Civil society is a transitional state that is intended to give way to political society each time. The return to civil society can be seen as a situation in which a nation has declared its independence from a tyrant and has agreed to create a new government to replace the old one. If a seceding nation creates a constitution before it secedes there may be no need to revisit civil society. Civil society remains a more energetic force in Althusius than in Locke. In some ways Althusian civil society is similar to our contemporary understanding of civil society. For Althusius and Locke there are multiple forms of associations that are no less legitimate nor less important than political associations. Althusius shows how a person's identity is shaped by each type of association they are a part of, whereas Locke shows that sovereignty remains with the people, albeit in different constructions, depending upon the type of association. What Althusius sees as identity Locke sees as sovereignty.

9. In 1990 a Yeltsin-led Russia had already decided that all Soviet law that contradicted Russian law was to be considered null and void in Russia.
10. "[W]here the Soviet Union once held sway, referendums have been used repeatedly to express nationalist claims and establish the legitimacy of new nations and constitutions. In Russia especially, the 1993 referendum played a vital role in President Boris Yeltsin's battle with Parliament over economic reform" (Butler and Ranney 1994d: 259).
11. The idea that centralized-decentralization is problematic is not unique to my evaluation or to Ethiopia. As Donna Lee Van Cott (2008) argues, in Bolivia, an inflexible and involuntary process of decentralization brought on by the central government stymied deliberation and diminished representation.
12. The Marxist regime overtook the Haile Selassie regime in 1977 after it could not successfully address the famine or military conflict with Eritrea and Somalia. To overcome these problems the new government "replaced the royalist ideology with scientific socialism and the emperor's elites with a new party" (Marcus 1994: 203). What the new regime neglected to consider is that the famine was the result of a centrally controlled

agriculture system that had once been successful under Haile Selassie when he allowed it to follow decentralized capitalist tenets.

13. Note how Brussels is treated similarly in Belgium.

14. I have in mind here the work of Nancy Fraser and Axel Honneth who disagree on matters of recognition but who both ultimately end up making the individual the most important component of their theories.

15. The local entity may have an additional measure proposed as to whether it would like to form its own state, country, or join with another state. Of course, if it would need the consent of the national government to form itself into a new state and the consent of the state it wishes to join should it choose that option. Procedures for each of these options could be drafted as well, but I will focus primarily at the state level.

16. The legislators would know that the support of the people is fundamental to a successful secession which makes this override unlikely. Moreover, the legislature also knows that if it seceded without the support of the people that the people in the new state could push for secession in various regions of the newly developed nation. Thus, the new nation would be born in, and continue to remain in, a state of instability.

CHAPTER 7

Exiting the Echo Chamber

The concern throughout has been how to make government more humane in the sense that it treats humans as the human condition requires. A government that allows for human flourishing without imposing an artificial view of how humans ought to associate is what federalism is designed to accomplish. Along the way there has been an emphasis on deliberative decision making. To restate why such an emphasis has been put on deliberative decision making I rely on the words of Habermas:

> Modern law is formal, because it rests on the premise that anything that is not explicitly forbidden is permitted. It is individualistic, because it makes the individual person the bearer of rights. It is coercive, because it is sanctioned by the state and applies only to legal or rule-conforming behavior . . . It is positive law, because it derives from the decisions of a political legislature . . . it is procedurally enacted law . . . A legal order is legitimate when it safeguards the autonomy of all citizens to an equal degree. The citizens are autonomous only if the addressees of the law can also see themselves as its authors. And its authors are free only as participants in legislative processes that are regulated in such a way and take place in forms of communication such that everyone can presume that the regulation enacted in that way deserve general and rationally motivated consent. (Habermas 1994: 121–2)

The theory of federalism I have set forth is designed to accomplish this task.

For federalism to work, and for deliberative decision making to work, there must be a willingness to work through problems in a way that has become foreign. Policy decisions need not be based upon the need to press one's agenda at the expense of the agenda of the other.

> Civic peace requires self-restraint, and even a bit of self-denial. For it to work, we must be willing not to litigate certain cases. Compromise cannot always mean splitting the difference. Sometimes it means letting the other side win, and even ignoring injustice in the name of peace. After so many years of shouting, it will take a while to learn the virtues of self-restraint. (Samuelson 2006: 3)

Samuelson is not advocating that we remain apathetic in the face of injustice, but rather, if something we do not like is occurring, but it is something we can live with, we should not object if the consequence of our objection will be worse than doing nothing. We can, and should, live with a little discomfort from time-to-time if the situation calls for it. "A workable federal system requires forbearance on the part of the political class . . . Until then, I'm okay, you're okay might not be a workable political program" (Samuelson 2006: 2). It may not always be necessary to impress your views or your claims upon others. More than forbearance is the need for humility, and renouncing the modernist need for control. Modernity tells us that we can control our environment to create predictable outcomes. Modernity does not allow for variation for the presence of an alternative mode of operation that produces desirable results undermines the modernist notion that it has the answer and there can only be one answer.

For federalism to work people need to live according to representative institutions and need to refrain from pressing their claims through the judiciary if the representative branch of government does not provide them with what they want. A commitment to the rules of the game and to deliberative procedures on behalf of the public is paramount. Swiss environmental reform illustrates this point in addition to showing how the referendum can be used as an agenda-setting mechanism and a public education system which does not yield immediate results. Activists and radicals must learn from their failed attempts, and the lesson is generally one of moderation. When there is a referendum there is discussion among the general public, politicians, and the press. This brings the issue to the attention of those who might have otherwise ignored it and it forces those who advocate the position to modify it for majority consumption and approval. In the 1980s when environmental groups pushed for restrictions they failed. But their failed attempts generated discussion in the public and parliament. Eventually, many of the restrictions sought in the 1980s were adopted a decade or so later, with some modifications. It is not that the population became radical environmentalists, but the discussion made the people aware of the problems facing the environment and policy-advocates had to propose initiatives that people could live with (Fossedal 2002: 102). Had the Swiss not had an attachment to their representative system of government, and the reformers sought change through the court or bureaucracy rather than the path it chose, environmental reform would not have received such widespread support or legitimacy, nor would the positive psychological effects have been realized.

James Q. Wilson has documented the rise of polarization in the United States and its probable causes.[1] To this list David Gelertner adds the collapse of federalism (Gelertner 2006). "True federalism accommodates profound national disagreement by allowing each state to tailor the local climate to suit itself. Federalism is an escape valve that lets polarizing bitterness blow off into the stratosphere" (Gelertner 2006: 1). In the United States, because it lacks federalism-enhancing mechanisms, important political disputes are made national disputes, which means the moderating effect of federalism is lost. In

an era where deep fundamental moral questions divide the nation, the nation is in need of a revival of federalism. Federalism supplies the expansion joints that make America supple rather than brittle; make it a bridge that can ride out hurricanes without falling to pieces, that can sustain enormous twisting, turning, and tearing forces without cracking. (Gelertner 2006: 2)

In federalism different views can be accommodated at the local and state level. Once an issue becomes national there can be no accommodation; one side will lose.[2]

Federalism can moderate politics by accommodating different views. This chapter will show why this is to be expected from a federal system by first examining the political theory of John C. Calhoun. By drawing on empirical research, the following section will show how a federal system that integrates deliberative decision-making procedures will moderate politics. The final section of this chapter will show why, and how, a federal regime should be implemented in both Israel and Iraq.

John C. Calhoun

A look at John C. Calhoun serves as both a summary and an introduction. The previous three chapters have discussed how a government can implement a negative power and why doing so is important. Calhoun is perhaps the foremost American defender of the negative power. But, because of his affiliation with the Antebellum South, and being on the losing side of many political battles, he and his theory of the concurrent majority do not receive the serious attention they deserve.[3] Therefore, reviewing Calhoun's most philosophical work, *A Disquisition on Government*, will provide a new articulation of my previous arguments while also giving a critical assessment of an overlooked thinker.

Calhoun was concerned with majority rule for the threat it posed to the defeated minority and the affect it had on politics and individuals. For Calhoun, a majority rule system created a zero-sum game in which the players would look to dominate the other side and secure victory through whatever means they could. The resulting political order was one in which compromise and deliberation were set aside in favor of polarization, the promotion of special interests, and the domination of the minority by the majority. Calhoun proposed a solution, one similar to what I have proposed in the earlier chapters. By reviewing Calhoun's theory of the concurrent majority, the reader will begin to see the dangers associated with a majority-rule system, the importance of federalism, and how the federal preserving mechanisms I advocate in the three previous chapters can be utilized to decrease polarization and ethnic tensions.

Like most of the other philosophers under consideration in this book, Calhoun begins his political theory with an account of human nature. And like the others, Calhoun determines that man is a social being and in society man is able to reach his fullest potential. In fact, outside of society, Calhoun determines, as Aristotle does, man is unable to raise above the level of "the brute creation" (Calhoun 1992: 5). The second characteristic of human nature is that humans are "so constituted as to feel more intensely what affects him directly, than what affects him indirectly through others . . . his direct or individual affections are stronger than his sympathetic or social feelings" (Calhoun 1992: 6). Because men naturally exist in a social state, and because they are partial to their own interests, Calhoun concludes that there must be government for there to be peace, for without it, men's nature will create violence and disorder.

> It follows, then, that man is so constituted, that government is necessary to the existence of society, and society to his existence, and the perfection of his faculties. It follows, also, that government has its origin in this twofold constitution of his nature; the sympathetic or social feelings constituting the remote—and the individual or direct, the proximate cause. (Calhoun 1992: 7)

Because of this second feature of man's nature, when creating communities, men will develop their own culture, language, and priorities, thus making it difficult for different communities to relate to one another. In relating to one another, communities will mimic individual interaction.

> Between these there is the same tendency to conflict—and from the same constitution of our nature—as between men individually; and even stronger—because the sympathetic or social feelings are not so strong between different communities, as between individuals of the same community. (Calhoun 1992: 11)

This characteristic of communities, as it is derived from human nature, will serve as later support for Calhoun's claim that government ought to be decentralized, but when action by a central authority becomes necessary, it should only be done with the consent of each local community in order to avoid abuse of government power.

Like Locke, Calhoun is suspicious of government even though he deems it necessary and proper. Calhoun understands that a government is capable of abusing its powers and creating disorder. This is because, as Locke also saw, government is populated by the same people who made it necessary.

> The cause is to be found in the same constitution of our nature that makes government indispensable. The power which it is necessary for government to possess, in order to repress violence and preserve order, cannot execute themselves. They must be administered by men in whom, like others, the individuals are stronger than the social feelings. (Calhoun 1992: 9)

It is through constitution that the abuses of government power are prevented. Just as government is in place to perfect and protect society, so too is the constitution in place to perfect and protect government.

After he has established the need for government, and government's ability to turn tyrannical, he turns his attention to how such a turn can be prevented.

Calhoun, without direct reference to Hamilton, Jay, or Hamilton, criticizes the argument put forth in *The Federalist Papers*. Calhoun argues,

> It cannot be done by instituting a higher power to control the government and those who administer it. This would be but to change the seat of authority, and to make this bigger power, in reality, the government; with the same tendency, on the part of those who might control its powers, to pervert them into instruments of aggrandizement. (Calhoun 1992: 10)[4]

Calhoun's argument can be used against modern proponents of international feder-alism and advocates of states' rights. In each instance trust is placed with the govern-ment, albeit at a different level, to protect the people. Calhoun draws our attention to this logical fallacy. For Calhoun, if you cannot trust one level of government you cannot trust another.

Calhoun is not naïve, and he knows that government must be equipped with certain powers in order to do its job. Therefore, one cannot stop the abuse of govern-ment by curtailing its powers to such a degree that it will be unable to do what is necessary. Government abuse cannot be prevented by shifting the seat of power or by limiting government power, for the only degree to which government power can be limited that will prevent its abuse would effectively neuter the government which would make the limitation on its power self-defeating. For Calhoun,

> [p]ower can only be resisted by power—and tendency by tendency. Those who exercise power and those subject to its exercise—the rulers and the ruled—stand in antagonistic relations to each other. The same constitution of our nature which leads rulers to oppress the ruled . . . will, with equal strength, lead the ruled to resist, when possessed of the means of making peaceable and effective resistance. (Calhoun 1992: 12–13)

This formulation will sound familiar to those who have read *Federalist Papers* #10 and #51, but Calhoun has something different in mind. While the U.S. Constitution is designed to prevent majority tyranny through delay, the numerical majority still decides what gets done. In Calhoun's estimation, allowing rule by the numerical majority will assure government abuse since the majority will seek to remain in power through whatever means it can, and execute its will through the means at its disposal. When a numerical majority is allowed to rule through representatives,

> [p]arty conflicts between the majority and minority . . . can hardly ever terminate in compromise—the object of the opposing minority is to expel the majority from power; and the majority to maintain their hold upon it. It is, on both sides, a struggle for the whole—a struggle that must determine which shall be the governing, and which the subject party—and, in character, object and result, not unlike those that be competitors for the scepter in absolute monarchies. (Calhoun 1992: 61)

Or, as he puts it earlier,

> [t]he conflict between two parties, in the government of the numerical majority, tends necessarily to settle down into a struggle for the honors and emoluments of the government; and each, in order to obtain an object so ardently desired, will, in the process of the struggle, resort to whatever measure may seem best calculated to effect this purpose. (Calhoun 1992: 32)

Because the government cannot be stripped of its powers, nor can adding successive levels of government on top of one another reduce the threat any more than a reliance on the will of the numerical majority, there must be some other mechanism. Calhoun proposes a negative power on government and those who administer its powers.

> From what has been said, it is manifest, that this provision must be of a character calculated to prevent any one interest, or combination of interests, from using the powers of government to aggrandize itself at the expense of others . . . This . . . can be accomplished . . . by dividing and distributing the powers of government, give to each division or interest, through its appropriate organ, either a concurrent voice in making and executing the laws, or a veto on their execution. It is only by such an organism, that the assent of each can be made necessary to put the government in motion; or the power made effectual to arrest its action, when put in motion—and it is only by the one or the other that the different interests, orders, classes, or portions, into which the community may be divided, can be protected, and all conflict and struggle between them prevented—by rendering it impossible to put or to keep it in action, without the concurrent consent of all . . . The necessary consequence of taking the sense of the community by the concurrent majority is, as has been explained, to give to each interest or portion of the community a negative on the others. It is this mutual negative among its various conflicting interests, which invests each with the power of protecting itself—and places the rights and safety of each, where only they can be securely placed, under its own guardianship. (Calhoun 1992: 21–2, 28)

This method must be combined with universal suffrage, argues Calhoun, in order to prevent the rulers from oppressing the ruled just as the concurrent consent will prevent any one faction from oppressing the other. "It may be readily inferred, from what has been stated, that the effect of the organism is neither to supersede nor diminish the importance of the right of suffrage; but to aid and perfect it" (Calhoun 1992: 23).

The most serious objection to the concurrent majority system that Calhoun must confront can also be raised against my endorsement of NVS in the previous three chapters. The system of concurrent majority is impractical because getting so many diverse interests to consent to a single policy is impossible.[5] The concurrent majority will lead to stagnation and the government will cease to exist. Calhoun agrees that this will be the case in most instances. "It is true, that, when there is no urgent necessity, it is difficult to bring those who differ, to agree on any one line of action" (Calhoun 1992: 49). But Calhoun revises this statement by arguing that not all matters are trivial, and when matters are so dire that action is required there will be compromise and consent by all sides. "When something must be done— and when it can be done only by the united consent of all—the necessity of the case will force to a compromise—be the cause of that necessity what it may" (Calhoun 1992: 49). Calhoun's argument rests on the idea that government is preferable to no government, and man is naturally inclined to be social, which means that if inaction will lead to anarchy, the competing interests will work to prevent it by compromising on a particular policy if not doing so will mean anarchy.

> The necessity of unanimity, in order to keep the government in motion, would be far more urgent, and would act under circumstances still more favorable to secure it. It is so much so that, to suspend its action altogether, even for an inconsiderable period, would subject the community to convulsions and anarchy. (Calhoun 1992: 50)

Or—to state it a bit differently, and less cataclysmically—when the costs of using one's veto to force inaction are higher than consenting to policy in order to allow action, a group or interest will choose to consent or withhold its veto. Government action is therefore limited to those things that are absolutely necessary. Therefore, if there are things that people want done, but are not necessary, they must do so through means other than the government. This is, in my estimation, one reason why NVS will force a revitalization of civil society. People will have to organize in other ways to get what they want, they will not be able to lobby the government successfully to get what they want, but only what is necessary.

The proposition of war can serve as an illustration of Calhoun's argument. If there is a civil war occurring in some far-off land (FOL) there may be some people in nation U who say the army of nation U should be sent to help. If nation U is governed by a concurrent majority, and the opposition utilizes its veto right, no troops will be sent to FOL by nation U. But the victorious regime in FOL then develops a strong army with animosity toward nation U, often invoking rhetoric that it will attack. Even more people in nation U approve of sending troops to FOL but still there are those who object. But when FOL has troops on the shores of nation U, and killing the citizens of nation U, there will be enough support for declaring war against FOL that a veto will not be invoked. Calhoun writes:

> Impelled by the imperious necessity of preventing the suspension of the action of government, with the fatal consequences to which it would lead, and by the strong additional impulse derived from an ardent love of country, each portion would regard the sacrifice it might have to make by yielding its peculiar interest to secure the common interest and safety of all, including its own, as nothing

compared to the evils that would be inflicted on all, including its own, by pertinaciously adhering to a different line of action. So powerful, indeed, would be the motives for concurring, and, under such circumstances, so weak would be those opposed to it, the wonder would be, not that there should, but that there should not be a compromise. (Calhoun 1992: 51)

Additionally, we must not confuse consensus with unanimity nor must we create a false dichotomy by saying that one must either vote for a particular measure or veto it. One may always refrain from voting or vetoing. The difference is subtle but it is one that must be made as it has caused a great deal of misunderstanding of Calhoun. Read writes,

> Calhoun did not merely argue that each interest should be consulted and given fair opportunity to make its case to the public. Nor was consensus merely a goal toward which legislators should aim ... He meant that consensus was a requirement for any political action at all. The consensus rule was to be enforced by guaranteed veto rights. (Read 2009: 160)

This reading of Calhoun has some validity, but Read takes it to mean that Calhoun was in favor of unanimity on all government action: this is a false reading.

Support is different from refraining to veto, and this is a point missed by critics of concurrent majority and what makes the concurrent majority different from unanimity. In unanimous government everyone must express positive support and there can be no dissenters. In a concurrent majority system the minority can block policy it is opposed to, but the majority does not need support and agreement from the minority. There is a tipping point at which the minority will exercise its veto. The majority only needs to make enough concessions to keep from going beyond the tipping point but does not need to go so far as to make the minority part of the majority. Think of the filibuster in the U.S. Senate. A senator may oppose a proposed bill so strongly that she is willing to exercise the right of filibuster which will then halt action. The only way to stop the filibuster and get the bill to a vote, if there are not 60 senators willing to override the filibuster, is to deliberate with the disgruntled senator to see what can be changed in the bill to stop the filibuster. The senator will not be asked to vote for the bill but only asked not to filibuster. So if there is a health care bill with a section concerning abortion funding, the opposing senator may be neutral on the prescription drug sections but fundamentally opposed to the abortion funding section. The majority in the Senate may then be willing to strike the abortion funding section from the bill in order to get the health care bill passed, which the senator can vote for or against—or even refrain from voting—so long as she does not filibuster.

Calhoun provides an additional means of justification for the federal preserving mechanisms I outline in the three previous chapters. What Calhoun goes on to argue of the concurrent majority, which also provides the foundation for the new argument advanced in this chapter, is that the negative that forces consent will provide for the common good by allowing all interests to be represented through productive, rather than combative, means. In a government of the numerical majority the government becomes a means by which the majority seeks to satisfy its appetite. That is, the government becomes an instrument of the majority in which the interests of the majority alone are represented. This being the case, the interests of the majority will not be reasoned, for they need not confront or address opposition. or compromised, for they need not heed the concerns of the opposition; and thus their interests will become more extreme, because that is the nature of groups which mirrors the nature of man. Rule by the numerical majority works to divide the country and forces the people to align themselves with their party more than their country. The concurrent majority system does not have these problems.

> By giving to each interest, or portion, the power of self-protection, all strife and struggle between them for ascendency, is prevented; and, thereby, not only every feeling calculated to weaken the attachment to the whole is suppressed, but the individual and the social feelings are made to unite in one common devotion to country. Each sees and feels that it can best promote it own prosperity by con-ciliating the goodwill, and promoting the prosperity of the others. And hence, there will be diffused throughout the whole community kind feelings between its different portions; and, instead of antipathy, a rivalry amongst them to promote the interests of each other, as far as this can be done consistently with the interest of all. (Calhoun 1992: 37–8)

Calhoun's exuberance for this system can be off-putting at first, but he does state his position more soberly at a later point.

> [B]y giving to each portion of the community which may be unequally affected by its action, a negative on the others, prevents all partial or local legislation, and restricts its action to such measures as are designed for the protection and the good of the whole. In doing this, it secures, at the same time, the rights and liberty of the people, regarded individually; as each portion consists of those who, whatever may be the diversity of interests among themselves, have the same interest in reference to the action of the government. (Calhoun 1992: 46)

The concurrent majority, unlike the numerical majority, is able to achieve a greater commitment to the common good because it forces reasoned deliberation. That is, Calhoun's concurrent majority serves as an early precursor to deliberative democracy. James Read's understanding of Calhoun's understanding of himself is accurate when he writes, "Its [the concurrent majority] purpose was not merely negative—to prevent action in opposition to one group's interests—but positive: to facilitate deliberation and the creation of a true common good" (Read 2009: 5). In a system of numerical majority, "principles and policy would lose all influence in the elections; and cunning falsehood, deception, slander fraud, and gross appeals to the appetites of the lower and most worthless portions of the community, would take place of sound reason and wise debate" (Calhoun 1992: 33). Calhoun does not seek to follow Madison and Hamilton by allowing factions to fight it out in the political arena, but instead he seeks to elevate the debate that occurs in the political arena. If each interest had a veto then one must convince the others that their interests would be represented as well, for, "in governments of the concurrent majority, each portion, in order to advance its own peculiar interests, would have to conciliate all others, by showing a disposition to advance theirs . . ." (Calhoun 1992: 52). Calhoun elaborates on this point by going back to his first principles.

> When traced to its source, this difference [between the numerical and concurrent majority] will be found to originate in the fact, that, in governments of the concurrent majority, individual feelings are, from its organism, necessarily enlisted on the side of the social, and made to unite with them in promoting the interests of the whole, as the best way of promoting the separate interest of each; while, in those of the numerical majority, the social are necessarily enlisted on the side of the individual, and made to contribute to the interest of the parties, regardless of that of the whole. (Calhoun 1992: 52)

Calhoun's theory is one of limited government. He seeks to narrow the scope of government to the point where it only does what is absolutely necessary. The government should act, and be authorized to act, when it is necessary, not when some interest needs its desires fulfilled.

> When something must be done,—and when it can be done only be the united consent of all,—the necessity of the case will force to a compromise;—by the cause of that necessity what it may . . . this will unite the most opposite and conflicting interests, and . . . blend the whole in one common attachment to the country.

The government does not have to act and individuals do not have to lobby or solicit the government for everything it desires. The only thing the government should do, according to Calhoun, is what is necessary. That is, those things that cannot be done through communal cooperation or individual ambition are the proper domain of government action. Calhoun narrows the scope of necessity by showing that those things that will unify our agreement on government action are those things that affect us all the same. If we all agree that the government must do something on a certain question it means we have all agreed that the individual, or the community, cannot do it without another actor facilitating the activity. This is the unifying component of the theory in that it exposes the true nature of the human condition to each citizen. Citizens, through their shared needs—that they realize are shared through the consensus and deliberative inducing mechanisms outlined by

Calhoun—come to recognize their shared humanity. Thus, citizens become more than fellow citizens and instead become fellow humans in those instances in which government must act. Calhoun has turned politics into a humanizing force.

Even still, political scientists who consider Calhoun often do so negatively, as is the case with James Read. Read, like others, argues that Calhoun's system of concurrent majority will not work and therefore Calhoun should not be taken seriously as a thinker except as an example of what thoughts not to have. Read provides three examples of when the veto power, when implemented, failed: Yugoslavia's 1974 Constitution, Northern Ireland's Good Friday Peace Accord, and South Africa's proposed constitution after apartheid.

Of course, Read's employment of Yugoslavia against Calhoun is only valid if Yugoslavia had implemented a concurrent majority system, which it did not. Yugoslavia still left power in the hands of a centralized state and the communist party which could overturn a lower level veto. The system itself was severely flawed not because it incorporated a minority veto, but because it only paid lip service to federal principles without actually implementing them.

Oddly, Read concludes from his examination of Yugoslavia that a concurrent majority will not work while simultaneously arguing that other factors were to blame for Yugoslavia's failures. The single biggest problem from Read's evidence seems to be a poorly constructed constitution whose poor construction had little to do with the inclusion of minority veto. First, not every republic in Yugoslavia had a formal veto power. Second, according to Read, there was still national supremacy. Third, "the constitution left entirely unclear who, if anyone, was empowered to enforce this theoretical supremacy of the federal constitution" (Read 2009: 213). The minority veto is but one part of the constitution yet it gets all the blame from Read even though he is unable to provide evidence to justify his claim and the evidence he does present, points away from the minority veto.

As for his other two examples, they are even less difficult to deal with. Of Northern Ireland Read writes, "[i]t is too early to judge whether the Good Friday Agreement will bring about lasting peace and effective government in Northern Ireland" (Read 2009: 208). In other words, his evidence is inconclusive. Equally important, the veto of which he speaks is not implemented in a way consistent with Calhoun's tenets in that Ireland and Britain are two separate countries.

As for South Africa, the minority veto was never incorporated into the constitution so there is no evidence for or against the minority veto; rather, there is political rhetoric about why it was not chosen. The rhetoric is what Read uses as evidence that the minority veto will not work. One of the three major parties in South Africa in the early 1990s suggested a strong form of federalism in which the national constitution was dependent upon the regional constitutions. "In terms of the IFP notion of federalism, the different regions would constitute autonomous states whose constitutions would dictate interpretation of the 'federal' constitution" (Klug 2000: 104). This type of arrangement would help maintain sovereignty in the subnational regions, by giving the subnational governing units the power of veto in fact, if not in name. If such an arrangement governed the relationship between Native American tribes and the national government of the United States, one could safely assume that Supreme Court decisions that have effectively stripped Native American tribes of their sovereign immunity would not have occurred. But, such a system was never implemented in the United States or South Africa. Thus, one can only know for certain that without it, the minority has been deprived of fundamental rights.

South Africa is an interesting case, however, for when we examine it we again see why central planning cannot adequately account for ethnic diversity and why granting a minority veto authority is a good idea. In 1959 the South African Parliament passed the Bantu Self-Government Act. This act identified certain nations within South Africa that could gain political independence on terms decided by the South African government. This Act was the government's attempt to quell ethnic opposition to its current policies without going so far as to grant full citizenship, and the rights contained therein, to opposition groups.

The boundaries of the bantustans were created by the central government. The South African government used property registers rather than census results to draw the lines. Once the bantustans were created, they were given their own flag and other national symbols. The lines that were drawn were done so without respect for traditional boundaries or ethnic cleavages, they merely served as a "gerrymandering" of sorts so that the white government could maintain its power. "The bantustans were not a basis for national self-determination but a means of turning an African majority/white minority relationship into one of a 'nation of minorities', so that around five million whites could maintain rule over twenty-four million Africans" (Egan and Taylor 2003: 106).

The most frightening aspect of what occurred in South Africa, which resulted from centralized planning, was that the government forced all African people to move to their ethnic bantustan. The government recruited ethnologists to figure out where each person belonged and moved them there through force if necessary. Millions of people were uprooted and resettled to new areas in order to fulfill the government's newly created bantustan mission. The result of this policy was the continuation of white control of South Africa and the rise of poverty and illness within the bantustans.

Politically, the governmental structures of the bantustans were unilaterally imposed by the central state, and had "no real power to affect the key issues within South African society." . . . Within the bantustans the power rested not with the people, but with the bureaucratized authority of chiefs and officials . . . "There is no sovereignty then. No autonomy. No democracy. No self-government. Nothing but a crude empty fraud." (Egan and Taylor 2003: 104)

It confounds the reader why Read would choose an instance of when the veto was proposed but never implemented as a way of disproving Calhoun. Read would have been more fair if he had attacked Calhoun on his own terms by showing that the examples Calhoun relies on—the jury system, Polish Diet, Roman Republic, Iroquois Confederacy—were in some way defective. This would have been a poor strategy for Read because the examples Calhoun uses support Calhoun convincingly.

Since the majority that controls the central government relies on the system for its power, it is unwilling to alter it in any significant way, but instead it seeks to pacify opposition while pushing through their own policy objectives. Through incremental measures, however, the majority is free to do what it wants with the minority once it has limited the minority's ability to participate. A minority veto would prevent this incremental repression. Moreover, a federal structure in which the local interests are consulted before drawing geographical boundaries around ethnic groups, in which they also have a voice during the time of the drawing, would prevent some of the problems inherent within central planning. There would certainly be conflicts between local interests over geographical boundaries, but working the problems out at the negotiation table before the lines are drawn would be preferable to years of violence that would force a revision of the boundaries at a later date.

The benefits of granting a minority veto have been well explicated in this book, including in this section. What deserves further discussion, and serve as the final argument for federalism, is the ability of a properly constructed federal state to diminish ideological polarization.

Polarization, Participation, Deliberation

It is theorized that deliberation among people with diverse opinions increases tolerance, moderation, and helps individuals refine their opinions. Alternately, isolation increases polarization by hardening opinions and decreasing tolerance (Sunstein 2008; 2009). Polarization is not a problem isolated to the general population as it is a problem within government as well (Hetherington 2001; McCarty, Poole, and Rosenthal 2006; Sinclair 2006). Calhoun predicted this.[6]

> As the society becomes more diverse, the individuals' own social networks become less diverse. More than ever, perhaps, the child of an affluent professional family may live, learn, and play with only similar children; the elderly factory worker may retire and relax only among other aged members of the working class. (Fischer 1999: 219)

I do not think it is the diversity of society that allows for this but the size of the society in that people can sequester themselves into whichever corner they like. But Fischer's point still remains valid in that isolation, which produces the echo chamber, is a fundamental problem regardless of its cause. When we sequester ourselves we generally do so by forming associations with people like ourselves.[7] This is problematic for several reasons, the first being that it produces an echo chamber in that only those ideas that are already accepted by the group are discussed, which means the ideas are not sharpened through challenge. To prevent this

John Stuart Mill advocates free speech. "If the opinion is right, they are deprived of the opportunity of exchanging error for truth; if wrong, they lose what is almost as great a benefit, the clearer perception and livelier impression of truth produced by its collision with error" (Mill 1956: 21). It is through reason-giving that our views become sharpened. When we are forced to justify our positions we are forced to develop a more sophisticated account of why we think the way we do (Green, Visser, and Tetlock 2000; Mutz 1998; Burnstein and Sentis 1981). Of course, opponents of deliberative democracy deny that people have complete theories in mind when making an argument, absent confrontation however, there will be no theory or reasoning of any kind.

> [B]y considering a given issue from different viewpoints, by making present to my mind the standpoints of those who are absent . . . The more people's stand-points I have present in my mind while I am pondering a given issue, and the better I can imagine how I would feel and think if I were in their place, the stronger will be my capacity for representative thinking and the more valid my final conclusions . . . (Arendt 1968: 241)

The echo chamber that isolated homogeneous groups find themselves in tend to produce more extreme views as well.[8] Isolation produces intolerance. As Mark Twain wrote, "nothing so liberalizes a man and expands the kindly instincts that nature put in him as travel and contact with many kinds of people . . ." A more academic version of this statement is offered by Seyla Benhabib who argues that contact and interaction with those who are not similar to us is, "essential for us to comprehend and to come to appreciate the perspective of others" (Benhabib 1992: 140; see also Allport 1954; Pettigrew and Tropp 2000). Therefore, deliberation between diverse groups should be encouraged because, in addition to bringing about a way of strengthening one's position, being exposed to diverse viewpoints will temper and moderate one's position (Barabas 2004).[9] Consequently, deliberation between diverse groups will confer legitimacy upon a policy because each side has expressed itself and heard the rationalization for the other side (Manin 1987; Fearon 1998). This point was addressed earlier by Montesquieu who wrote, "I say it, and it seems to me that I have written this work only to prove it: the spirit of moderation should be that of the legislator; the political good, like the moral good, is always found between two limits" (XXIX.1).

Politics does not end at deliberation, for people must act. As the authors of *Democracy at Risk* (2005) would have it, political participation and civic engagement will lead to more responsive politics and an improved quality of life for its citizens. Therefore, the results of political participation are enhanced by deliberation since the citizens who participate are sophisticated and tolerant. However, we find that this conclusion cannot be reached too hastily for research has found that deliberation has a negative impact on participation. Diana Mutz (2006) shows that there is a paradox between deliberation and participation. As deliberation increases, participation tends to decrease. This means that those who we would most like to participate, those who are more tolerant and have more sophisticated opinions, are less likely to participate. The result tends to be, then, that politics is dominated by ideologues (Prior 2007). Mutz attributes this phenomenon to the fact that when individuals are confronted with a multitude of divergent opinions they become less sure of their own and are unwilling to act upon their, now, unsteady set of beliefs. Second, Mutz argues that individuals are unwilling to engage in conflict with those in their social network and will therefore disengage from political participation in order to avoid conflict. I suppose there is a third explanation that Mutz does not consider. When one becomes tolerant of another's position one loses the animus for his or her participation. If I tolerate someone else's position, or the policy that results from their position, then it is less important for me to act against it. Unless I truly oppose or support something to the extent that I cannot stand to see the other side win, then I will not become active politically. It is possible that tolerant individuals can work their differences out among themselves rather than going to the government for assistance.

Mutz also ignores the fact that methods of political engagement and participation are more varied than simply voting. By only measuring political participation in terms of voting, she underestimates the extent to which individuals participate. If I engage in a dialogue with my neighbor, or go to a town hall meeting in which an issue is being discussed, and we resolve the conflict without government action, we have not ceased our participation or engagement, but have decided to resolve our conflict without going to the government. One of the reasons government exists is to settle disputes. If individuals can settle their disputes by deliberating with one another, and thus becoming more tolerant, this should hardly be characterized as political apathy. Thus, deliberation and the model of deliberation that I set up in the previous chapters is not prior to the political or apolitical, but it is a form of political participation that does not necessitate positive action from the government.

There are also those who might object to my model of participatory government on the grounds that it is simply unworkable due to the size and complexity of modern nation-states. This concern has been addressed in previous chapters but deserves further consideration, albeit briefly. Those who argue that nations are too large for deliberative and participatory government have failed to grasp the structural possibilities and have instead opted for a view that governments can only change in the direction of the bigger (Bryan 1999; Cohen and Sabel 1997). It is possible to devolve power, and it is possible to create institutions and procedures within large systems that allow them to act like small systems (Fung 2004).

Critics of participatory democracy, particularly when participation is predicated upon a model of deliberation, argue that in environments with deep cultural, ethnic, and economic cleavages deliberative forums can be transformed into forums of "domination, paralysis, or chaos." While there are strong theoretical claims to refute these objections, there is also empirical evidence that shows "appropriate external supports can make participatory decision-making fair even under trying circumstances of factionalism and inequalities of power" (Fung 2004: 173).

As Fung points out, there are too few accounts of how public policy and institutional design might reverse trends of civic deterioration. The suggested procedures I outline for NVS incorporate civic building mechanisms in addition to predicting that deliberative procedures will indirectly build a stronger civil society by decreasing reliance on government. Moreover, with delay procedures in place there is much less the government can do, which means people must rely on themselves and nongovernmental actors if they wish for something to be done.

Israel and Iraq

My emphasis on scale at the beginning of this book was designed to, in part, dispute advocates of federalism who think federalism is effective at resolving disputes and forming consensus because of homogeneity (Delahunty 2007). The thought is that because people in a small community are the same, conflicts tend to be minimized. This concept of why federalism works is overturned by the peaceful yet diverse federal societies of Switzerland and Belgium, and the existence of violent conflict in small, diverse, nonfederal states like Israel and Sri Lanka. Of course, homogeneity is likely to breed peace in that if there is no difference there is no reason for conflict. But no society, no matter how small, can be so homogeneous. This is why federalism should be seen as a way of reconciling tensions since it is "made for people of fundamentally different views."[10] Political scientists have also concluded that

> in countries that have higher degrees of ethno-linguistic fractionalization, the ethno-federal sample shows significantly higher quality of government scores than diverse states that have adopted a unitary/integrationist model of power-sharing. The results support the notion that the impact of federal institutions on the quality of government is contextualized and nuanced and that, given a diverse population, certain institutions such as ethno-federalism can encourage better governance among various groups than its integrationist rival. (Charron 2009: 587)

Like Calhoun argued of the concurrent majority, Delahunty makes the observation that "Federalism often seems to sustain loyalty to the nation-state rather than to weaken it: by defusing potential internal conflicts along creedal, ethnic or linguistic lines, it lends the nation-state greater resilience, tenacity and strength" (Delahunty 2007: 4).

Scale is not the only component of federalism. I have argued throughout that equipping a minority interest with a formal-political voice will help lead to conflict reconciliation, decreased threats to minority interests, a strengthened civil society, and maintenance of the proper scale. In the course of developing this argument I touched on the question of recognition and what federalism has to contribute to that dialogue.

Recognition is generally conceived as culturally based (Gutmann and Thompson 1999). Meanwhile, federalism is generally conceived of as geographically dependent.

These are both errors. To think that one can only be recognized according to a cultural identity, or that federalism cannot work unless competing groups are geographically based, is to misunderstand recognition and federalism. First, recognition is not exclusive to ethnic, religious, or gender distinctions. Second, federalism does not have to be seen as a remedy for only cultural conflict or as simply a regional solution. There can be other sources of conflict that have nothing to do with ethnically defined culture. One need only think of the economic-based cleavages that have developed in Iraq or Belgium. Certainly the economic disagreements in Iraq and Belgium are exacerbated by the ethnic cleavages, but it is disparity in oil distribution in Iraq that is standing in the way of developing an ethnically based federal structure. In Belgium the economic disparity between the French-speaking and Dutch-speaking regions is what led to the latest rounds of devolution and not conflict over culture.

Taylor (1994) criticizes Kymlicka, and his idea of federalism, for developing a system in which the survival and perpetuation of a given culture will go on indefinitely. From Taylor's view, identities can change and shift and to institute measures designed to lock in current cultures is to act contrary to a politics of recognition. For Taylor,

> nonrecognition or misrecognition . . . can be a form of oppression, imprisoning someone in a false, distorted, reduced mode of being. Beyond simple lack of respect, it can inflict a grievous wound, saddling people with crippling self-hatred. Due recognition is not just a courtesy but a vital human need. (Taylor 1994: 25)

Taylor may be right in his estimation of Kymlicka, but he is not right about federalism. Federalism can be designed in such a way that recognition can be fluid to the same degree identity is fluid.

The intention of the remainder of this chapter is to show how a federal design can be adapted to new situations. However, what I offer is an outline rather than a policy prescription. What is needed is the development of a system that recognizes each group as that group seeks to be recognized are institutions that allow for self-determination without the risk of turning tyrannical, and a space for deliberation that facilitates human connections as much as an exchange of ideas.

In addressing Israel and Iraq I rely on the argument developed throughout that reform from a centralized authority is rarely successful and usually does more harm than good. According to Fathali Moghaddam, "most governments, particularly superpowers, are likely to exaggerate their abilities to re-shape the present, even against the direction of deep cultural and historical trends . . ." (Moghaddam 2008: 166). The reform toward federalism cannot be instituted from an outside actor. While mediators and consultants can be employed with success, the decision to federate, and how to federate, must always remain with those who have the most familiarity with the issues and the largest stake in the decision.

Israel

While the Israeli-Palestinian conflict seems somewhat intractable as each side has valid claims, it can be said that the involvement of the UN after World War II to set up a Jewish state, while not actively pursuing a Palestinian state, did not help matters and is yet one more illustration of how the top-down development of a nation is conducive to nothing else but producing conflict and disruption.

This section is critical of some aspects of Israeli politics. However, this is not to deny the legitimacy of Zionists claims, nor deny that Jews need a safe-haven in the form of a nation-state. Nor is this to choose sides on the matter of who is at fault with regard to the persistent violence in the region. All this section shows is that there are aspects of Israeli politics that lead to mistreatment of the Arab minority. In denying full recognition and cultural expression in Israel for Arabs, the Israeli government violates the principles it has tried to secure for Jews. The point of this section is to show how Zionists and Arabs can coexist while leaving the possibility open that they may not be able to coexist in the same state.

The political problems in Israel reflect the need for recognition of two different cultures in the same country.

> A country's unity is expressed in and sustained by its citizens' shared sense of history; by their recognition of national holidays, ceremonies, symbols and myths; by their participation in a range of informal customs covering virtually every aspect of life, includes modes of dress, styles of music, patterns of work and leisure, attitudes toward gender, sex and sexuality, and tastes in food and drink. (Scheffler 2007: 93–4)

While Scheffler is referring to the problem immigrants may have in transitioning to a new country, his observation is applicable to the Palestinians in that prior to 1948, what is now Israel was a Palestinian state and Palestinians became outsiders in their own land and the nonstate components of identity and citizenship were replaced by Jewish symbols and nonstate components of citizenship. Because Palestinian Arabs are the minority, and their culture and identity are denied a full expression under Jewish rule, corrections must be made to current Israeli policy for the minority group to be represented in government and through policy.[11]

> The reasoning underlying the demand for special rights and accommodations for ethnic and cultural minorities is that minority cultures are seriously disadvantaged by the fact that the majority culture is reflected through the official language, official holidays, and state symbols and is dominant in all aspects of everyday life and that consequently minority members suffer serious harms. (Stopler 2007: 323)

Israel has institutionalized political disparity by passing legislation and constitutional measures that limit the extent to which Palestinians can influence policy.

For instance, legislation was passed in 2003 that "restricts the right of Palestinian Arab citizens of Israel who marry Palestinian Arabs from the occupied territories to bring their spouses to live with them in Israel" (Stopler 2007: 330). But this is less of a challenge to Arab parity and recognition than 7A of the Basic Law that establishes that Israel is a Jewish state and prohibits candidates for the Knesset from denying that Israel is a Jewish state. Thus, even if a Palestinian party were able to gain a majority in the Knesset, it would be unable to make laws that recognized Arabs as being equal to Jews, culturally, within Israel, as Jewish culture is the constitutionally sanctioned culture of Israel. The establishment of a dominant culture through law and constitution is one thing, for law may not be put into practice effectively, but "Israel is a Jewish state and all its national symbols, including the flag, the national anthem, holidays, memorial days, names of places, streets and sites, and the national heroes are purely Jewish" (Stipler 2007: 349). There must be equal recognition for there to be political parity, and political parity is necessary for there to be just laws. "Overall, in these regimes Jews exercise preponderant political as well as military and police power, while Arabs either are a minority, or if a majority, are in a dependent, controlled political position" (Weingrod 2003: 119).

Nancy Fraser argues that "justice requires social arrangements that permit all adult members of society to interact with one another as peers" (Fraser 2003: 36). Unfortunately, in Israel, social arrangements do not permit adult members to interact as peers since there is an institutionalized preference for Jewish heritage and culture. Fraser's argument is that there must be a redistribution of material resources in order to create an environment in which people can interact as peers. Those in favor of material redistribution argue that "Social arrangements that institutionalize deprivation, exploitation, and gross disparities in wealth, income, and leisure time fail the objective condition of participatory parity by denying some people the means and opportunities to interact with others as peers" (Stopler 2007: 319). However, a focus on material redistribution as a means of achieving political equality is unnecessary—if not insufficient—if the proper political mechanisms are in place. Regardless of economic parity, there cannot be equal participation if the government will not allow it. By providing groups with a bargaining chip to, or by giving a voice to, a group through institutionalized political means will do far more to advance the cause of political parity. Granting a group, such as Arab Palestinians, the power of NVS, Jewish officials must give equal weight to, and recognition of, their needs in a way that economic parity cannot guarantee. If it is true that "the intersubjective condition of participatory parity requires that institutionalized patterns of cultural value express equal respect for all participants and ensure equal opportunity for achieving social esteem," then we must avoid economic solutions in favor of political solutions as the economic solutions abstract the cultural concerns in a way inconsistent with what may be nonmaterial grievances and claims. By focusing on economic parity culture is rendered one dimensional. If the focus shifts to political parity, which allows culture to express its multifaceted character, better representation is afforded to that group, and true interaction among peers is possible.

It may seem that the obvious solution is to grant Palestinians their own state so that they have the power to govern themselves, or to institute a federal structure that isolates the competing groups from one another's influence. "Self-government rights seek to preserve the minority culture and its capacity to develop . . . Self-government rights enable the minority itself to shape aspects of life relevant to those individuals" (Saban 2005: 909). Self-government does not have to be atomistic or isolating. And while I hold out that separate nations should be left as an option, it should only be chosen when all other solutions have failed. Rather than an atomistic version of self-government, minority groups, or regions, should be equipped with the tools necessary to ensure self-determination—which might look like self-government—within a federal scheme. "Providing minority groups with these rights decentralizes power, and bestow part of that power on the minority" (Saban 2005: 909). Although I agree with the sentiment expressed by Saban, I disagree with the extension of the idea that minority groups should be granted near immunity over matters relating to its culture, education, and economics. Part of developing a multicultural society is figuring out ways different groups can live together. This does not mean that values and institutions have to be compromised, as some things can operate independently, but having the goal be to establish a system in which each group governs itself independent of the other will do little to relieve future conflicts at points where the groups must come into contact. No group can isolate itself from another entirely. Separation is limited in what it can accomplish. Moreover, no minority group is homogeneous and therefore there will be opposition views expressed by members of that group and therefore conflict will arise within that group as well, further dividing that group into minority and majority groups. Therefore, this group, if we extend Saban's idea of self-government, should be further subdivided into smaller and smaller groups until only homogeneous groups remain—which might mean only individuals are left. Saban's solution encourages individualism and denies the importance of community. Competing groups and interests must learn how to work with one another, and government systems which grant self-determination should be crafted so as to use deliberative decision-making procedures to protect one group from having its right to self-determination limited by another.

The first recommendation for Israel would be to rewrite those parts of the constitution that set up Jewish culture as the state supported culture. Equal recognition cannot be achieved until this is done.[12] If this cannot be done then a separate state may be necessary. Given that it is unlikely Israel will rewrite its constitution along these lines it may be necessary to adopt the less than ideal solution of creating separate states within Israel. The system Saban suggests can work and the downside can be limited, so long as institutions are in place that allow for groups to work together when necessary. Of course, the decision on which areas to give to each group should be determined by the interested groups. However, peaceful negotiation does not always seem to be the strong suit of the leaders in this region. The people of Israel and Palestine should be given a prominent role in the negotiations over how to divide the state. But prior to negotiations, mediated meetings should be held between members of these groups so that they can express their concerns and recommendations. Measures should be taken to make sure that each side correctly understands what the other side is arguing and to help keep the meetings focused. Such meetings have been successful in other countries,

> [h]owever, in the Israeli-Palestinian case these [people-to-people] initiatives have failed to deliver tangible long-term results due to limited funding, disparities in power and resources between Israeli and Palestinian representatives [to the meetings], a lack of political and financial support by officials on both sides, scarce involvement of the grassroots, language limitations . . . (Mikhelidze and Pirozzi 2008: 20)

Of course, what made these initial attempts at small-deliberative bodies ineffective can be improved in future attempts if one looks to the success that was had, albeit at a small level, in Sri Lanka and elsewhere. Funding does not seem to be insurmountable due to the international interest in resolving the Israeli-Palestinian dispute, but high levels of funding are not necessary so long as the small-deliberative bodies are well organized. There were not a lot of resources spent on the successful efforts in Sri Lanka to create similar groups. Language limitations were overcome in Sri Lanka and can be overcome in Israel as well. The disparity between the two groups does not have to limit efforts given what Archon Fung and Olin Wright find. Moreover, the power disparities derive from the political disparity that exists in Israel, so a move to institute political parity in government will trickle down to the local level, but efforts to produce parity will be better served if action is taken at both the national and local levels. Grassroots organizations that exist in the civil sphere can work as links between the people and the government to bring about greater cooperation in an effort to produce parity.

> Mid-range actors engaging at grassroots level seek to empower local communities to make decisions and formulate their own goals in conflict resolution and to strengthen their capacity to address these goals and needs. It is important that all groups, including the marginalized, should be involved in this process. However, effective peacebuilding requires the coordination between actors at all levels, including also between mid- and top-level actors. (Mikhelidze and Pirozzi 2008: 20)

If this can be done, and it may take years, then a federal scheme in which self-government is guaranteed within a federal scheme may be instituted. While I advocate the use of NVS as a way to preserve self-determination, such measures may not be necessary so long as a nation is able bring together disparate groups in small-deliberative meetings at the subnational level. If two groups—or however many—are divided into two distinct geographical regions then an echo chamber will likely form and future conflict will inevitably result.

The case for NVS has been articulated extensively already and need not be recounted here. But, it can be assumed that a federal regime such as that seen in the United States, supplemented with NVS, may be an acceptable option for Israel. The point to make clear in this section is that redrafting a constitution, or implementing institutional mechanisms, will prove insufficient if the people are not willing to work together. But, this is not to blame the citizens of Israel, or the noncitizen inhabitants, it is only to suggest that the people must lead the way because of the unlikelihood of rewriting the Israeli constitution.

Iraq

"As violence raged in the summer of 2006, seventy-eight percent of Iraqis opposed the division of Iraq along ethno-sectarian lines" (Williams and Simpson 2008: 201). Polls in 2007 and 2008 show that this sentiment has not changed, particularly as if the question is whether the divisions should be drawn forcibly or imposed by the United States. (Williams and Simpson 2008: 202, 203). The first requirement of any division, even if not ethno-sectarian, is to involve the people who will be affected by the process. Perhaps it would be possible, following the peace workshops in Sri Lanka, the procedures used in Chicago or Porto Alegre, to bring the members of the different ethnic groups together at the regional level and then at the national level. The region would be determined, for the purposes of holding forums, by drawing a radius of X kilometers around any town with a population of Y.[13] These towns would then host forums on how regions should be drawn. In the first forum there might be made a list of concerns and recommendations. Then at the second meeting, one official—or three, the number is not particularly important—would be elected to represent the region at the national forum where the regional boundaries would be drawn. At the national level the representatives would voice the concerns and recommendations of their regions. When the national level devises a plan, it will be sent to the regions for certification by general vote. Initiating the process this way not only confers legitimacy upon the procedure, and brings disparate groups together in a deliberative format so that polarization is decreased, but it takes into account that "Iraqi identity is rooted in a complex history, and not simply upon ethno-sectarian characteristics" (Williams and Simpson 2008: 204). Quoting Visser from the Norwegian Institute for International Affairs, Williams and Simpson write, "to many Iraqis, the entho-religious community is but one of several possible foci of identity . . . Instead, villages, towns and regions have shaped identities" (Williams and Simpson 2008: 205). The problems associated with a centralized division of a nation have been seen in Ethiopia, Iraq, the former Soviet Union, and elsewhere. By giving the people, at a local level, the ability to draw the political boundaries in their country, perhaps some of the problems seen in these other countries can be avoided.

The objection to the federalization of Iraq has less to do with decentralization and federalism than it does with ethno-centric divisions arbitrarily conceived.

The Iraqis are rightly skeptical of a Western force looking to reorganize its structure. Following the collapse of the Ottoman Empire after World War I three Ottoman provinces were pulled together by the British to form a protectorate. Basra, Baghdad, and Mosul—the three provinces pulled together—had different histories and cultures that made their unification unnatural. By combining different cultures and religious sects into one unified state, the British laid the groundwork for unrest. "But religious identities are not easily contained by 'official' boundaries and formal laws. Southern Iraq is developing into a Shi'a Islamic republic, with enormously important oil resources . . ." Iraq is not the only country that has to deal with economic disparity nested within cultural conflict. Belgium has successfully dealt with this problem by producing solutions that were both ethnically and geographically based. The solutions adopted by Belgium were discussed in Chapter 6. Some of Belgium's success is attributable to its willingness to solve problems in ways that do not include litigation or legislation. For example, with a large influx of Muslim immigrants to Europe, including Belgium, there has been a clash of cultures. One area that has received media attention is the wearing of headscarves by Muslim women. While some countries have tried to address the problem through legislation or litigation, such as France, where headscarves have been banned, Belgium has attempted to resolve conflict through dialogue outside of the legal system and there has been much less conflict and backlash as a result. Even apart from this most recent development,

> Belgium has displayed the ability to be open to adaptation. The structures and institutions have shifted, but Belgium has remained united and effective. Through the ethnic conflict prior to 1960, through the linguist conflict post-1960, and the economic conflict that incorporated the other two, Belgium has been able to adapt. The willingness to adapt—even institutions—is a key component to federalism. (Swenden and Jans 2009: 16)

In looking for ways that Iraq can be organized we must be creative with our approach, including the drawing of regional boundaries. "Two major reasons for the failure of United States policy in Iraq after the 2003 invasion of that country are the lack of appreciation for the importance of cultural continuity and tradition, and the enormous weight of history in the Near and Middle East region" (Moghaddam 2008: 170). This is not a problem unique to the United States; rather, it is an inescapable consequence of centralized reform as only those living in the country, and in the localities, can be familiar with the tradition and history of a place.

Ethnicity in Iraq is not defined by religion alone, and conflict is not then a result of religion and economic disparity. Responding to those who characterize religion as the major source of Iraqi identity, Peter Munson argues, "These are only segments of Iraqi identity, competing for dominance with other characteristics: Iraqi nationalism, Arab identity, Islamic identity, tribal and family allegiance, profession, urban or rural provenance, and socio-economic condition" (Munson 2009: 17–18). This makes the Iraqi people no different than the people of any other nation. But due to the artificial nature in which the Iraqis have been united, there are problems in Iraq that exist in few other countries. Regional boundaries need to be drafted by those who live there, and they need not be permanent fixtures in the federal structure. Geographic boundaries can change as populations shift and redefine themselves. Moreover, the manner in which the population is represented in parliament can be done even without regional divisions and still remain federal. While this would take a great deal of creativity, it is not out of the question. But for the sake of discussion, let us assume that the manner in which I have chosen to draw regional boundaries has been completed.

Once regional boundaries have been formed crafting the rest of the federal structure can continue. I will provide an example only of how the parliament might be constructed. Perhaps one of the ways the national parliament can be structured is through a three-house legislature in which one house is elected through ethnically closed elections—so long as this has been determined to be the primary manner of identification. In election for this house one could only vote for members representing their ethnic group. The seats would be divided upon ethnic population with no reference to region. Therefore, one ethnic group may only get to vote on 12 seats. In voting on those 12 seats there might be upwards of 40 candidates from which the voter ranks his or her top 12.[14] The second house will be an open election which has no geographic or ethnic restrictions. The house might contain another 100 members which means the ballot might have over 200 names. The voter would rank his or her top five preferences. There would have to be run-off and contingency plans in place if 100 different choices were not made.

The third house would represent the geographic interests. These members would be voted upon by the regions that were drawn by the previous forums. One representative per region. This house would have only veto authority. Once a bill passed the other two houses in identical form, the third house could execute a veto through two-thirds vote, or however many the regional forums decided. If a veto is utilized then a conference is called in which representatives from each of the three houses meet to decide if a compromise can be made. A compromised bill would then have to pass through another vote in each of the three houses by a simple majority.

This division of the parliament can be altered and manipulated depending upon the desire of the people. For instance, there may be no geographic house, but instead a house based on occupation if that is how the voters choose to be identified. Or, what I have made the ethnic house may be given veto power instead of the geographic house. The point is that there are many ways in which people can be represented and national institutions constructed. Federalism is not an intractable problem. Of course one would have to give consideration to the judiciary, bureaucracy, local, regional, and executive components, but the work can be done so long as we feel confined only by the desire to create a just and equitable system and do not feel the need to craft institutions and constitutions the way they have been previously. I would encourage any constitutional project, however, to include NVS provisions and procedures that demand deliberation and direct participation. NVS provisions are important in Iraq, as elsewhere, for preventing majority tyranny, but in Iraq in particular, given that there are nomadic minorities that compose a very small segment of the population, self-defense mechanisms for an otherwise unrecognized minority are vital for preventing discriminatory practices.

Federalism, and the subsequent devolution of power, should be done prudently.

> Critical to the sustainability of the political and economic stability of the state is for power to be transferred from the central government to the governorates. Key to maintaining the stability is ensuring that power is devolved only where appropriate, asymmetrically, and in a gradual manner that is consistent with each government's ability to accept such power. (Williams and Simpson 2008: 231)

The point made by the authors is accurate, but implementing such a system is difficult as it may be in the political advantage of certain regions to deem other regions unfit for devolved power. The manner in which this is determined is fundamental. It would be difficult to create benchmarks, for benchmarks would have to be regionally sensitive. That is, you could not have a mandatory minimum of literacy or public utilities for the region may not find those a top priority, nor may they reflect the inability for self-rule but instead be indicators of the need for self-rule. To devolve power asymmetrically would require that the region still be given representation at the national level and that it has the power of NVS. For without the ability to stop policy that might negatively affect it, it would have no other way of forcing fair treatment or recognition. Such regions, if given the power to secede, would force fair treatment and assessment by the other regions if they desire not to lose that region.

Of course, determining the proper distribution of powers and responsibilities between the national and subnational would take considerable attention. But with the proper institutional mechanisms and representation, it would be but another policy matter to be ironed out in a deliberative format.

No nation is incapable of self-government. Federalism provides the best remedy for polarized nations and a means of resolving conflict. We need only be creative in how we craft it so that we can be sensitive to the unique needs and preferences of the place and people. The goal should be to create a good government for that country, not in how well we can follow a given model. We should use previous attempts as lessons, not as restrictions on what we are capable of.

My discussion of Israel and Iraq are suggestions that open the reader to new possibilities more than it is an outline of formal policy prescriptions. More than formal structures are necessary to make a system work, but formal structures can enhance the informal components if developed properly. By instituting procedures and institutions that encourage decentralization and deliberative decision making, civil society can be invigorated, which then creates a space for resolving disputes independent of direct government involvement. The intention is to depolarize politics by bringing people into closer contact with one another and limiting the need to appeal to the government to bring about resolutions. When the government is the primary forum through which disputes are settled, the state can be turned into a coercive body; for those who seize control can exert undue influence.

Conclusion

Nations such as Iraq and Israel will never see peace so long as they opt for top-down solutions. In order to be effective, policy—which seeks to promote peace—must be seen as legitimate by those who are to be governed by the policies—something top-down solutions can never achieve, particularly in heterogeneous societies. Policies will only be seen as legitimate if each side feels that its concerns are properly reflected in the final policy outcome. This requires that those in the minority feel as though they had the ability to influence policy and the majority did not create a policy that was threatening to the minority. The majority cannot feel as though it was held hostage by the minority either, for the majority does have a right to rule. The only way all these needs can be balanced is if there is deliberation, and for there to be deliberation there must be an incentive to deliberate. Federalism is the only system that provides incentives for deliberation. Therefore, it is federalism, which is our last, best hope.

Notes

1. The reader should keep in mind Montesquieu's teaching as expressed in Chapter 2, that extremism will lead to a nation's downfall.
2. When disputes are taken to the political arena the stakes are raised, which means the tendency to polarize increases.
3. One obvious exception to this trend is Cheek (2004). Because I did not find it necessary to discuss Plato's or Aristotle's relationship to, or thoughts on, slavery I do not find it necessary to discuss Calhoun's. I have not argued for a complete adoption of the thought of any theorist in this book, for if I had, then it would be necessary to address all dimensions of that thinker, including the biographical. But, as stated earlier, I have merely tried to present my reading of a particular thinker as it relates to a particular question, taking what I need to develop my own theory, and move on.
4. In his *A Discourse on the Constitution and Government*, Calhoun rejected Madison's formulation of a partly federal, partly national system in *Federalist* #39. The issue for Calhoun was the division of sovereignty. One cannot divide sovereignty. Powers can be divided between various levels and departments, but when it came to sovereignty, and whether something could be partly federal and partly national, he expressed his disagreement by saying that one might as well speak of a half a triangle or half of a square. One cannot hope to create a federal structure, in which the national government does not usurp the power of the subnational parts, unless sovereignty is granted to the subnational levels. The only way they may have sovereignty is to have the necessary tools, such as the power of veto, secession, and nullification.

5. Ralph Lerner criticizes Calhoun for inconsistency as he, in Lerner's view, makes "self-interest . . . the warp and woof of every significant political act," which then produces a system that produces policy in the common good by turning "irreducible self-interest [in]to enlarged patriotism by way of dread of stalemate and anarchy." Read agrees with Lerner that "One cannot imagine Hobbesian men effectively administering a consensus-based political order." Read and Lerner have constructed self-interest as to be something hedonistic and narrow. Government and cooperation can be in someone's self-interest even if unmotivated by altruistic means. Locke and Hobbes both make the point that man can be safer and more productive living in a government than outside of it; therefore, man will give up some of his freedom to do so. Lerner and Read seem to be saying that a self-interested actor would not give up any freedom and therefore never enter any contract, let alone become a citizen of a nation with laws. The contradiction they accuse Calhoun of is not Calhoun's contradiction but rather the apparent contradiction that exists within human nature. Calhoun is simply reporting what he sees, he does not seek to invent a human but take humans how they are and implement a system that works best for them. Lerner and Read have taken aim at the wrong target.

6. "Deliberation theorists often deplore the perceived polarization of American politics, which they believe leads to hardened opinions, diminishing tolerance for opposing points of view, and increasing dissensus" (Lawrence, Sides, and Farrell 2010: 141).

7. "Individuals prefer social contexts populated by others who share their core political values and avoid social discourse with people who disagree with them profoundly over politics" (Lawrence, Sides, and Farrell 2010: 144).

8. "Ultimately, homophily within networks likely coincides with polarization—that is, the divergence of competing partisans or ideologues, such that individuals who initially leaned to the left find themselves moving farther left over time, and individuals who initially leaned to the right move farther right . . . both sides of the ideological spectrum inhabit largely cloistered cocoons of cognitive consonance, thereby creating little opportunity for a substantive exchange across partisan or ideological lines" (Lawrence, Sides, Farrell 2010: 144).

9. These seem to be contradictory consequences, but only if we assume that a strong view is synonymous with intolerance. As the research demonstrates, one can have a strong view, but also be open to hearing the views of others without feeling the need to impose their view on the other group.

10. *Lochner v. New York*, 198 U.S. 45 (1905) (Holmes, J. dissenting).

11. The nature of identity conflict demonstrates the need of political participation and civic engagement. But not only must there be participation and engagement, these activities must lead to outcomes. First, citizens will become apathetic and seek other avenues for change if they cannot affect change through sanctioned political activities. Second, outcomes that result from, and therefore reflect, participation and engagement will have greater legitimacy than those that do not. Legitimacy is of great importance when dealing with identity conflict.

12. Had the Palestinian minority had a veto over constitutional language during the time the constitution was drafted and ratified such a provision would probably have been absent.

13. Modifications would have to be made to make the model workable of course.

14. It is possible for some to identify with no ethnic group. There could be seats allotted for these identifiers as well.

Bibliography

Allport, Gordon W., *The Nature of Prejudice*, Garden City: Doubleday, 1954.

Althusius, Johannes, *Politica*, ed. and trans. Frederick S. Carney, Indianapolis: Liberty Fund, 1995.

Amar, Akhil Reed, "Of Sovereignty and Federalism," *Yale Law Journal* 96.4 (1987): 1425.

Ansell, Christopher and Jane Gingrich, "Trends in Decentralization," *Democracy Transformed? Expanding Political Opportunities in Advanced Industrial Democracies*, eds. Bruce Cain, Russell J. Dalton, and Susan Scarrow, Oxford: Oxford University Press, 2003.

Arendt, Hannah, *Between Past and Future: Eight Exercises in Political Thought*, New York: Viking Press, 1968.

Aristotle, *Nicomachean Ethics*, trans. H. Rackham, Cambridge: Loeb Classical Library, 1934.

—, *The Politics*, trans. Carnes Lord, Chicago: Chicago University Press, 1984.

Aroney, Nicholas, "Subsidiarity, Federalism and the Best Constitution: Thomas Aquinas on City, Province and Empire," *Law and Philosophy* 26.1 (Winter 2007): 161–228.

Augustine, Saint Bishop of Hippo. *De Civitate Dei*, New York: Modern Library, 1983.

Bachrach, Peter and Morton S. Baratz, "Two Faces of Power," *American Political Science Review* 56.4 (December 1962): 947–52.

Baiocchi, Gianpaolo, "Participation, Activism, and Politics: The Porto Alegre Experiment," *Deepening Democracy: Institutional Innovations in Empowered Participatory Governance*, eds. Archon Fund and Erik Olin Wright, New York: Verso, 2003.

Bakke, Kristin M. and Erik Wibbels, "Diversity, Disparity, and Civil Conflict in Federal States," *World Politics* 59.1 (October 2006): 1–50.

Barabas, Jason, "How Deliberation Affects Policy Opinions," *American Political Science Review* 98.4 (Fall 2004): 687–701.

Barber, Benjamin R., *Strong Democracy: Participatory Politics for a New Age*, Berkeley: University of California Press, 1984.

Barreto, Matt A., Gary M. Segura, and Nathan D. Woods, "The Mobilizing Effect of Majority-Minority Districts on Latino Turnout," *American Political Science Review* 98. 1 (February 2004): 65–75.

Bednar, Jenna, *The Robust Federation: Principles of Design*, New York: Cambridge University Press, 2009.

Bellamy, Richard and Dario Castiglione, "Building the Union: The Nature of Sovereignty in the Political Architecture of Europe," *Theories of Federalism: A Reader*, ed. Dimitrios Karmis and Wayne Norman. New York: Palgrave Macmillan, 2005.

Benhabib, Seyla, *Situating the Self*, New York: Routledge, 1992.

Benoist, Alain, "The First Federalist: Johannes Althusius," *Telos* 118.1 (Winter 2000): 25–58.

Biaggini, Giovanni, "Federalism, Subnational Constitutional Arrangements and the Protection of Minorities in Switzerland," *Federalism, Subnational Constitutions, and Minority Rights*, eds. Tarr, G. Alan, Robert F. Williams, and Joseph Marko, Westport: Praeger, 2004.

Brady, Henry and Cynthia S. Kaplan, "Eastern Europe and the Former Soviet Union," *Referendums around the World: The Growing Use of Direct Democracy*, eds. David Butler and Austin Ranney, Washington, DC: AEI Press, 1994.

Brancati, Dawn, "Decentralization: Fueling the Fire or Dampening the Flames of Ethnic Conflict and Secessionism?" *International Organization* 60.3 (Summer 2006): 651–85.

Brettschneider, Corey, "The Value Theory of Democracy," *Politics, Philosophy, and Economics* 5.3 (October 2006): 259–78.

Bryan, Frank M., "Direct Democracy and Civic Competence: The Case of Town Meeting," *Citizen Competence and Democratic Institutions*, eds. Stephen L. Elkin and Karol Edward Solton, University Park: Penn State University Press, 1999.

Buchanan, Allen, *Secession: The Morality of Political from Fort Sumter to Lithuania and Quebec*, Boulder: Westview Press, 1991.

—, *Justice, Legitimacy, and Self-Determination*. Oxford: Oxford University Press, 2004.

Buchanan, James and Gordon Tullock, *The Calculus of Consent: Logical Foundations of Constitutional Democracy*. Ann Arbor: University of Michigan Press, 1962.

Buckle, Stephen, "Natural Law," *A Companion to Ethics*, ed. Peter Singer, Oxford: Blackwell Publishing, 1991.

Burnstein, E. and K. Sentis, "Attitude Polarization in Groups," *Cognitive Responses in Persuasion*, eds. Richard E. Petty, Thomas M. Ostrom, and Timothy C. Brock, Hillsdale: Lawrence Erlbaum, 1981.

Butler, David and Austin Ranney, eds., *Referendums around the World: The Growing Use of Direct Democracy*, Washington, DC: AEI Press, 1994a.

—, "Theory," *Referendums around the World: The Growing Use of Direct Democracy*, eds. David Butler and Austin Ranney, Washington, DC: AEI Press, 1994b.

—, "Practice," *Referendums around the World: The Growing Use of Direct Democracy*, eds. David Butler and Austin Ranney, Washington, DC: AEI Press, 1994c.

—, "Conclusion," *Referendums around the World: The Growing Use of Direct Democracy*, eds. David Butler and Austin Ranney, Washington, DC: AEI Press, 1994d.

Cairns, Huntington, "Plato's Theory of Law," *Harvard Law Review* 56 (1942): 359–87.

Calhoun, John C., "A Disquisition on Government," *Union and Liberty: The Political Philosophy of John C. Calhoun*, ed., Ross M. Lence, Indianapolis: Liberty Fund, 1992.

Cameron, Charles M., *Veto Bargaining: Presidents and the Politics of Negative Power*. Cambridge: Cambridge University Press, 2000.

Carney, Frederick S., "Introduction," in Althusius, Johannes, *Politica*, ed. and trans. Frederick S. Carney, Indianapolis: Liberty Fund, 1995.

Charron, Nicholas, "Government Quality and Vertical Power-Sharing in Fractionalized States," *Publius* 39.4 (Fall 2009): 585–605.

Cheek, H. Lee, *Calhoun and Popular Rule: The Political Theory of the Disquisition and Discourse*, Columbia: University of Missouri Press, 2004.

Cohen, Gideon, "The Developments of Regional and Local Languages in Ethiopia's Federal System," *Ethnic Federalism: The Ethiopian Experience in Comparative Perspective*, ed. David Turton, Athens: Ohio University Press/Addis Ababa, Ethiopia: Addis Ababa University Press, 2006.

Cohen, Jean L. and Andrew Arato, *Civil Society and Political Theory*, Cambridge: MIT Press, 1992.

Cohen, Joshua, "Deliberation and Democratic Legitimacy," *Deliberative Democracy: Essays on Reason and Politics*, eds. James Bohman and William Rehq, Cambridge: MIT Press, 1997.

Cohen, Joshua and Charles Sabel, "Directly Deliberative Polyarchy," *European Law Journal* 3.4 (December 1997): 313–42.

Condorcet, Marie Jean Antoine Nicolas de Caritat, "Observations on the Twenty-Ninth Book of the *Spirit of the Laws*," trans. Thomas Jefferson, New York: Burt Franklin, 1814.

Conlan, Timothy, "From Cooperative to Opportunistic Federalism: Reflections on the Half-Century Anniversary of the Commission on Intergovernmental Relations," *Public Administration Review* 66.4 (September/October 2006): 663–76.

Conyers, A. J., *The Long Truce: How Toleration Made the World Safe for Power and Profit*, Dallas: Spence Publishing, 2008.

Davis, Kenneth Culp, "Sovereign Immunity Must Go," *Administrative Law Review* 22 (1970): 383.

Delahunty, Robert J., "Federalism and Polarization," *St. Thomas Journal of Law and Public Policy* 1.1 (Winter 2007): 1–33.

DeVotta, Neil, *Blowback: Linguistic Nationalism, Institutional Decay, and Ethnic Conflict in Sri Lanka*, Stanford: Stanford University Press, 2004.

Doernberg, Donald L., *Sovereign Immunity or The Rule of Law: The New Federalism's Choice*, Durham: Carolina Academic Press, 2005.

Druckman, James N. and Kjersten R. Nelson, "Framing and Deliberation: How Citizens' Conversations Limit Elite Influence," *American Journal of Political Science* 47.4 (October 2003): 729–45.

Dubois, Sebastien, "The Making of Nations in Belgium and Western Europe in Historical Perspective (Fifteenth-Twentieth Century): National Ideology, Ethnicity, Language and Politics," *Promoting Conflict or Peace through Identity*, ed. Nikki Slocum-Bradley, Burlington: Ashgate Publishing, 2008.

Duncan, Kyle, "Subsidiarity and Religious Establishments in the U.S. Constitution," *Villanova Law Review* 52 (2006): 67.

Edelman, Murray, *Politics as Symbolic Action: Mass Arousal and Acquiescence*, New York: Academic Press, 1971.

Edrisinha, Rohan, Lee Seymour and Ann Griffiths, "Adopting Federalism: Sri Lanka and Sudan," *Handbook of Federal Countries, 2005*, eds. Ann L. Griffiths and Karl Nerenberg, ed., Montreal & Kingston: Forum of Federations/McGill-Queen's University Press, 2005.

Egan, Anthony and Rupert Taylor, "South Africa: The Failures of Ethnoterritorial Politics," *The Territorial Management of Ethnic Conflict*. 2nd edition., ed. John Coakley, Portland: Frank Cass, 2003.

Elazar, Daniel J., "Althusius' Grand Design for a Federal Commonwealth," *Politica*, Johannes Althusisus, ed. and trans. Frederick S. Carney, Indianapolis: Liberty Fund, 1995.

Elster, Jon, "The Market and the Forum: Three Varieties of Political Theory," *Deliberative Democracy: Essays on Reason and Politics*, eds. James Bohman and William Rehq, Cambridge: MIT Press, 1997.

Fearon, James, "Deliberation as Discussion," *Deliberative Democracy*, ed. Jon Elster, Cambridge: Cambridge University Press, 1998.

Feeley, Malcolm M. and Edward Rubin, *Federalism: Political Identity and Tragic Compromise*, Ann Arbor: University of Michigan Press, 2008.

Fischer, Claudia S., "Uncommon Values, Diversity and Conflict in City Life," *Diversity and Its Discontents*, eds. N. J. Smelser and J. C. Alexander, Princeton: Princeton University Press, 1999.

Fiseha, Assefa, "Theory versus Practice in the Implementation of Ethiopia's Ethnic Federalism," *Ethnic Federalism: The Ethiopian Experience in Comparative Perspective*, ed. David Turton, Athens: Ohio University Press/Addis Ababa, Ethiopia: Addis Ababa University Press, 2006.

Fletcher, Matthew L., "The Comparative Rights of Indispensible Sovereigns," *Gonzaga Law Review* 40.1 (2005): 1–126.

Fossedal, Gregory A., *Direct Democracy in Switzerland*, New Brunswick: Transaction Publishers, 2002.

Fraser, Nancy, "Social Justice in the Age of Identity and Politics: Redistribution, Recognition, and Participation," *Redistribution or Recognition: A Political Philosophical Exchange*, eds. Nancy Fraser and Axel Honneth, London: Verso, 2003.

Friedrich, C. J., "Introductory Remarks," *Politica Medhodice Digesta of Johannes Althusius*. New York: Arno Press, 1979.

Fruehwald, Scott, "The Supreme Court's Confusing State Sovereign Immunity Jurisprudence," *Drake Law Review* 56.2 (2008): 1–67.

Fung, Archon, *Empowered Participation: Reinventing Urban Democracy*, Princeton: Princeton University Press, 2004.

Fung, Archon and Erik Olin Wright, "Thinking about Empowered Participatory Governance," *Deepening Democracy: Institutional Innovations in Empowered Participatory Governance*, eds. Archon—Fung and Erik Olin Wright, New York: Verso, 2003.

Gelertner, David, "Back to Federalism: The Proper Remedy for Polarization," *Weekly Standard* 11.28, April 10, 2006.

Gerber, Elisabeth R., "Legislative Response to the Threat of Popular Initiatives," *American Journal of Political Science* 40.1 (Winter 1996): 99–128.

—, *The Populist Paradox: Interest Group Influence and the Promise of Direct Legislation*, Princeton: Princeton University Press, 1999.

Gladwell, Malcolm, "How David Beats Goliath," *The New Yorker*, May 11, 2009.

Goldman, Ralph M. "The Advisory Referendum in America," *Public Opinion Quarterly* 14.2 (1950): 303–15.

Goodin, Robert E., "Democratic Deliberation Within," *Debating Deliberative Democracy*, eds. James S. Fishkin and Peter Laslett, Oxford: Blackwell Publishing, 2003.

Greaves, Edward, "Constructing Affirmatively Empowered Participatory Regimes: The Making of Public Space in Urban Popular Municipalities of Santiago, Chile," *Polity* 39.3 (July 2007): 305–34.

Green, Melanie C., Penny Visser, and Phillip E. Tetlock, "Coping with Accountability Cross-Pressures: Low-Effort Evasive Tactics and High-Effort Quests for Complex Compromises," *Personality and Social Psychology Bulletin* 26.4 (Fall 2000): 1380–91.

Griffiths, Ann L. and Karl Nerenberg, eds., *Handbook of Federal Countries, 2005*. Montreal & Kingston: Forum of Federations/McGill-Queen's University Press, 2005.

Gudina, Merera, "Contradictory Interpretation of Ethiopian History: The Need for a New Consensus," *Ethnic Federalism: The Ethiopian Experience in Comparative Perspective*, ed. David Turton, Athens: Ohio University Press/Addis Ababa, Ethiopia: Addis Ababa University Press, 2006.

Guinier, L., *The Tyranny of the Majority: Fundamental Fairness in Representative Democracy*, New York: The Free Press, 1994.

Gutmann, Amy and Dennis Thompson, *Democracy and Disagreement*, Cambridge: Belknap Press of Harvard University Press, 1996.

—, "Democratic Disagreement," *Deliberative Politics*, ed. Stephen Macedo, New York: Oxford University Press, 1999.

Habermas, Jurgen, trans. Shierry Weber Nicholsen, "Struggles for Recognition in the Democratic Constitutional State," *Multiculturalism*, ed. Amy Gutmann, Princeton: Princeton University Press, 1994.

Hale, Henry E., "Divided We Stand: Institutional Sources of Ethnofederal State Survival and Collapse," *World Politics* 56.2 (January 2004): 165–93.

Hardin, Russell, "Deliberation: Method, Not Theory," *DeliberativePolitics*, ed. Stephen Macedo, New York: Oxford University Press, 1999.

Hayward, Clarissa R., "The Difference States Make: Democracy, Identity, and the American City," *American Political Science Review* 97.4 (November 2003): 501–14.

Hetherington, Marc, "Resurgent Mass Partisanship: The Role of Elite Polarization," *American Political Science Review* 95.3 (2001): 619–31.

Hill, Ronald J., "The Dissolution of the Soviet Union: Federation, Commonwealth, Secession," *The Territorial Management of Ethnic Conflict*. 2nd edition., ed. John Coakley, Portland: Frank Cass, 2003.

Himmelfarb, Gertrude, *The Roads to Modernity: The British, French, and American Enlightenments*, New York: Vintage Books, 2004.

Hobhouse, L.T., *Liberalism*, New York: Oxford, 1964.

Hollinger, David, *Postethnic America: Beyond Multiculturalism*, New York: Basic Books, 1995.

Hooghe, Liesbet, "Belgium," *The Territorial Management of Ethnic Conflict*. 2nd edition., ed. John Coakley, Portland: Frank Cass, 2003.

Hosking, Geoffrey, *Russia and the Russians: A History*, Cambridge: The Belknap Press of Harvard University Press, 2001.

Houston, Horace K., "Another Nullification Crisis: Vermont's 1850 Habeas Corpus Law," *The New England Quarterly* 77. 2 (June 2004): 252–72.

Hug, Simon, "Occurrence and Policy Consequences of Referendums: A Theoretical Model and Empirical Evidence," *Journal of Theoretical Politics* 16.3 (Summer 2004): 321–57.

Hug, Simon and Geogre Tsebelis, "Veto Players and Referendums Around the World," *Journal of Theoretical Politics* 14.4 (Fall 2002): 465–515.

Imtiyaz, A. R. M. and Ben Stavis, "Ethno-Political Conflict in Sri Lanka," *Journal of Third World Studies* 25.2 (Fall 2008): 135–52.

Kahn, Jeffrey, *Federalism, Democratization, and the Rule of Law in Russia*. Oxford: Oxford University Press, 2002.

Kant, Immanuel, *Critique of Pure Judgment*, trans. Werner S. Pluhar, Indianapolis: Hackett Publishing, 1987.

—, *Groundings for the Metaphysics of Morals*, 3rd edition, trans. James W. Ellington, Indianapolis: Hackett Publishing, 1993.

Karmis, Dimitrios and Wayne Norman, eds., *Theories of Federalism*, New York: Palgrave Macmillan, 2005.

Kaufman, S. J., *Modern Hatreds: The Symbolic Politics of Ethnic War*, Ithaca: Cornell University Press, 2001.

Kiewiet, Roderick D. and Matthew D. McCubbins, "Presidential Influence on Congressional Appropriations Decisions," *American Journal of Political Science* 32 (1988): 713–36.

Klug, Heinz, "How the Centre Holds: Managing Claims for Regional and Ethnic Autonomy in a Democratic South Africa," *Autonomy and Ethnicity: Negotiating Competing Claims in Multi-Ethnic States*, ed. Yash Ghai, Cambridge: Cambridge University Press, 2000.

Kobach, Kris W., "Switzerland," *Referendums around the World: The Growing Use of Direct Democracy*, eds. David Butler and Austin Ranney, Washington, DC: AEI Press, 1994.

Kramer, Larry, *The People Themselves: Popular Constitutionalism and Judicial Review*, New York: Oxford University Press, 2003.

Kunesh, Patrice H., "Tribal Self-Determination in the Age of Scarcity," *South Dakota Law Review* 54 (2009): 398–418.

Kymlicka, Will, "Is Federalism a Viable Alternative to Secession?," *Theories of Secession*, ed. Percy B. Lehning, New York: Routledge, 1998.

—, "Emerging Models of Multination Federalism: Are They Relevant to Africa," *Ethnic Federalism: The Ethiopian Experience in Comparative Perspective*, ed. David Turton, Athens: Ohio University Press/Addis Ababa, Ethiopia: Addis Ababa University Press, 2006.

Lasch, Christopher, "The Communitarian Critique of Liberalism," *Community in America*, eds. Charles Reynolds and Ralph Norman. Berkeley: University of California Press, 1988.

Lawler, Peter Augustine, *Postmodernism Rightly Understood: The Return to Realism in American Thought*, Lanham: Rowman and Littlefield, 1999.

Lawrence, Eric, John Sides, Henry Farrell, "Self-Segregation or Deliberation? Blog Readership, Participation, and Polarization in American Politics," *Perspectives on Politics* 8.1 (March 2010): 141–57.

Lecours, Andre, "Belgium," *Handbook of Federal Countries, 2005*, eds. Ann L. Griffiths and Karl Nerenberg, Montreal & Kingston: Forum of Federations/McGill-Queen's University Press, 2005.

Lehning, Percy B., ed., *Theories of Secession*, New York: Routledge, 1998.

Lemieux, Scott E. and David J. Watkins, "Beyond the 'Countermajoritarian Difficulty': Lessons from Contemporary Democratic Theory," *Polity* 41.1 (Winter 2009): 30–62.

Levy, Jacob T., "Federalism, Liberalism, and the Separation of Loyalties," *American Political Science Review* 101.3 (Fall 2007): 459–77.

Locke, John, *Second Treatise of Government*, ed. C. B. MacPherson, Indianapolis: Hackett Publishing, 1980.

Lustick, Ian S., Dan Miodowink, and Roy J. Eidelson, "Secessionism in Multicultural States: Does Sharing Power Prevent or Encourage It?" *American Political Science Review* 98.2 (May 2004): 209–29.

Macedo, Stephen, "Introduction," *DeliberativePolitics*, ed. Stephen Macedo, New York: Oxford University Press, 1999.

Malesevic, Sinisa, "Ethnicity and Federalism in Communist Yugoslavia and Its Successor States," *Ethnic Federalism: The Ethiopian Experience in Comparative Perspective*, ed. David Turton, Athens: Ohio University Press/Addis Ababa, Ethiopia: Addis Ababa University Press, 2006.

Malhotra, Deepak K. and Sumanasiri Liyanage, "Assessing the Long-Term Impact of 'Peace Camps' on Youth Attitudes and Behaviors: The Case of Ethno-Political Conflict in Sri Lanka," Harvard NOM Research Paper No. 03–24, 2003.

Manin, Bernard, "On Legitimacy and Political Deliberation," *Political Theory* 15.3 (1987): 338–68.

Marcus, Harold G., *A History of Ethiopia*, Berkeley: University of California Press, 1994.

McCarty, Nolan, Keith Poole, and Howard Rosenthal, *Polarized America: The Dance of Ideology and Unequal Riches*, Cambridge: MIT Press, 2006.

McCoy, Charles S. and J. Wayne Baker, *Fountainhead of Federalism: Heinrich Bullinger and Covenantal Tradition*, Louisville: Westminster/John Knox Press, 1991.

McGinnis, John O. and Ilya Somin, "Federalism vs. States' Rights: A Defense of Judicial Review in a Federal System," *Northwestern University Law Review* 99: 1 (Winter 2004): 89–130.

Mikhelidze, N. and N. Pirozzi, *Civil Society and Conflict Transformation in Abkhazia, Israel/Palestine, Nagorno-Karabakh, Transnistria and Western Sahara*. MICROCON Policy Paper 3, Brighton: MICROCON, 2008.

Mill, John Stuart, *Considerations on a Representative Government*, ed. Currin V. Shields, Arlington, TX: Liberal Arts Press, 1953.

—, *On Liberty*, Indianapolis: Bobbs-Merrill, 1956.

Miller, Fred D., "The Rule of Reason in Plato's Statesman and the American Federalist," *Social Philosophy and Policy* 24.2 (Fall 2007): 90–129.

Moghaddam, Fathali M., "Religion and Regional Planning: The Case of the Emerging 'Shi'a Region'," *Promoting Conflict or Peace through Identity*, ed. Nikki Slocum-Bradley, Burlington: Ashgate Publishing, 2008.

Montesqueiu. *Spirit of the Laws*. eds. Anne M. Cohler, Basia C. Miller, and Harold S. Stone, Cambridge: Cambridge University Press.

Munson, Peter J., *Iraq in Transition: The Legacy of Dictatorship and the Prospects for Democracy*, Washington, DC: Potomac Books, 2009.

Mutz, Diane C., *Impersonal Influence*, Cambridge: Cambridge University Press, 1998.

—, *Hearing the Other Side: Deliberative versus Participatory Democracy*, Cambridge: Cambridge University Press, 2006.

Niven, David, "The Mobilization Solution? Face-to-Face Contact and Voter Turnout in a Municipal Election," *Journal of Politics* 66. 3 (August 2004): 868–84.

Norman, Wayne, *Negotiating Nationalism: Nation-Building, Federalism, and Secession in the Multinational State*, Oxford: Oxford University Press, 2006.

Ober, Josiah, "Natural Capacities and Democracy as a Good-in-Itself," *Philosophical Studies* 132 (2007): 59–73.

O'Connell, Brian, *Civil Society: The Underpinnings of American Democracy*. Foreword by John W. Gardner. Hanover: University Press of New England, 1999.

Oliver, J. Eric, "City Size and Civic Involvement in Metropolitan America," *American Political Science Review* 94.2 (June 2000): 361–73.

O'Neill, Onora, "Justice and Boundaries," *Political Restructuring in Europe: Ethical Perspectives*, ed. W. J. A. Macartney, London: Routledge, 1994.

Pangle, Thomas L., *Montesquieu's Philosophy of Liberalism: A Commentary on* The Spirit of the Laws, Chicago: University of Chicago Press, 1973.

Pateman, Carole, *Participation and Democratic Theory*, Cambridge: Cambridge University Press, 1970.

Patz, Tom, "Ethiopia," *Handbook of Federal Countries, 2005*, eds. Ann L. Griffiths and Karl Nerenberg, Montreal & Kingston: Forum of Federations/McGill-Queen's University Press, 2005.

Pettigrew, Thomas F. and Linda R. Tropp, "Does Intergroup Contact Reduce Prejudice? Recent Meta-Analytic Findings," *Reducing Prejudice and Discrimination: The Claremont Symposium on Applied Social Psychology*, ed. Stuart Oskamp, Mahwah: Erlbaum, 2000.

Phillips, Derek L., "Social Participation and Happiness," *American Journal of Sociology* 72.5 (March 1967): 479–88.

Phillips, Kevin, *Bad Money: Reckless Finance, Failed Politics, and the Global Crisis of American Capitalism*, New York: Viking, 2008.

Plato, *Plato: Complete Works*, eds. John M. Cooper and D. S. Hutchinson, Indianapolis: Hackett Publishing, 1997.

Polanyi, Karl, "Aristotle Discovers the Economy," *Primitive, Archaic and Modern Economies: Essays of Karl Polanyi*, ed. G. Dalton, Boston: Beacon Press, 1968.

Pommerhene, Werner W., "Institutional Approaches to Public Expenditure: Empirical Evidence from Swiss Municipalities," *Journal of Public Economics* 9.2 (Summer 1978): 255–80.

Prior, Markus, *Post-Broadcast Democracy: How Media Choice Increases Inequality in Political Involvement and Polarizes Elections*, New York: Cambridge University Press, 2007.

Putnam, Robert, *Bowling Alone: The Collapse and Revival of American Community*, New York: Simon and Schuster, 2001.

Rahe, Paul A., *Soft Despotism, Democracy's Drift: Montesquieu, Rousseau, Tocqueville and the Modern Project*, New Haven: Yale University Press, 2009.

Rawls, John, *Collected Papers*, ed. Samuel Freeman, Cambridge: Harvard University Press, 1999.

Read, James H., *Majority Rule versus Consensus: The Political Thought of John C. Calhoun*, Lawrence: University Press of Kansas, 2009.

Rousseau, Jean-Jacques, *The Social Contract*, trans. Maurice Cranston, London: Penguin Books, 1968.

Saban, Ilan, "Minority Rights in Deeply Divided Societies: A Framework for Analysis and the case of the Arab-Palestinian Minority in Israel," *International Law and Politics* 36 (2005): 885–1003.

Sale, Kirkpatrick, *Human Scale*, New Catalyst Books, 1980.

Samuel, Ana J., "The Design of Montesquieu's *The Spirit of the Laws*: The Triumph of Freedom over Determinism," *American Political Science Review* 103:2 (May 2009): 305–21.

Samuelson, Richard, "Can Federalism Solve America's Culture War?" *Real Clear Politics*, April 26, 2006.

Sandel, Michael, "On Republicanism and Liberalism," interviewed by Leif Werner and Chong-Min Hong, *The Harvard Review of Philosophy*, volume VI (Spring 1996): 66–76.

Scheffler, Samuel, "Immigration and the Significance of Culture," *Philosophy and Public Affairs* 35.2 (Summer 2007): 93–125.

Schmidt, Manfred G., "The Impact of Political Parties, Constitutional Structures and Veto Players on Public Policy," *Comparative Democratic Politics: A Guide to Contemporary Theory and Research*, ed. Hans Keman, London: Sage Publications, 2002.

Scott, Kyle, *Dismantling American Common Law: Liberty and Justice in Our Transformed Courts*, Lanham: Lexington Books, 2007.

—, *The Price of Politics: Lessons from* Kelo v. City of New London, Lanham: Lexington Books, 2009.

Setala, Maija, *Referendums and Democratic Government: Normative Theory and Analysis of Institutions*, New York: St Martin's Press, 1999.

Shapiro, Ian, "Enough Deliberation: Politics is about Interests and Power," *Deliberative Politics*, ed. Stephen Macedo, New York: Oxford University Press, 1999.

Shortell, Christopher, *Rights, Remedies, and the Impact of State Sovereign Immunity*, Albany: SUNY Press, 2008.

Silberbauer, George, "Ethics in Small-Scale Societies," *A Companion to Ethics*, ed. Peter Singer, Oxford: Blackwell Publishing, 1991.

Sinclair, Barbara, *Party Wars: Polarization and the Politics of National Policy Making*, Norman: University of Oklahoma Press, 2006.

Sisk, Gregory C, "A Primer on the Doctrine of Federal Sovereign Immunity," *Oklahoma Law Review* 58.3 (Fall 2005): 439–68.

—. *Litigation with the Federal Government*. 4th Edition, Philadelphia: The American Law Institute, 2006.

Sobei, Mogi, *The Problem of Federalism: A Study in the History of Political Theory*, London: Allen and Unwin, 1931.

Stauffer, Thomas, Nicole Topperwien, and Urs Thalmann-Torres, "Switzerland," *Handbook of Federal Countries, 2005*, eds. Ann L. Griffiths and Karl Nerenberg, Montreal & Kingston: Forum of Federations/McGill-Queen's University Press, 2005.

Stein, Janice Gross, David R. Cameron, and Richard Simeon with Alan Alexandroff, "Civic Engagement in Conflict Resolution: Lessons for Canada in International Experience," *The Referendum Papers*, ed., David R. Cameron, Toronto: University of Toronto Press, 1999.

Stopler, Gila, "Contextualizing Multiculturalism: A Three Dimensional Examination of Multicultural Claims," *Journal of Law and Ethics of Human Rights* 1 (2007): 309–53.

Strauss, Leo, *The City and Man*, Chicago: University of Chicago Press, 1964.

—, "On the *Minos*," *Roots of Political Philosophy: Ten Forgotten Socratic Dialogues*, ed. Thomas L. Pangle, Ithaca: Cornell University Press, 1987.

Sunstein, Cass, "Constitutionalism and Secession," *University of Chicago Law Review* 58.4 (Fall 1991): 633–70.

—, *The Partial Constitution*, Cambridge: Harvard University Press, 1996.

—, "Agreement without Theory," *DeliberativePolitics*, ed. Stephen Macedo, New York: Oxford University Press, 1999.

—, "Should Constitutions Protect the Right to Secede?" *Journal of Political Philosophy* 9.3 (Fall 2001a): 350–5.

—, *Designing Democracy: What Constitutions Do*, New York: Cambridge University Press, 2001b.

—, "Neither Hayek nor Habermas," *Public Choice* 134.1 (2008): 87–95.

—, *Republic.com 2.0*. Princeton: Princeton University Press, 2009.

Swenden, Wilfried and Maarten Theo Jans, "'Will it Stay or Will it Go?' Federalism and the Sustainability of Belgium," *The Politics of Belgium: Institutions and Policy under Bipolar and Centrifugal Federalism*, eds. Marleen Brans, Lieven de Winter, and Wilfried Swenden, New York: Routledge, 2009.

Taylor, Charles, "The Politics of Recognition," *Multiculturalism: Examining the Politics of Recognition*, ed. Amy Gutmann, Princeton: Princeton University Press, 1994.

Tiebout, Charles M., "A Pure Theory of Local Expenditures," *Journal of Political Economy* 64.5 (October 1956): 416–24.

Tirucelvam, Neelan, "The Politics of Federalism and Diversity in Sri Lanka," *Promoting Conflict or Peace through Identity*, ed. Nikki Slocum-Bradley, Burlington: Ashgate Publishing, 2008.

Topperwien, Nicole, "Participation in the Decision-Making Process as a Means of Group Accommodation," *Federalism, Subnational Constitutions, and Minority Rights*, eds. Tarr G. Alan, Robert F. Williams, and Joseph Marko, Westport: Praeger, 2004.

Tsebelis, George, *Veto Players: How Political Institutions Work*, New York/Princeton: Russell Sage Foundation/Princeton University Press, 2002.

Tushnet, Mark, *Taking the Constitution Away from the Courts*, Princeton: Princeton University Press, 1999.

Twain, Mark, "Letter to San Francisco Alta California," dated May 18, 1867, published June 23, 1867.

Van Cott, Donna Lee, *Radical Democracy in the Andes*, New York: Cambridge University Press, 2008.

VanDrunen, David, "Aquinas and Hayek on the Limits of Law: A Convergence of Ethical Traditions," *Journal of Markets and Morality* 5.2 (Fall 2002): 315–37.

Vischer, Robert K., "Subsidiarity as a Principle of Governance: Beyond Devolution," 35 *Indiana Law Review* 35.1 (2001): 103–42.

—, "The Good, the Bad, and the Ugly: Rethinking the Value of Associations," *Notre Dame Law Review* 79.3 (2004): 949–1021.

—, "Subsidiarity and Suffering: The View from New Orleans," *Journal of Catholic Legal Studies* 45.1 (Winter 2007): 183–94.

Waldron, Jeremy, *Law and Disagreement*, Oxford: Oxford University Press, 1999.

Walzer, Michael, *On Toleration*, New Haven: Yale University Press, 1997.

Ward, Lee, "Montesquieu on Federalism and Anglo-Gothic Constitutionalism," *Publius* 37.4 (Fall 2007): 557–77.

Weingrod, Alex, "Israel: Ethnic Conflict and Political Exchange," *The Territorial Management of Ethnic Conflict*. 2nd edition, ed. John Coakley, Portland: Frank Cass, 2003.

Wellman, Christopher, "A Defense of Secession and Political Self-Determination," *Philosophy and Public Affairs* 24.2 (Summer 1995): 142–71.

Wertheimer, Alan, "Internal Disagreements: Deliberation and Abortion," *Deliberative Politics*, ed. Stephen Macedo, New York: Oxford University Press, 1999.

Williams, Paul R. and Matthew T. Simpson, "Rethinking the Political Future: An Alternative to the Ethno-Sectarian Division of Iraq," *American University International Law Review* 24.2 (Summer 2008): 191–247.

Williams, Robert F. and G. Alan Tarr, "Subnational Constitutional Space: A View from the States, Provinces, Regions, Lander, and Cantons," *Federalism, Subnational Constitutions, and Minority Rights*, eds. G. Alan Tarr, Robert F. Williams, and Joseph Marko, Westport: Praeger, 2004.

Wolin, Sheldon, "Foreward," *Federalism: Origin, Operation, Significance*, ed. William H. Riker, New York: Little Brown and Co, 1964.

Wood, Gordon S., *The Radicalism of the American Revolution*, New York: Vintage Books, 1991.

—, *The Creation of the American Republic, 1776–1787*, Chapel Hill: The University of North Carolina Press, 1998.

Wong, David, "Relativism," *A Companion to Ethics*, ed. Peter Singer, Oxford: Blackwell Publishing, 1991.

Young, Iris Marion, "Difference as a Resource for Democratic Communication," *Deliberative Democracy: Essays on Reason and Politics*, eds. James Bohman and William Rehq, Cambridge: MIT Press, 1997.

—, "Self-Determination and Global Democracy: A Critique of Liberal Nationalism," *Designing Democratic Institutions*, eds. Ian Shapiro and Stephen Macedo. New York: New York University Press, 2000a.

—, "Hybrid Democracy: Iroquois Federalism and the Postcolonial Project," *Political Theory and the Rights of Indigenous Peoples*, eds. Duncan Ivison, Paul Patton, and Will Sanders, Cambridge: Cambridge University Press, 2000b.

Zimmerman, Joseph F., *The Referendum: The People Decide Public Policy*, Westport: Praeger, 2001.

Zurn, Christopher, *Deliberative Democracy and the Institutions of Judicial Review*, Cambridge: Cambridge University Press, 2007.

Index